SO-AHH-245

1975
36

The Audience in the Poem

Dorothy Mermin

❧THE❧

Audience in the Poem

FIVE VICTORIAN POETS

RUTGERS UNIVERSITY PRESS
NEW BRUNSWICK, NEW JERSEY

The publication of this book was aided by the Hull Memorial Publication Fund of Cornell University.

Library of Congress Cataloging in Publication Data

Mermin, Dorothy, 1936–
The audience in the poem.

Includes bibliographical references and index.
1. English poetry—19th century—History and
criticism.   2. Monologue.   3. Authors and readers.
4. Reader-response criticism.   I. Title.
PR599.M6M47   1983   821'.8'09   82-23188
ISBN 0-8135-0988-2

Copyright © 1983 by Rutgers, The State University
All rights reserved
Manufactured in the United States of America

For Jonathan and Elizabeth

Contents

Acknowledgments		ix
Introduction		1
ONE	Tennyson	16
TWO	Browning	47
THREE	Arnold	83
FOUR	Clough and Meredith	109
Conclusion		145
Notes		157
Index		175

Acknowledgments

I am very grateful to Lord Tennyson, who gave me permission on behalf of the Tennyson trustees to quote unpublished Tennyson manuscripts, and to the librarians of Trinity College, Cambridge, and the Houghton Library. Manuscripts owned by Harvard University are published by permission of the Houghton Library.

For permission to reprint material that first appeared in scholarly journals I am grateful to the editors. I have used all or part of these articles: "Tennyson's *Maud*: A Thematic Analysis," *Texas Studies in Literature and Language*, 15 (1973), 267–277; "Poetry as Fiction: Meredith's *Modern Love*," *English Literary History*, 43 (1976), 100–119; "Speaker and Auditor in Browning's Dramatic Monologues," *University of Toronto Quarterly*, 45 (1976), 139–157; "Ironic Translation in *Fifine at the Fair*," *Victorian Newsletter*, 54 (Fall 1978), 1–4.

And I am most grateful to my colleagues and students in the Cornell English department whose skepticism, criticism, encouragement, and friendship have contributed to the writing of this book.

Introduction

WHEN TENNYSON WROTE "St Simeon Stylites" in 1833 he inaugurated a mode of poetic discourse that was to flourish richly in the next few decades. Simeon has been on his pillar for thirty years and is getting impatient. He describes his sufferings to God and explains that it is time for his reward, but God does not reply. Finally, however, Simeon turns to address the people who have gathered at the base of the pillar, and they respond with immediate enthusiasm; calling him "saint," they revive his faith in his perversely fostered sanctity and point his speech toward its triumphant conclusion. The poem thus becomes not only the first full-fledged Victorian dramatic monologue, but the first as well in a briefer but extremely distinguished line of Victorian poems containing auditors whose responsiveness determines the poems' movement and meaning. Although the auditors in "St Simeon Stylites" appear late and rather unexpectedly, the essential characteristics of such poems are already present in this one: the auditors' response significantly affects the course of the speaker's utterance, and the poem is concerned with the speaker as both an imaginative and a social being, and with the ways in which social beings communicate their private imaginative visions to other people.

Tennyson wrote two more poems of this kind in 1833, probably a month or two later: "Ulysses" and part of "Tiresias." Browning, who admired "St Simeon Stylites" very much, published his first collection of short poems in 1842; two of them, "My Last Duchess" and "Count Gismond," had auditors. Arnold did not want to emulate either Tennyson or Browning, but when his first book appeared in 1849 it ended with "Resignation," in which a poet explains his ideas about life to a sister who refuses to accept them. The peculiarity of these poems and their significant relation to each other are blurred by their

1

generic diversity—most but not all of them are dramatic monologues, and some are more clearly dramatic monologues than others—and by their evident similarity to such works as "The Sun Rising" or "Gerontion." But what differentiates them as a group from poems that they otherwise very much resemble—what makes "Resignation," for instance, crucially different from its progenitor, "Tintern Abbey," or "Ulysses" from "Tithonus," or "My Last Duchess" from "Johannes Agricola in Meditation"—is the presence of an auditor from whom the speaker wants (and often gets) a response: not as a consequence of the completed utterance, but while he is speaking. When the auditor is human, adult, alive, awake, physically present, and able to hear and respond—not God, nor a mythological figure, nor a real or fictional reader of words on paper—the poem is a representation of speech. The auditor's silent presence directs our attention to what we do not usually expect to find in poems, and take for granted in dialogue and drama: that the speaker is understood to be speaking out loud, not to the reader or to himself but to someone who could answer or interrupt or do something unexpected before he has finished speaking. His words are intended to have an immediate effect on his auditor—they are primarily instrumental rather than expressive—and both his utterance and the poem's meaning are significantly affected by the auditor's responses or refusal to respond. "Tintern Abbey" would be such a poem if it were conceivable (as of course it is not) that at any moment Dorothy Wordsworth might argue or try to change the subject or simply turn away; the felt possibility of such interruption, whether it actually occurs or not, marks the presence of the distinctively Victorian auditor.

Such poems hardly occur at all in English literature outside the Victorian period. The closest forerunner is Coleridge's "The Eolian Harp," in which the auditor's pious rebuke makes the poet moderate his eloquent imaginative speculations. There are more distant parallels in Renaissance love and seduction poems, particularly Donne's; but even "The Flea" is a witty tour de force with an auditor who acts neatly on cue, between stanzas. Moreover, Victorian poems of this sort appear, flourish, ramify, and disappear again in the course of a few decades. In the 1833 manuscripts of "St Simeon," "Tiresias," and "Ulysses" we can see the first auditors emerging in the course of composition as distinct elements that are never fully assimilated into the poem as a whole: Simeon's auditors work against the tone established in the first part of the poem, Ulysses' language falters as he seems to shift from soliloquy to a public statement about Telemachus, and in "Tiresias" (which Tennyson left unfinished for half a century) our awareness that the speaker is urging a young man to go out and die makes his personal reminiscences seem, despite their obvious thematic importance, digressive and unfeeling. After 1833 Tennyson only used this strategy with substantial alterations, in *Maud*, "The Holy Grail," and "Rizpah," and a few very minor late works. Browning, of course, wrote many such monologues, but most of them, including the best and most famous ones, belong to the years 1842 to 1855. The best of his relatively few later ones (*"Dîs Aliter Visum,"* "Mr. Sludge, 'The Medium'," and *Fifine at the Fair*) become increasingly longer and more convoluted, pressing the dramatic situations they enact past the limits of verisimilitude and their analyses of communication beyond the scope of most readers' attentiveness. Arnold wrote only a few, and none after 1853 ("Dover Beach" was published in 1867 but written much earlier). Arnold exploits the auditor more thoroughly and consistently than Tennyson does, but most of his auditors are less vividly alive and responsive than Browning's, for Arnold is more openly concerned with the difficulties of communication than Tennyson is, and more single-mindedly determined than Browning to try to imagine ways of overcoming those difficulties. The only other short Victorian poem of any note at all that exploits this strategy is the title poem of the first volume of Pre-Raphaelite poetry, William Morris's *The Defense of Guenevere* (1858), in which the speaker's words are blatantly manipulative and shamelessly deceptive and the poem implicitly denies that poetry is a way of speaking or that poets should try to communicate anything true or useful at all.

These poems appear early in the careers of the three major Victorian poets, and reflect a time of general uncertainty about the nature and future of poetry. Tennyson and Browning were working free of Romantic influences and looking for new ways to speak in a new world, and Arnold was not only experimenting with poetic forms and subjects but beginning to formulate the principles that were to dominate poetic theory for the rest of the century. Meanwhile, the novel was in the process of displacing poetry as the central literary expression of the age. In these few decades Victorian poetry and the Victorian novel as we know them came into being. By 1833 Wordsworth and Coleridge were pretty much silent; Byron, Shelley, and Keats were dead; and it was generally agreed that a new kind of poetry was needed for a new age. A few loud voices had already announced that poetry would probably be trampled to death by the march of mind. Bentham found little use for it, Macaulay said it flourished best in primitive societies, and Carlyle thought that prose could do more work than verse and silence more than either. But W. J. Fox, writing in the *Westminster Review* in 1831, expressed the happier view that was central to the critical discourse of the next few decades: poetry, he asserted, can assimilate new intellectual discoveries and "can act with a force, the extent of which it is difficult to estimate, upon national feelings and character, and consequently upon national happiness."[1]

The requirements for a poetry fit for so high a destiny were articulated by the major writers and periodical reviewers in the following years; these requirements must often have seemed to poets who took them seriously—and Tennyson, Browning, and Arnold did—mutually contradictory. Poets should address themselves to the concerns of an age that was generally agreed to be unpoetical. They should express the simple passions of the heart, the affections binding man to man, in a society that was becoming increasingly conscious of its own complexities, class hostilities, and fragmentation. They should provide beauty for a world getting uglier day by day, without seeming to condemn or withdraw from that world. Hardest of all, perhaps, they should speak deep and important truths in a manner everyone could understand; open their hearts simply and unaffectedly to a multitude of readers; and express their deepest thoughts and feelings without being introspective, morbid, or impure.[2]

The difficulties of this program spring from its combination of two antithetical theories of poetry: what M. H. Abrams has called the "expressive" theory of romanticism, which emphasizes the poet as source and validation of the poem, and the older "pragmatic" theory, which is concerned with the effect of the poem on its readers.[3] For while the early Victorians read and wrote in the light cast by the great Romantics, their deepest hopes and fears about poetry centered on its power to communicate. This is what lies behind their apparent obsession with the content of poetry. John Sterling, for example, wondered why Tennyson wrote about Ulysses instead of Drake, Columbus, or Vasco da Gama, since "their feelings and aims lie far nearer to our comprehension— reach us by a far shorter line."[4] Critics objected with tedious predictability, often in the indignant tones of someone who has unexpectedly been snubbed, that the early works of Tennyson and Browning were affected and obscure, and unfamiliar words annoyed them exceedingly; they wanted language simply to carry thought and feeling from writer to reader. Even those who stood out from the "pragmatic" consensus defined the value, if not the nature, of poetry in terms of what it communicates and how directly it does so. Arthur Hallam said that poetry should "communicate the love of beauty to the heart"; John Stuart Mill, who differentiated poetry from eloquence by its unconsciousness of an audience, still assumed that the object of both is "to act upon the emotions"; Carlyle interrupted an eloquent elaboration of the theme that poetry is pure expressiveness, pure song, with an impatient statement of his real concern: "What we want to get at is the *thought* the man had, if he had any." And in 1853 Arnold wrote to Clough: "I am glad you like the Gipsy Scholar—but what does it *do* for you? . . . 'The complaining millions of men' . . . want . . . something to *animate* and *ennoble* them—not merely to add zest to their melancholy or grace to their dreams."[5]

If poetry were to affect the destinies of the nation it had to animate and ennoble the "complaining millions," not just the poet's friends. The question of whether good poetry can be widely popular is frequently, often anxiously, canvassed; Hallam and Mill thought it could not be, and did not much care— although Hallam's essay on Tennyson opens and closes with just that subject. But most of the critics who thought of poetry primarily as communication assumed that a poet had only to choose widely accessible subjects and emotions, and express them plainly enough, to win a large audience; this is the essential argument of Arnold's Preface of 1853. In general, furthermore, the larger the audience was assumed or hoped to be, the more intimately the poet was expected to address it. Wordsworth had said in the preface to *Lyrical Ballads* that a poet is "a man speaking to men"; Francis Garden, in a formulation typical of the 1830s and 1840s, reduced "men" to the singular and the poet's speech to one side of a friendly conversation: poetry "is discourse; it is utterance; it is man speaking to man, man telling man his thoughts and feelings."[6] The poem with an auditor, one might say, takes this formulation literally, but combines it with Mill's antithetical expressive one—that poetry is unconscious of an audience, overheard not heard.[7] The speaker speaks to someone, but not to us, and we overhear him.

English tradition offered few useful examples of how one Victorian individual could speak in poetry to another. Browning found a suitable tone and manner in Donne for a while, but that was part of Browning's eccentricity. The Romantics had established feeling and imagination as the essential qualities of poetry, making the socially poised speaking voices of Augustan verse sound like prose to nineteenth-century ears, and in any event the cultivated irony and easy allusiveness of the Augustans were unsuitable for young poets addressing the more diffuse Victorian audience.[8] Coleridge's conversation poems might have served as models if the Victorian poets had been able to sustain a faith in the benignity and truth of the poetic imagination, the value of their own experience, and the validity of lofty personal utterance. Tennyson's, Browning's, and Arnold's first poems with auditors are in one way or another ironically concerned with central Romantic values: "St Simeon Stylites" mocks a conspicuously isolated visionary, the Duke of "My Last Duchess" scorns the beauty and pathos of natural innocence, and the poet in "Resignation" sees inhuman dreariness in Wordsworth's own natural world. The best Romantic poetry seemed too inward, too asocial, by Victorian standards; and yet the criteria of inwardness and spontaneity were so deeply established that much of Wordsworth seemed too moralized and controlled to be poetry. For the introduction of the pragmatic theory was accompanied by a narrowing of Romantic poetics to focus on the doctrine of sincerity that was being widely and effectively promulgated by Carlyle. Carlyle conceived of sincerity as the source and measure of all value, a mode of vision, of speech, and of action: sincerity meant living by one's inner vision of the truth of things, speaking and acting from those depths of self in which one participates in the deep mysteries of the universe. Sincere speech is thus by definition *true*; and because others recognize it to be so by the response it awakens in the depths of their own beings, it is effective: it works.[9]

Such an affirmation of the value of poetry in a scientific, mechanistic age must have been very attractive—although Carlyle himself always advised poets to write prose. But it presented difficulties. The Victorian idea of sincerity, springing as it did from the Romantic and Puritan emphasis on the solitary soul confronting the universe or God, is impossible to reconcile with awareness of an audience. The logical conclusion of the doctrine of sincerity is stated (not surprisingly) by John Stuart Mill when he says that if art is aware of an audience, it is eloquence, not poetry. Thus there is a real contradiction in the simultaneous demands for unself-conscious sincerity and deliberate communication—sharpened by the awkward fact that sincerity can finally be measured only in terms of how well an impression of sincerity is communicated. This contradiction, which underlies in one form or another the complexities and tensions of almost every Victorian poem with an auditor, is set forth very plainly in *Pippa Passes*. Like Shelley's poet-nightingale, Pippa sings to cheer her own solitude; she too is the unacknowledged legislator of her world: her songs, overheard, change hearts. But Browning could not be Pippa, and Pippa could not create *Pippa Passes*. Without the context Browning provides for her, her songs crumble into facile and meaningless optimism; they are premised on innocence and ignorance, and if she possessed Browning's knowledge of sin and his pragmatic intention she could not sing them.

We feel a similar difficulty in "Ulysses." Ulysses sounds not only patronizing but insincere as soon as it appears that he is not just talking to himself, and his richly self-absorbed language turns awkward and loose: "This is my son, mine own Telemachus . . . Well-loved of me . . . Most blameless is he." But both Browning and Arnold deliberately explore the contradiction: more often than not the auditors seem to be there for just that purpose. In general, the more sincerely and disinterestedly speakers try to persuade their auditors, the less they succeed. "Two in the Campagna" and "The Buried Life" are both about the difficulty of being sincere at all when one most wants to be, and Browning's speakers succeed best in their purposes either when they do not care what the auditor really thinks of them, as in "My Last Duchess" and "Andrea del Sarto," or when, like Bishop Blougram and Mr. Sludge, they are insincere.

Lyric poetry, which Matthew Arnold in a typical Victorian formulation calls "the direct expression of personal feeling,"[10] was vulnerable to attack on two opposite fronts: for being aware of an audience, and for not responding to the audience's needs. *In Memoriam* XXI shows Tennyson's sense of the dilemma. It defines the poem as purely expressive, sung at the grave on rustic pipes "to him that rests below." But the use of pastoral convention already contradicts the idea of spontaneous private utterance, and the poet adds that travelers sometimes overhear him and make different objections: that his song is enervating, or that it is meant to be overheard and is thus a mere "parade of pain," or that "private sorrow's barren song" is worthless anyway. In reply to these contradictory attacks, he asserts the sincerity of his poem, though not its worth to others: "I do but sing because I must, / And pipe but as the linnets sing." On the whole, however, the effect of the concurrent demands for sincerity and for communication was at least as much to inhibit as to encourage direct personal expression. Reviewers naturally assumed that what moved them was sincere and what did not was factitious. Tennyson's "A Farewell," James Spedding wrote in 1842, shows "how truly the poet's feeling vibrates in sympathy with nature; otherwise how should so simple a tone out of his heart awaken such an echo in our own?"[11] Such a criterion, as Hallam and Mill pointed out and as Spedding's essay unwittingly demonstrates, favors the lowest common emotional and intellectual denominator. For insofar as sincerity was regarded as a form of vision or an expression of the deep common heart of humanity, it encouraged readers to dismiss feelings and values that they did not think true or valuable, to distrust introspection and idiosyncracy, and to prefer the familiar to the strange.

7

Tennyson, Browning, and Arnold, who of course found all sorts of peculiar and unacceptable impulses in their hearts, were extremely sensitive to approval and disapproval both. Tennyson was notoriously distressed by hostile criticism; Browning was too, though he would not admit it, and both tried and feared to "speak out." Arnold wrote sadly in 1858 that "if the opinion of the general public about my poems were the same as that of the leading literary men . . . I should gain the stimulus necessary to enable me to produce my best—all that I have in me, whatever that may be." [12] But they did not want people to see into their hearts, to apply Carlyle's biographical methods to them. "With this key / Shakespeare unlocked his heart," Wordsworth said of the sonnet; Browning's response—"If so, the less Shakespeare he!"—expresses the fear both that avid hordes are ready to rush in, and that indeed the doors are already wide open. *In Memoriam* is studded with doubts about its own propriety, and in later years Tennyson insisted that the "I" of the poem was not just the poet himself. Browning frequently felt it necessary to insist that all those people who sounded just like him were not him at all; he said it most adroitly, as if by the way, in "One Word More." Arnold tried to hide his private life (as did Tennyson and Browning), but he seems to have sent his poems forth pretty much undisguised—in the void they discover, there is little worth bothering to conceal. He and his family insisted, of course, that "Marguerite" was entirely fictional.

Poems with auditors are peculiarly suitable for both evading and exploring this situation. If the speaker is characterized as someone other than the poet, the poet can disavow his words, and dramatic context can always justify them. Furthermore, the speaker turns his back to the reader and enacts an attempt to communicate with someone whose responses he can immediately perceive and try to counter or control. Thus the poet can incorporate into the poem the reader he wants or fears, and try out ways of talking to him. He can objectify possible relationships between artist and audience, and show how different relationships produce different kinds of speech. Poems with auditors are about communication, regarding the individual as part of society and speech in terms of its effect on an audience, and mimicking, in the relation of speaker to auditor, the ambivalence with which Tennyson, Browning, and Arnold regarded their prospective readers.

The poets were confident of their own superiority, although they needed public approbation and shrank from indifference and hostility. Speech in these poems is the mark of power—when differences of status are indicated the speaker is usually superior (even Fra Lippo Lippi has a Medici patron)—

and the auditors are necessarily subordinate insofar as they are audience, not actors. The speaker exists as a voice, while the auditors are voiceless and exist only as the speaker's utterance recognizes them. But auditors have power too: the power to resist. They can remain unpersuaded, unmoved, hostile, or just indifferent; like the Bishop's sons or Andrea del Sarto's wife, they can refuse to listen, they can even walk away. The speaker's utterance defines itself in terms of the auditor, whose presence thus creates the possibility that the speaker might not be able to speak. The poems move between the opposite but complementary versions of the relation between poet and audience that Tennyson expressed in companion poems published in 1830: the poet's word is said to shake the world in "The Poet," but the presence of a sophist would blight the garden of "The Poet's Mind" and stop the fountains of his song.

In retrospect we can see that most of the qualities critics looked for in poetry during the 1830s and 1840s were those of the emerging Victorian novel. When Scott died in 1832 he had made the novel both popular and respectable; by the end of the next decade novelists were presenting the middle classes and the working poor instead of the aristocrats and criminals who had flourished in the fiction of the thirties, and presenting them in nineteenth-century England. No conflict was as yet apparent between quality and popularity or between present needs and available tradition: the best novels of the 1840s were best-sellers, and the novel, unlike poetry, had a usable past.[13]

The novel was becoming what poetry aspired to be: it spoke to and about ordinary nineteenth-century people, and large numbers of them listened. What they heard, moreover, was a speaking voice, man (or woman) talking to man. Bulwer-Lytton, who although perhaps not a very good novelist could perceive and emulate the achievements of his betters, explained in 1838 that in a novel (as opposed to a play) "we address ourselves to the one person."[14] During the years in which we find strong and persistent demands for communication from critics, and auditors in poems, we hear in novels the friendly voices of narrators welcoming and guiding us in their fictional worlds. And serial publication gave individual readers a chance to respond and at least to think they were being attended to, particularly when the first parts were published before the last were written.[15]

Reviewers of poetry in these decades paid an extraordinary amount of attention to the slightest hints of narrative and characterization. They praised anything that could be described as an affecting "incident" of common life, they liked to find nice people in poems, and they liked the people to seem familiarly real. Tennyson's early poems about women received a lot of notice, mostly favorable; even Arthur Hallam, who pointed out that Tennyson creates moods rather than characters, rhapsodized over Mariana and the likes of airy fairy Lilian without appearing to notice any significant difference between them. James Spedding commended "the depth of the pathos which [Tennyson] can evoke from the commonest incidents," and Leigh Hunt praised "Godiva" but added that Tennyson should have told us more about the heroine's feelings and those of the villagers who did not peep.[16] Occasionally reviewers seem to be thinking about the formal aspects of a poem and use metaphors like "delineation" from the visual arts—but they clearly thought of painting too, as most of their contemporaries did, in terms of narrative and portraiture, incident and characterization. Here, for instance, is Charles Kingsley introducing a Bellini portrait in 1848: "Now, this old man [the Doge in the painting, not Bellini] is a very ancient friend of mine, and has comforted my heart, and preached me a sharp sermon too, many a time. I never enter that Gallery without having five minutes' converse with him."[17] Not only is the picture a person; it talks and (we gather from "converse") listens.

Poems with auditors have many of the novelistic qualities that the reviewers wanted. Most of them enact an incident and all suggest one, many elaborately characterize the speaker and some characterize the auditor as well, many recount past incidents, and several contain the rudiments of a fictional autobiography. But we should be wary of reading them as innocently as Kingsley read the Doge. For not only is a short monologue an unsuitable medium for telling any story more complex than a romantic, pathetic, or melodramatic anecdote, its powers of characterization are highly limited and specialized. A monologue cannot depict character as the novel does, as a process of becoming, or incident as part of such a process. It can present a character in an act of self-definition, but it cannot really depict people living (as opposed to speaking) as social beings who both find and create a self as they experience the social world. The monologue lacks the resources to develop the temporal dimension, the notion of life as a continuing process of growth and change, that pervades all of Victorian thought and is essential to the Victorian novelist's sense of character. Mr. Farebrother in *Middlemarch* says: "character is not cut in marble—it is not something solid and unalterable. It is something living and changing, and may become diseased as our bodies do."[18] But if the speaker in a dramatic monologue were to enter a novel, he would have to be a minor figure whose nature does not change, or a Dickens grotesque, or a hero who has gotten stuck at the beginning of his career and never achieved his education. For the incidents that monologues enact are not formative or educative: they can reveal the speaker's character but they do not alter it.

The elaborate characterization of a speaker is itself a signal that the poet is interested in communicating with his readers. As T. S. Eliot says, "The mere fact that he is assuming a role, that he is speaking through a mask, implies the presence of an audience: why should a man put on fancy dress and a mask only to talk to himself?"[19] A dramatic monologue with or without an auditor is a performance: it requires an audience. The more richly the poet characterizes the speaker in a short poem, the more we admire his professional skill; if the characters unwittingly expose their own folly or vice, we enjoy in addition the sense of a tacit understanding between the poet and ourselves, a flattering tribute to our cleverness, virtue, and judgment.[20] In such poems the presence of auditors doubles the emphasis on communication that is already implicit in the form. The highly specialized concern of these poems is not to do something that novels and plays can do much better, but to establish poetry in the context of the overwhelmingly social world of nineteenth-century fiction and consider how and to what effect one can speak publicly of imaginative visions and private feelings in that world.

At the end of the line of poems with auditors stand four large, strange works that develop their basic strategy to explore a direct confrontation between the needs of poetry and the standards and values of prose fiction: *Maud* (1855), *Amours de Voyage* (1855), *Modern Love* (1862), and *Fifine at the Fair* (1872). Like the shorter poems, these make a group that at least in the Victorian period forms a unique type. *Fifine at the Fair* is a dramatic monologue with an auditor that has grown grotesquely beyond the limits of credibility. The other three consist of present-tense utterances that take place in a series of clearly defined present moments, with intervals between them in which other people react to what the speakers have done or said or imagined and thus define in turn the dramatic situation of the next utterance: these intervals contain the element that is represented in the shorter poems by the silence of the auditors.

As in the shorter poems, the speakers are conceived both as poetical and as social beings, constantly trying to superimpose imaginative patterns on the world, and yet constantly responsive to the changing and unexpected responses of other people. The poems tell stories of marriage, or courtship thwarted just short of marriage—that is, they deal with love in its double nature as the most personal and private of emotions, and as the most important legal bond normally contracted by social beings. And since these two aspects of love correspond to the two aspects of poetry—the expressive and the pragmatic, the visionary and the social—with which the shorter poems are concerned, they work out in their plots the same issues and conflicts. Their use of language shows a constant awareness that against the novelistic ethos of humaneness, moderation, relativism, and common sense that suffuses Victorian fiction and forms the narrative context of these poems, poetry was apt to sound selfish, absolutist, even violent—and worst of all, just silly. The poems are obtrusively contemporary in theme and setting and atmosphere and often use obtrusively poetical language, and by the incongruities that result the protagonists frequently call into question their own emotional honesty and verbal sincerity. The poets' attitude toward their speakers is correspondingly ambiguous, a mixture of ironic distancing and intense engagement that produces a tone at once unique, highly variable, and very difficult to define: the four poems sound alike because they all sound similarly peculiar. Furthermore, each poem appears to be rooted in a crucial episode of the poet's own social and passionate life, and the element of autobiography seems to add a final intensity and complication to the problem of reconciling poetic impulse, imagination, and desire with the realities of social life.

Most poems with auditors are usually classified as dramatic monologues, and almost all critics would put the rest in that category too if they thought that the speaker was deliberately characterized as someone other than the poet. The Victorians wrote dramatic monologues of many sorts without grouping them at all consistently under that name or any other—as a glance at Browning's and Arnold's classifications of their own poems will show—and many attempts have since been made to define the form, its function, its sources, and its significance in literary and intellectual history. The "perfect" dramatic monologue has been described as one containing "speaker, audience, occasion, revelation of character, interplay between speaker and audience, dramatic action, and action which takes place in the present";[21] this is informative but too restrictive to have been very useful. Most studies, in fact, take "revelation of character" as the single essential and defining criterion. The most influential as well as the broadest in scope has of course been Robert Langbaum's *The Poetry of Experience*, with its brilliant analysis of dramatic monologues as products of a relativistic age that is overwhelmingly concerned with human character. Langbaum's formulation of the "tension between sympathy and moral judgment" in the reader's response has done much to save us from the assumption that we read poems mostly for the pleasure of feeling smarter and better than their speakers, but it inevitably puts the highest value on characterization at its most striking and extreme: "most successful dramatic monologues deal with speakers who are in some way reprehensible." [22] Park Honan's definition—"'a single discourse by one whose presence is indicated by the poet but who is not the poet himself'"—despite its deliberate generality focuses even more exclusively on characterization: it would presumably not include, for instance, "Dover Beach," although a man looking out of a window at Dover and talking to a woman cannot be identical with a man writing a poem on a piece of paper, wherever he may be. [23] That there is much to be learned from focusing on other aspects of the monologue form and on more than one writer has been shown in A. Dwight Culler's analysis of "Ulysses" and *Maud* as late examples of monodrama, a form that presents the varied emotions of a solitary figure and is essentially musical and expressive, and by Alan Sinfield's location of the form "on the border between" fiction and self-expression. [24]

But none of these approaches is able to make much sense of auditors. Langbaum concludes that the presence or absence of auditors is finally of no importance since the speaker is always really talking to himself. Honan finds that in the twenty Browning poems he studies "the auditor element may be said to be an objectified representation of some aspect of the speaker's own being." Culler asks us to imagine music in the background of "Ulysses" and inquires: "With these accompaniments would one worry about Penelope or little Telemachus?" [25] And yet Tennyson forces us to worry about Telemachus (who surely is not "little"), although he does not guide us to a firm conclusion, and it is just this obscure persistence of the auditor element—it does not seem to account for itself, but it is still obstinately there—that makes it call so urgently for explanation. Langbaum dismisses auditors and dramatic situations alike with the interesting general observation that in dramatic monologues "the motive for speaking is inadequate to the utterance . . . the utterance is in other words largely gratuitous," and that "the speakers never accomplish anything by their utterance, and seem to know from the start that they will not." [26] This is by no means always true—the speeches of Tiresias and Mr. Sludge, for instance, accomplish a good deal—but the fact that it often *is* true surely suggests a quite different conclusion: if the dramatic situations with all their distracting specificity have so little real function, matter so much less than their prominence in the poems seems to indicate, then why are they there at all? Some of them appear in poems which, like "The Buried Life," show no interest whatever in characterization. Sinfield, on the other hand, suggests that the auditor points up the fictionality of the speaker,[27] but auditors most often appear with speakers whom no one could possibly take to be the poet himself, while Arnold's auditor poems are not dramatic monologues and hardly fictionalize the speakers at all. The presence of auditors is adequately accounted for, however, if we assume that the poet does not create the dramatic situation and the utterance to display the character, but rather that he invents the character and the situation to define the status of the utterance and to let us watch what it does.

Too much emphasis on either characterization or the lyrical element and too strong an insistence on erecting barriers between dramatic monologues and dramatic lyrics obscure the fact that in writing poems with responsive auditors the three major Victorian poets more or less simultaneously invented a new kind of poem at the beginnings both of Victorian poetry and of their own careers. The brilliant success with which most of these poems exploit their peculiar formal strategy has led us to take that strategy for granted, seldom considering that it was very rare even at the height of its brief popularity and that it is very unwieldy except in some special and peculiar sorts of dramatic situations. There are actually so few such poems that it will be possible to take account of all of them, as well as some interesting further developments, in this study: an undertaking made more attractive by the fact that they include a very large portion both of the best Victorian poems and of those that have generated the most interesting controversy and the most widely divergent readings. The same considerations, moreover, apply to the longer poems in which the auditor element appears: while there are other long poems composed of lyrics set against the background of an implied narrative—"Switzerland," for instance, "James Lee's Wife," or *The Angel in the House*—no others enact the protagonist's engagement with other people or present the use of language and literary convention as an essential aspect of such engagement.[28] And here too the form calls for explanation partly because of its apparent awkwardness: it is so evidently ill-suited to the job of telling a complicated story that does not follow a familiarly conventional plot. As with the shorter poems with auditors, the wonder is not that there are so few of these, but that there are so many and that they are so good.

The chapters that follow trace the history of Victorian poems with auditors through the careers of the three major poets, beginning with Tennyson's revi-

14

sions of "St Simeon Stylites" in 1833 and considering *Maud* and *Fifine at the Fair* as developments of their authors' earlier monologues, and then turn to Clough and Meredith. This organization violates chronology and breaks up the group of longer poems, but it has the advantage of providing a double focus for *Maud* and *Fifine*. Considering all these poems together, short and long alike, enables us to see how a distinctive new strategy developed in response to a new literary situation: how major poets first explored the problem of being a poet in an age when the tone and values of mimetic fiction were coming to represent the literary norm. Grouping the poems in this way cuts across categories that have become habitual in critical thinking, especially dramatic monologue and dramatic lyric. It brings to our attention elements that do not seem very significant until we begin to see how consistently they recur, such as the tendency to associate speech itself with power and aggression. And it shows us multifarious relations between works that we do not generally think about together except in the broadest and most general terms.

⋙ ONE ⋘

Tennyson

TENNYSON WROTE "ST SIMEON STYLITES" in the fall of 1833, probably just before Arthur Hallam died, and "Ulysses" and part of "Tiresias" soon after the news of Hallam's death had reached him.[1] The speaker in each is an old man—a saint, a prophet, a hero—who dreams dreams and pursues visions. Until the moment enacted in the poem, the intensity of his experiences and his concentrated yearnings have served increasingly to cut him off from the world of ordinary human beings. Simeon is high on a pillar, Tiresias's prophecies have gone unheeded, and Ulysses bitterly feels himself an alien at his own still hearth. Isolation, failure, and bodily decrepitude have weakened and disheartened them. But the poems present each in his moment of power and triumphant social reintegration, breaking out of self-enclosure by the act of successfully imposing his visions on his auditors. Simeon is proclaimed not only healer but saint; Tiresias, attended to at last, saves Thebes; Ulysses' mariners follow him away to seek a newer world. From the point of view of the three speakers themselves, this is all to the good, a happy end to isolation and paralysis. For their auditors, however, the advantage is more dubious. Simeon leads his admirers deeper into foolish superstition; Tiresias persuades a young man to kill himself; Ulysses is taking his mariners to their death, and perhaps—since Tennyson's source for the poem is Dante's *Inferno*—to hell.

In these poems, speech is action. Each includes an utterance that causes things to happen and that is itself an event. In contrast to later dramatic monologues, which tend to show habitual behavior and recurrent or typical situations ("My Last Duchess," for instance, or "The Love Song of J. Alfred Prufrock"), the events in these poems are unique ones that decisively alter

16

both the speakers' lives and—certainly in "Tiresias," in the dramatic situation of "Ulysses" if not so clearly in its tone, and to some extent in "St Simeon" too—the lives of the auditors as well. The decisive event takes place during, and as the direct and immediate consequence of, the utterance that is the poem; it is the speaker's successful communication of his private vision to his auditors. The poems, then, suggest both that such communication of vision is possible, and that for the hearers it can be very dangerous.

A famous episode from Tennyson's undergraduate years provides a suggestive introduction to these poems, a paradigm of how he conceived of the relation between a poet and his audience and of how nervous the conception made him. The center of his intellectual and social life at Cambridge was the society known as The Apostles, and Hallam Tennyson reports: "'Ghosts' was the subject of an essay written by my father for the Society, but he was too shy to deliver it."[2] He therefore had to resign his membership (and was made an honorary member instead). But the essay is not so much about ghosts as about telling ghost stories: it first describes with comic gusto the immense power of a storyteller over his listeners, and then presents the beginning of a discussion that was no doubt intended to sound like a meeting of the society itself.

If any of my friends have the power of telling deep, horrible agreeable ghost stories, he will not only be sure of auditors & numerous ones too but he will feel himself in possession of Power greater than that of the Caesars—a Power over the inmost recesses of the human mind, a despotism voluntarily submitted to, with shuddering & with delight: every cheek is blanched, every eye fixed upon the narrator: he speaks in a simple manner of a high matter: he speaks of life & death & the things after death: he lifts the veil but the form behind it is shrouded in deeper obscurity: he raises the cloud but he darkens the prospect: he unlocks with a golden key the iron grated gates of the charnel-house; he throws them wide open: & forth issue from the inmost gloom the colossal Presences of the Past majores humano some as they lived, seemingly pale with exhaustion & faintly smiling; some as they died in a still agony, like the dumb rage of the Glaciers of Chamouny, a fearful convulsion suddenly frozen by the chill of Death & some as they were buried, with dropped eyelids, in their cerements & their winding sheets. The circle becomes gradually more contracted: his listeners creep closer to each other: they are afraid of the drawings of their own breath & the beatings of their own hearts: his voice alone like a mountain stream on a still night fills up & occupies the silence: he stands as it were on a vantage-ground he becomes the minister & expounder of human sympathies: his words <u>find</u> the heart like the arrows of truth: those who laughed before have long ago become solemn & those who were solemn before feel their hair bristle & their flesh creep with a sense of unutterable mystery.

The rest of the second surviving page of the manuscript is crossed out but clearly legible.

"And wherefore" says one "granting the intensity of the feeling wherefore this fever & fret about a baseless vision?" "Do not assume" responds another "upon the authority of a quotation from Shakespeare that any vision is baseless. There is rhyme & reason for every thing. The impressions [the next page has been torn away].[3]

Like the three 1833 monologues, this essay imagines the storyteller communicating vision and exercising power through the spoken word. The act of communication is personal, intense, successful, and charged on both sides with danger. While the speaker displays his despotic power and barely disguised aggression (described in gloating hyperbole only partially mitigated by humor) the eyes of his audience are fixed upon him and their circle tightens about him. And the mixture of fear and affectionate intimacy that the fragment describes is reflected in Tennyson's behavior: he was too shy to read his essay, encircled by such eyes.

The awkward jocularity does not mean that Tennyson took the subject lightly: on the contrary, it probably indicates that he was more serious than he cared to admit. A ghost story, after all, is a less dignified version of Tennyson's own theme in his many poems about the visionary world and reunion with the dead, with a particular emphasis on the element of fear and danger. Perhaps he recalled the account in the preface to *Frankenstein* of Shelley and Byron and a few other friends reading ghost stories aloud in Geneva—that preface repudiates belief in "supernatural terrors" but defends their value for art.[4] Moreover, Tennyson is apparently quoting from Ovid's account of a perfectly dignified ghost,[5] the charnel-house ghoulishness seems to echo "Adonais" and "The Triumph of Life,"[6] and the allusions to *The Tempest* that open the discussion remind us of Prospero, the benevolent despot of imagination who renounced his power to call up spirits.[7] The return of the dead is a main concern—almost an obsession—of Tennyson's poetry, early and late; "Hark! the dogs howl," which Hallam Tennyson called the "germ of *In Memoriam*," strikingly recalls the ghosts essay:

The vapour labours up the sky,
Uncertain forms are darkly moved,
Larger than human passes by
The shadow of the man I loved.
(18–21)

("Forth issue from the inmost gloom the colossal Presences of the Past majores humano.")[8] But the most compelling testimony to Tennyson's feelings about such matters is another incident recorded by his son: "My father told me that within a week after his father's death [in March 1831] he slept in the dead man's bed, earnestly desiring to see his ghost, but no ghost came. 'You see,' he said, 'ghosts do not generally come to imaginative people.'"[9]

The teller of ghost stories, then, has a subject that Tennyson took with profound if enigmatic seriousness. The mode of oral presentation accords with Tennyson's lifelong practice, from the children's elaborate rituals of storytelling at Somersby Rectory to the Laureate's famous recitations.[10] For his Cambridge friends he would recite and improvise poems,[11] and when he launched the first of the *Idylls of the King*, the "Morte d'Arthur," he framed it with "The Epic" (probably written 1837–1838), which tells how the poet reads his work aloud to a circle of friends and how the friends respond. Testing the story— which presents a transhuman world of vision, imagination, magic, and hope for the return of the dead—by its effect on its audience, "The Epic" both jokes about it and affirms its worth and power. One listener falls asleep, but another justifies the poem and fulfills its desire by dreaming that night of King Arthur's return. "St Simeon Stylites," "Tiresias," and "Ulysses" consider the relationship between a visionary speaker and his auditors more thoroughly and seriously than the essay on ghosts or "The Epic" does, and with even deeper ambivalence.

The dark humor of "St Simeon Stylites" and the way it exploits the modulations of the speaking voice link this poem, in which Victorian auditors make their first appearance, to the essay on ghosts. The poem would have been suitable for the sort of comic performance with which Tennyson used to amuse his friends. (He particularly liked to impersonate Milton's Satan squatting like a toad at the ear of Eve, "Assaying by his Devilish art to reach / The Organs of her Fancy, and with them forge / Illusions as he list, Phantasms and Dreams.")[12] Simeon is always vociferously talking—arguing, exhorting, cajoling, explaining—but to different auditors at different times. He addresses God (1–130), the people standing around at the foot of the pillar (131–142), himself (143–157), the people again (157–194), himself and angelic phantoms (195–210), concluding with a brief exhortation to the people (211–218) and final instructions to the Lord (218–220). Despite some moments of self-forgetfulness and self-doubt, he is almost always conscious of being heard or overheard, so that the whole poem seems to be spoken aloud. He does not pray: he talks to God as if God were a person who needed explanations, reminders, and instructions.

> And I had hoped that ere this period closed
> Thou wouldst have caught me up into thy rest,
> Denying not these weather-beaten limbs
> The meed of saints, the white robe and the palm.
> (17–20)

He argues:

> O Jesus, if thou wilt not save my soul,
> Who may be saved? who is it may be saved?
> (45–46)

He is politely reproachful:

> Bethink thee, Lord, while thou and all the saints
> Enjoy themselves in heaven . . .
> (103–104)

God does not reply, nor does Simeon seem to expect him to. Simeon has had enough experience of supernatural responses, in fact, to make him wary of colloquy with the divine. Long ago instead of speaking he used to sing, an expressive activity that did not require or even allow any response: his hymns and psalms drowned out other noises (32–33), and the angel who sometimes came to "stand and watch" him sing was silent (33–34). Demonic visitors, in contrast, came closer and spoke up. There were devils who tormented him and "With colt-like whinny and with hoggish whine / . . . burst my prayer" (174–175); these he escaped by mortifying his flesh. But more articulate devils are less easily evaded; these represent not just the temptations of the flesh, but a bewildering parodic reflection of Simeon's own thoughts: "they prate /

Of penances I cannot have gone through, / Perplexing me with lies" (98–100). Thus even when he finally sees an angel who, after a bit of teasing, lets him have his crown of sanctity, he has a final fleeting doubt: "Ah! let me not be fooled" (209). (He is probably recalling that he has been embarrassingly fooled by a vision before. Gibbon records "a piece of ancient scandal": "the Devil, assuming an angelic form, invited him to ascend, like Elijah, into a fiery chariot. The saint too hastily raised his foot, and Satan seized the moment of inflicting this chastisement [an ulcer] on his vanity.")[13]

About the response of the crowd at his feet, however, there need be no such ambiguity, and Simeon accepts it as definitive. Here is true reciprocity, an interchange of gifts in which power bestowed returns intensified upon the giver. Simeon ends his fruitless address to God and speaks to the people, asking the halt and maimed to come forward and be cured.

> Yes, I can heal him. Power goes forth from me.
> They say that they are healed. Ah, hark! they shout
> "St Simeon Stylites."
> (143–145)

For the first time, finally, he is named a saint. He accepts the words as definitive, hearing them echoed from above and echoing them himself.

> They shout, "Behold a saint!"
> And lower voices saint me from above.
> Courage, St Simeon! This dull chrysalis
> Cracks into shining wings.
> (151–154)

This is the moment that Simeon has long and wearily awaited, and he does not turn back. His new and sudden delight, exaltation, and confidence last to the end of the poem.

The potential usefulness and significance of such responsive human auditors seem to have become apparent to Tennyson after he had already written most of the poem. There appear to be two different conceptions at work in it, almost two different poems. The first is a rather cheerful, conventionally English and Protestant mockery of extreme asceticism, with particular emphasis on the speaker's self-deceptions and self-seeking, and on the paradox of his exceedingly conspicuous retreat, his very public privacy. The second conception, on the other hand, emphasizes the imaginative energies that went into

Simeon's folly and impressed it so vividly on the minds of others; it also stresses the complicated interplay between the doubting visionary and the crowd that reassures him. In early drafts of the poem only the first conception appears: Tennyson is evidently enjoying himself, piling up absurdities to mock an easy target. The passages that Tennyson added to the first version, however, strike a consistently different note.[14]

The most significant additions are the response of the crowd (143–157) and Simeon's memory and fear of being deluded by devils (91–102, 166–182, 209).[15] The others seem designed mostly to work toward the creation of a tone of imaginative richness and beauty, moderating the grotesquerie that predominated earlier. They include such lines as these:

> A sign betwixt the meadow and the cloud
> (14)

> Or in the night, after a little sleep,
> I wake: the chill stars sparkle; I am wet
> With drenching dews, or stiff with crackling frost.
> (111–113)

> And you may carve a shrine about my dust,
> And burn a fragrant lamp before my bones.
> (192–193)

Except for the omission of two extremely grotesque images—the "scent" of an ulcer (from line 67) and bats that hung from Simeon's ears (from lines 160–161)—and some small improvements in wording, these three categories account for all the revisions after the first completed version. The effect is to diminish the merely satirical aspects of the poem and enhance its visionary ones. "Ah! let me not be fooled, sweet saints" (209) even echoes King Lear, another old man who was grotesquely exposed to the elements: "O, let me not be mad, not mad, sweet heaven" (I.v.40).

The manuscripts that let us follow the change in Tennyson's conception of the poem also suggest how the change might have come about. Tennyson cited two sources for the poem, William Hone's *Every-Day Book* and Gibbon's *Decline and Fall of the Roman Empire*, and the difference between Tennyson's first versions of the poem and his final one is essentially that between Hone's treatment of the subject and Gibbon's. The first drafts follow, in tone and in detail, Hone's cheerful account of the anchorite's foolish and nasty self-mortifications. But then, perhaps, Tennyson turned to the *Decline and Fall* (an obvious book to consult) and found a wider context and a much more interesting point of view. For in Gibbon's richly contemptuous account of the rise of monasticism Simeon is the chief representative not only of its folly but also of its popular success. "The monastic saints, who excite only the contempt and pity of a philosopher, were respected and almost adored by the prince and people. Successive crowds of pilgrims from Gaul and India saluted the divine pillar of Simeon."[16] Gibbon presents monasticism as a great popular movement, and the monastic ideal as silly and bad, but of immense imaginative potency. It is as the willing victims of this grotesque and tainted power— victims whose eager acquiescence Tennyson found vividly recorded as historical fact—that responsive auditors enter Victorian poetry.

Themes that are comically base in "St Simeon" become sad, serious, and even heroic in the poems Tennyson wrote just after he heard of Hallam's death. The saint's isolation from human society combined with a rather resentful desire for human recognition, his fortitude in extreme old age and desire for death, and his sense of tremendous moral superiority all reappear, qualitatively transformed, in Tiresias and Ulysses. It is as if "St Simeon Stylites" were a proleptic parody. When Tiresias laments the inefficacy of his wisdom—that is, the fact that no one seriously attends to it—he imagines for himself an apotheosis very much like Simeon's.

> O therefore that the unfulfilled desire,
> The grief for ever born from griefs to be,
> The boundless yearning of the Prophet's heart—
> Could *that* stand forth, and like a statue, reared
> To some great citizen, win all praise from all
> Who past it, saying, "That was he!"
>
> In vain!
> (78–83)

In early versions of this passage he imagines himself not only admired, not only sanctified, but actually deified by the admiration of a crowd.

> O therefore that the dumb & errant thought
> The secret purpose of the noble heart

23

Blighted from bearing [?] of action, could
Stand forth & like a solid statue set
Upon a pedestal collect all praise
Till contemplation made us Gods. In Vain. [17]

Tiresias wants to save the city of Thebes. But though he knows what must be done, he cannot himself do it. His vision, even more than Simeon's, has no virtue—can bear no fruit—until others recognize it. Inspired by that vision, though, Menoeceus not only can act to save the city; he can become what Tiresias vainly aspires to be. Tiresias promises him the persuasive power he himself so urgently desires:

> No sound is breathed so potent to coerce,
> And to conciliate, as their names who dare
>
> .   .   .   .
>
> Nobly to do, nobly to die. Their names,
> Graven on memorial columns, are a song
> Heard in the future.
>   (116–121)

The purport of this exhortation is, almost literally, a crude antiliterary cliché: actions speak louder than words. [18] "No sound is . . . so potent" as the name of a hero. But Tiresias is really concerned, as the cliché itself suggests, not to weigh the relative merits of speech and action, but to blur the distinction between them. Menoeceus's deed itself will be produced by the words Tiresias is saying—that is, paradoxically, by Tiresias's lament about his own uselessness. And that deed will make Menoeceus's name—the word itself, "graven" in stone—into a "song" which will in turn produce further deeds. The "examples" of heroic deeds

> reach a hand
> Far through all years, and everywhere they meet
> And kindle generous purpose, and the strength
> To mould it into action pure as theirs.
>   (122–125)

Tennyson revised, completed, and published "Tiresias" in the 1880s, but the part of the poem that is formally a dramatic monologue with an auditor, and which deals with the problem of communicating vision, was largely written in 1833. In the first part Tiresias tells how he lost his eyesight and acquired the gift of prophecy. This is notably undramatic: so much so, that we must almost forget the dramatic situation if Tiresias is not to seem simply long-winded, egocentric, and insensitive. The last part, which was written in the 1880s and is spoken after Menoeceus has gone, is straightforwardly a soliloquy, in which Tiresias expresses his wish to die. But at the center of the poem is a dramatic utterance explicitly addressed to the auditor and urgently concerned with his response which dates mostly from 1833. Here Tiresias describes his misery at being possessed of a vision he cannot communicate, and, communicating it at last, sends Menoeceus to his death.

First, however, he sets forth the ambiguous nature and dangerous consequences of vision as he himself experienced it. As in several other poems that Tennyson wrote in the early 1830s, an encounter with divinity is presented in sexual terms. Wandering in search of knowledge, "With some strange hope to see the nearer God" (28), Tiresias saw Athena coming naked from her bath and was blinded both in punishment and as proper consequence: "'Henceforth be blind, for thou hast seen too much'" (48). (We may recall that Tennyson's severe and recurrent hypochondria tended to focus on his eyesight.) The theme of blindness is doubled by references to Oedipus and the sphinx that suggest a further association of blindness with forbidden knowledge. The encounter with Athena does not appear in the surviving 1833 drafts, although it may have been on some of the pages that were torn out of the notebooks, but it is epitomized in the 1833 version of the opening lines: "I looked upon divinity unveiled / And wisdom naked."[19] Moreover, the notebook that contains the major 1833 drafts also contains, as if in its stead, "Semele," in which the vision of the divine becomes explicitly carnal and destructive knowledge.

> I wished to see Him. Who may feel
> His light and live? He comes.
> The blast of Godhead bursts the doors.
> (1–3)

Like Semele, Tiresias was both exalted and consumed by his vision; communicating it to Menoeceus, he exalts and destroys him too.

The completed poem repeatedly stresses the fact of this repetition, especially at the beginning and end of Tiresias's speech to Menoeceus. Tiresias first tells the story of Ares' anger against Thebes (11–17), and then recounts the effect that story had on him when he was a young man hearing it from an old one:

A tale, that told to me,
When but thine age, by age as winter-white
As mine is now, amazed, but made me yearn
For larger glimpses of that more than man.
(17–20)

The tale led him to Athena and his doom, just as his retelling of it preludes
the doom of Menoeceus. He makes a similar though more complicated connection when his long exhortation is almost completed and he sends Menoeceus to sacrifice himself at the cave where Oedipus once found the sphinx:

There blanch the bones of whom she slew, and these
Mixt with her own, because the fierce beast found
A wiser than herself, and dashed herself
Dead in her rage: but thou are wise enough,
Though young, to love thy wiser, blunt the curse
Of Pallas, hear, and though I speak the truth
Believe I speak it.
(145–151)

In the implied contrast, blind Tiresias is blind Oedipus, now seeking to be
absolved from the curse of his knowledge by a hearer who will believe his
words without resenting them and knowing, willing, but guiltless, choose
darkness for himself:

let thine own hand strike
Thy youthful pulses into rest and quench
The red God's anger, fearing not to plunge
Thy torch of life in darkness.
(151–154)

Dying to save Thebes, Menoeceus dies also to complete the work that Tiresias
cannot do.

"Ulysses" is a very much richer and more important poem than either "St
Simeon" or "Tiresias," but it is like them formally, thematically, and in details
of phrase and cadence. "To follow knowledge like a sinking star, / Beyond the
utmost bound of human thought" (31–32) comes from the draft of the begin-

ning of "Tiresias." More surprisingly, Ulysses' resonant exhortation to his mariners echoes Simeon's querulous argument with God.

> It may be that the gulfs will wash us down:
> It may be we shall touch the Happy Isles.
> ("Ulysses," 62–63)

> It may be I have wrought some miracles,
>
> .   .   .   .
>
> It may be, no one, even among the saints,
> May match his pains with mine.
> ("St Simeon," 134–137)

These two speakers are similarly determined, in similar language, to persevere. Ulysses' last words recall, in both content and cadence, Simeon's first ones.

> Although I be the basest of mankind,
> From scalp to sole one slough and crust of sin,
> Unfit for earth, unfit for heaven, scarce meet
> For troops of devils, mad with blasphemy,
> I will not cease to grasp the hope I hold
> Of saintdom, and to clamour, mourn and sob
> Battering the gates of heaven.
> ("St Simeon," 1–7)

> Though much is taken, much abides; and though
> We are not now that strength which in old days
> Moved earth and heaven; that which we are, we are;
> One equal temper of heroic hearts,
> Made weak by time and fate, but strong in will
> To strive, to seek, to find, and not to yield.
> ("Ulysses," 65–70)

The end of the later poem circles back to echo the beginning of the earlier one, so that in the last line of "Ulysses" we can hear not only Milton's heroically fallen archangel, but Tennyson's comically ascendant saint.

Unlike Simeon and Tiresias, Ulysses seems concerned less with affecting others than with articulating his feelings and fixing his own resolve. But Tennyson's hero is based on Dante's Ulisse, who is in the circle of hell reserved for evil counselors. Both heroes summon their men to follow them beyond the limits of the mortal world: Dante's Ulisse passes the Gates of Hercules, and arrives at the Mount of Purgatory, and Tennyson's Ulysses hopes to see Achilles in "the Happy Isles"—the world of visionary experience, the world of ghosts. Dante followed the Roman tradition of a Ulysses notorious for cunning and rhetorical skill. His Ulisse reports both his speech to his mariners and its powerful effect on them:

> With these few words I sharpen'd for the voyage
> The mind of my associates, that I then
> Could scarcely have withheld them.[20]

Our sense that Ulysses' auditors are also moved to follow him comes partly from our knowledge of what happens in the *Commedia*, partly from our unconscious assumption as we read that they will share our own responsiveness to the poetry, and most subtly and conclusively from the replacement in the last nine lines of "I" and "you" by "we" and "us"; there are six first-person plural pronouns in the first six of these final lines. "*My* purpose holds," Ulysses says, to sail "until *I* die." And immediately after: "It may be that the gulfs will wash *us* down" (my italics).

Dante records Ulisse's story as an admonition to himself as a poet:

> Then sorrow seiz'd me, which e'en now revives,
> As my thought turns again to what I saw,
> And, more than I am wont, I rein and curb
> The powers of nature in me, lest they run
> Where Virtue guides not; that if aught of good
> My gentle star, or something better gave me,
> I envy not myself the precious boon.
> (20–26)

Tennyson, too, probably saw Ulisse as a warning against the misuse of imaginative powers. Both in Tennyson's poem and in Dante's the speakers persuade, not through cleverness or cunning, but by eloquence—and their eloquence moves most (though not all) readers of the poems as well as the fictional auditors within them. (Even Carlyle, who was gruffly contemptuous of modern poetry, found himself moved *almost* to tears by Tennyson's poem.)[21] "Ulysses" resembles the episode in the *Inferno* most of all by the fact that many readers experience them both as raising, finally, the same problem: how freely should we respond to the speaker's noble eloquence? Are we to admire his heroic spirit, or condemn him for antireligious or antisocial pride—or both?[22]

Tennyson explicitly invited biographical readings of "Ulysses," and gave no hint whatsoever that he was out of sympathy with his hero: the poem "was written soon after Arthur Hallam's death, and gave my feeling about the need of going forward, and braving the struggle of life perhaps more simply than anything in 'In Memoriam.'"[23] In the context of Tennyson's reaction to Hallam's death "going forward," if it meant anything more than not committing suicide or pining away, meant doing what Hallam had regarded as Tennyson's true work: writing poetry. Ulysses' repudiation of his social responsibilities in Ithaca has disturbed many readers, but it is fully consonant with Hallam's views on poetry. In his essay on Tennyson's poems, Hallam says that good poetry will probably not, at the present time, be popular, since most readers are too dull and lazy to read it well. He regards it as the task of the reader, not the poet, to change: he certainly does not suggest that the poet should be a Telemachus, addressing himself with "slow prudence" to the improvement of national taste. The review stresses the notion, a commonplace at the time, that the freshness and vitality of a literature in harmony with the people belonged to the youth of the world and "the youthful periods of any literature."

> Hence the melancholy which so evidently characterises the spirit of modern poetry; hence that return of the mind upon itself and the habit of seeking relief in idiosyncrasies rather than community of interest. In the old times the poetic impulse went along with the general impulse of the nation; in these it is a reaction against it.[24]

Modern poetry is "old," like Ulysses; but "Old age hath yet his honour and his toil" ("Ulysses," 50), and "Some work of noble note, may yet be done" (52). Hallam says of Tennyson's poems: "How wonderful the new world thus created for us, the region between real and unreal."[25] Ulysses, heading into the unpeopled ocean, says, "'Tis not too late to seek a newer world" (57). For Tennyson as a poet, this is not a bad definition of "the struggle of life," or of the work the poem itself accomplishes: it makes a "work of noble note" of a subject that had been treated in the younger days of literature by Homer, Dante, and Shakespeare.

If it were not for the Telemachus passage, we would probably not think much about any antisocial or life-negating implications in Ulysses' speech. And that passage, like the response of the crowd in "St Simeon Stylites," seems not to have been part of Tennyson's first conception. The earliest manuscript goes directly from the opening soliloquy to the Dantesque exhortation to the mariners, with the Telemachus passage added at the end.[26] "This is my son" implies that both Telemachus himself and others are present; at this point in the poem we know nothing of the mariners, and since the tone is quite unlike that in which Ulysses spoke to himself or will speak to his men, it seems likely (there can be no certainty) that the others are ordinary Ithacans. Even this shadowy suggestion of their presence makes an enormous difference. For they incorporate into our experience of the poem the point of view of the ordinary social world, the humdrum common humanity from which Ulysses so vigorously asserted his separateness in the opening lines. Furthermore, we have now to consider not just what the speaker says, but the fact that he is speaking out loud under particular circumstances to particular auditors. Thus his contemptuous dismissal of his "agèd wife" (3) in the first part of the poem is less disturbing than what seems the bland condescension of praising to his face the sober virtues of his son.[27] For the barest suggestion that Telemachus might actually be listening makes Telemachus real to us in a way that Penelope in the opening is not.

Perhaps the most interesting thing about Ulysses' ceremonious farewell to ordinary people is that as soon as he addresses them directly his language, which in the rest of the poem is marvellously rich and expressive, fails him. Auditors represent the world that calls into question not only the values but also the language of poetry. The passage has a touch of the flatness and flaccidity, the lifeless pomposity that so often afflicts Tennyson's celebrations of decent communal virtues.

> This is my son, mine own Telemachus,
> To whom I leave the sceptre and the isle—
> Well-loved of me, discerning to fulfil
> This labour.
> (33–36)

The praise is so unconvincing that many readers quite reasonably suspect the presence of irony. But in tone, content, and vocabulary it is nearly indistinguishable from the ending of "The Two Voices," which is certainly not ironical.

> One walked between his wife and child,
> With measured footfall firm and mild,
> And now and then he gravely smiled.

The prudent partner of his blood
Leaned on him, faithful, gentle, good.
(412–416)

The main difference between this passage and the one from "Ulysses" is that the latter is rhythmically and syntactically more complicated. Both are notably inferior poetically to the rest of the poems in which they appear. As in much of "The Palace of Art" and "Oenone," the poetry does not manage to validate the assertions of the moral will: we hear moral but not aesthetic conviction.

It is reasonable to suppose that Tennyson could perceive the relative weakness of such passages—which is not to say that he deliberately wrote badly—and that such a perception contributed to his fear that genuine poetry and social responsibility might turn out to be incompatible. (In the early thirties he wrote quite a lot of political poetry, aiming for a tone of lofty impersonality, with mixed success.) Not only does the speech in praise of Telemachus leave most readers pretty cold, the poem does not show it as persuading any fictional auditors either. The total effect of the passage is to remind us that the greatness of aspiration, experience, and vision that makes Ulysses so potent a speaker in the rest of the poem also makes him unfit to fulfill his obligations as a social being: it dramatizes not only the cool formality with which he acknowledges the rights and values of ordinary decent people, but also their corresponding unresponsiveness. By its very attenuation, the dramatic character of the scene demonstrates the impassable gulf between the visionary speaker and the ordinary world. Ulysses is eloquent and persuasive only to those who have shared his experiences: "Souls that have toiled, and wrought, and thought" (46) with him, that like him "strove with Gods" (53). His praise of Telemachus is stiff and awkward, but he calls his men into the unknown as if with a magical incantation and with irresistible power.

The monologue that is most like these three, and thus most instructively different, is "Tithonus," begun like the others in the fall of 1833 and described by Tennyson as a "pendant" to "Ulysses." The criteria that make the first three a group exclude "Tithonus" on only one point: his auditor is not a human being. Tithonus too is old and tired, isolated from human society—literally, like Simeon, above it—because he has seen and known the divine, and filled with longing for death. But his words do not make anything happen. His speech represents just the opposite of a unique and decisive event: it is part of the eventless circularity, the endless diurnal recurrence, that has entrapped him. Eos is emotionally responsive, but to no effect; she is moved, but not to do anything. For not only is she not human, she is part of the natural world that can only repeat its patterns and has in effect no will to work on. The tears that express her pity are the mists and dews that rise with every dawn. Although she is separate from the speaker, she cannot be said to have or represent a point of view—certainly not a social or human one—or to suggest potential points of view to the reader. Instead of opposition "Tithonus" contains resonating parallels (Eos is lover, goddess, natural phenomenon, perhaps a symbol of art) and a single, coherent emotion. Tithonus does not want to attain, test, validate, justify, or communicate a vision: he wants to escape the one he has all too fully realized. No social world counterbalances the visionary one, no Ithaca or Thebes. There is only the primitive pastoral earth seen as a far-off object of hopeless desire: for Tithonus there is really no place but the vast and empty spaces through which he wanders like the sad ghost of his human self, "A white-haired shadow roaming like a dream" (8).

By 1833 Tennyson's finest and most distinctive poetic achievement had been precisely the creation of such lyrical spaces, in which beauty exists only by virtue of the inhabitants' isolation. In "The Lotos-Eaters," self-enclosure in art is rendered in brilliantly literal terms:

> if his fellow spake,
> His voice was thin, as voices from the grave;
> And deep-asleep he seemed, yet all awake,
> And music in his ears his beating heart did make.
> (33–36)

The Lady of Shalott eventually finds her loneliness intolerable, but when she leaves her tower the world that was bright in her mirror turns rainy and gray, and she dies. Those who do not leave their towers of art, however, are likely to find them filling up with phantoms and hallucinations, projections of madness and images of death. Mariana's house is haunted by old faces, old footsteps, old voices; the Palace of Art, more disagreeably, by phantasms, nightmares, shades, and corpses. Near the end of "The Palace of Art," the self-immured soul feels itself "Shut up as in a crumbling tomb, girt round / With blackness as a solid wall" (273–274); and then, in a beautiful simile, it is as if the tomb has crumbled away and the soul has emerged into a world beyond humanity or death:

As in strange lands a traveller walking slow,
In doubt and great perplexity,
A little before moon-rise hears the low
Moan of an unknown sea;

And knows not if it be thunder, or a sound
Of rocks thrown down, or one deep cry
Of great wild beasts; then thinketh, "I have found
A new land, but I die."
(277–284)

The death that the soul herself now fears is like Tithonus's death in life, an eternal self-consuming isolation. So she leaves the Palace of Art, with the hope that she might be able to return some day "with others" (295). When the auditors in the 1833 monologues accept the speakers' visions, they become such saving "others."

Simeon, Tiresias, and Ulysses want to achieve particular ends—sainthood, the safety of the city, a final voyage out—but each wants at least as urgently to escape from the prison of his isolated self. Tiresias uses the strangest and most painful image: he is one of those

Whom weakness or necessity have cramped
Within themselves, immerging, each, his urn
In his own well.
(85–87)

For Ulysses, to remain in Ithaca is to "store and hoard" (29) himself. When Simeon is acclaimed a saint, he uses a more conventional image for escape from self-constriction: "This dull chrysalis / Cracks into shining wings" (153–154). Their isolation was caused in the first place by the visions (in Simeon's case, perhaps just the desire for such visions) that removed them from the world of ordinary people into a world like Mariana's or the Palace of Art. But Mariana's isolation is not a narrowing of space but an expansion of herself to fill all the space available or imaginable in the poem; she cannot touch anyone else, the lover cannot come, because there is no boundary to cross and no one outside her consuming consciousness.[28] The Palace of Art is a mimic universe, complete in itself. Auditors in the 1833 monologues, in contrast, serve to define the speaker's space in relation to their own, and therefore to limit it. The crowd at Simeon's feet, Menoeceus, and Telemachus are outside the speaker's world and thus give it boundaries that the speaker is able, in the course of the poem, to break through. By consciously affecting other people the self touches something outside itself and feels that it is no longer solitary in a world of its own. The soul in "The Palace of Art" escapes only by leaving art entirely and renouncing its visions as falsehoods and nightmares; but responsive auditors allow the speaker to escape from himself while simultaneously affirming (for the speaker, at any rate) the truth of what he has wished and seen.

The hero of *Maud* is young, full of violent energy, and despite his poverty and disaffection very much a Victorian gentleman. Still, he significantly resembles Simeon, Tiresias, and Ulysses. Like them, he is totally isolated when the poem begins, stuck in a little world of "gossip, scandal, and spite" (I.109) that he despises as Ulysses does the "savage race" of Ithacans. He too can imagine happiness only in the lost past or beyond death, and desires at the end only to follow a visionary apparition into another world. He too, however, must first establish a community of shared vision with other people, and the poem ends, like "Ulysses," in the revived heroic fellowship of those who move together toward a noble death.

> We have proved we have hearts in a cause, we are noble still,
>
> . . . .
>
> I have felt with my native land, I am one with my kind,
> I embrace the purpose of God, and the doom assigned.
>   (III.55–59)

Maud began, like the three monologues, in 1833, and the history of its development repeats on a larger scale that of "St Simeon" and "Ulysses." The first short version of "Oh! that 'twere possible," written that year, is a purely lyrical expression of the central emotional impulses and the visionary experiences of the monologues. It is a poem of longing and fear, ghosts and hallucinations. The speaker is haunted, like Simeon, by a bewilderingly hostile phantom, a "dull mechanic ghost" (83).

> A shadow flits before me—
>   Not thou, but like to thee.
> Ah God! that it were possible
>   For one short hour to see

The souls we loved, that they might tell us
What and where they be.
(11–16)

He feels himself an outcast from a society he despises:

I loathe the squares and streets,
And the faces that one meets,
Hearts with no love for me.
(58–60)

The narrative background briefly adumbrated in 1833 is expanded in 1834 and more extensively in 1837. Still, in all these versions the poem remains a lyric, taking place in a continuous lyric moment. No one is there but the speaker, there is no dramatic context, and nothing happens in the course of the poem except the utterance itself.

To this lyric *Maud* adds, in effect, auditors, or the auditor element: that is, representatives of the ordinary world whose responses to the speaker's lyric and visionary impulse determine his utterance and his fate. *Maud* tells a long and complicated story in the present tense, through a sequence of lyrics, and between those lyrics the events of the story take place. Each lyrical moment is a response to the events that preceded it, and a cause of those that follow. The vision and feelings that the separate lyrics express get a response which in turn is incorporated into the poem. As in the shorter monologues, the poem's movement is not determined solely by the speaker, but is repeatedly altered by the behavior of other people with lives of their own who are quite capable of behaving in ways that the speaker neither expects nor wants. While the speaker's words are not themselves actions, they are the lyrical counterparts of his actions: his active encounters with the world consist of attempts to impose on others the visions and desires that the lyrics express. As in the three monologues, the speaker's most urgent need is for others to respond to him, and like the earlier speakers he harms whom he persuades; in fact, he kills.

Maud is Tennyson's richest, most intense and varied long lyric. It is also— and the extraordinary combination is at the heart of the poem's greatness, its strangeness, and its meaning—his central political poem and his most direct and sustained piece of social criticism.[29] *Maud, and Other Poems* (1855) was the first book Tennyson published as Poet Laureate. It is a book about England in the 1850s, though not quite the uplifting and celebratory sort of book that had been expected from the Laureate. It contains only eight poems; none of them is set anywhere but in contemporary England (or with the English army in the Crimea), and three besides *Maud* (the Wellington ode, the verses to Maurice, and "The Charge of the Light Brigade") deal with public affairs. *Maud* itself depicts the social and intellectual world of Tennyson and his friends, and its political, social, and scientific references are numerous, precise, and topical. In Part III—written, Tennyson said, "when the cannon was heard booming from the battleships in the Solent before the Crimean War"— fictional time and the time of writing coincide.[30]

The lyrical element is still more intense and concentrated. It is rarely diluted even in the interests of storytelling, although Tennyson added some passages in later editions to clarify the plot. There is no narrator, nor are there devices to make narration easy: no letter writing, no confidant to whom the hero might plausibly explain things. He doesn't write, he speaks, and when he speaks he is alone. His utterances are spontaneous, expressive, and usually (not always) unself-conscious: purely lyrical.

But the result of setting this intense lyricism so firmly against an ordinary contemporary background is to make lyricism itself, except for the very few times when the occasion is clearly adequate to the poetic intensity, seem morbid or mad—or at least unseemly. Tennyson called the hero "a morbid poetic soul"; in *Maud* "morbid" and "poetic" are synonymous, and Tennyson enthusiastically endorsed a commentary on the poem that defended the hero as a sensitive soul like Shelley or Keats reacting to a disagreeable world.[31] The hero does not inhabit a Palace of Art or a dim and far-off moated grange; he lives with two servants in contemporary England and is implicitly held up for judgment by conventional standards of social behavior. By such standards, he is absurd. Charles Kingsley tried to say this nicely:

> For mingled purity and passion, we know no love-poetry in the English language equal to this canto ["Come into the garden, Maud"], or perhaps to the thirteen pages preceding it: and yet, devil's advocate as we are—will not the world say that it is now and then rather the passion of a southern woman, than of an English man? . . . Mr. Tennyson means that his hero should be in earnest; the leap, the ring, the live melody of every line shows that; but would an Englishman in earnest talk thus?[32]

Less friendly reviewers amused themselves with easy sarcasm against the speaker's excesses. Tennyson's implicit defense was that these were signs of incipient lunacy—thus Hallam Tennyson reports, "My father would say that in calling heath 'blood'-red the hero showed his extravagant fancy, which is already on the road to madness," and many of Tennyson's additions to the poem after 1855 seem designed to drive home the same point.[33] But Coventry Patmore, who like Kingsley detested the poem but reviewed it politely, acutely and disapprovingly observed that the "element of a morbid mind" serves chiefly "as a means of pitching the tone of the work in a key of extraordinarily high poetic sensibility, and at once providing for the expression of thoughts and feelings with the strongest emphasis, and with almost total irresponsibility on the part of the writer."[34] For the hero is cursed, as he himself says, with a "passionate heart and morbid eye" (III.32)—but that heart and that eye produce both the poem's lyrical potency and a picture of the world whose accuracy Tennyson never really disavowed.[35]

Nature's cruel life is depicted as it is in the darkest moments of *In Memoriam*, but with no resistance of the will or testimony of the heart against it.

> For nature is one with rapine, a harm no preacher can heal;
> The Mayfly is torn by the swallow, the sparrow speared by the shrike,
> And the whole little wood where I sit is a world of plunder and prey.
> (I.123–125)

The poem defines this as morbid, the projection of inner conflict and remembered strife; but it does not suggest as *In Memoriam* does about similar formulations that it is inaccurate. Nor, when the hero reaches a happier vision of nature, does he define that vision as truer: on the contrary. He sees the stars "Go in and out as if at merry play" (I.629)—but it is only "as if," and the phrase "merry play" is borrowed from Spenser's *Epithalamion* and is part of a brief recreation of nature in terms of mythic and literary allusion. Even when the speaker is asserting a momentary triumph over the darker vision, he cannot deny its truth. Once, he says, he would have preferred not to know the "sad astrology" (I.634) that tells of man's "nothingness" (I.638); now the love that has come to him as a "countercharm of space and hollow sky" (I.641) makes that astrology tolerable, but it does not prove it wrong.

Nor did Tennyson really disavow the poem's social criticism, despite the attacks it provoked, except for what seemed to be slurs on particular individuals. Its violence does not always seem inappropriate.

> When the poor are hovelled and hustled together, each sex, like swine,
> . . . .

And chalk and alum and plaster are sold to the poor for bread,
And the spirit of murder works in the very means of life,

. . . .

When a Mammonite mother kills her babe for a burial fee,
And Timour-Mammon grins on a pile of children's bones.
(I. 34–46)

The language is overwrought, no doubt—but if such things are to be admitted
to poetry at all, what would be a sane tone in which to describe them? The
hero's vision is morbid, but the society is still more deeply diseased. He resolves to pull himself together and overcome his "morbid-hate and horror
. . . / Of a world in which I have hardly mixt" (I. 264–265). But love is an
unwelcome intruder in a society in which marriages are made for rank and
money, and rank and money come from speculation and treachery and the
oppression of the poor. The happy endings of both *The Princess* and *In Memoriam* are made by the protagonists' loving reintegration into society, symbol-
ized chiefly by marriage.[36] But the hero of *Maud* discovers that he cannot
avoid being morally and psychologically implicated in society, that society itself is neither loving nor good, and that he cannot be redeemed until the society is. Almost the first effect of his dawning love is to make him feel his
essential identity with the world he despises: "Till I well could weep for a time
so sordid and mean, / And myself so languid and base" (I. 178–179).

Maud, however, seems to him an almost entirely symbolical being, with no
essential connection to the people around her, no discernible personality, and
nothing to do but love. He loves her as the embodiment of the beauty, innocence, and wholeness of the past: Eden, his own childhood, the heroic age of
chivalry. We are shocked into laughter when he speaks of her as if she were a
real girl with real dresses ("The habit, hat, and feather, / Or the frock and
gipsy bonnet," I. 804–805) whom he can actually touch ("I kissed her slender
hand, / She took the kiss sedately; / Maud is not seventeen, / But she is tall
and stately" I. 424–427). As an ideal image of the idealized past she can exist
only in imagination or in death, not in mortal flesh in England.

When the poem begins, the hero is obsessed by his family disaster, seeing
all of nature and society as discolored by its garish light. Then Maud comes—
from the innocent, happy time before his father was ruined and died and his
mother pined away. Appropriately, her beauty first seems just "Dead perfec-
tion" (I. 83); at night her image haunts him, "ghostlike, deathlike" (I. 95), and
when he flees into the garden he finds death there too: "The shining daffodil

dead, and Orion low in his grave" (I.101). His early association of Maud with death is more than proleptic and more than a morbid symptom: she represents the lost past that their love will attempt to revive. This is made particularly clear in Sections VI and VII, where the lover's thoughts move backward through the layers of the past and associate Maud first with their fathers' feud, then with his mother, then with their own friendship as children, until he reaches the farthest, most dreamlike depths of his memory and finds there both an end and a beginning. When Maud was born, he recalls, their fathers had agreed that they should marry; by loving and being loved by Maud he hopes to revive that originating moment and redeem the past by fulfilling its broken promise. Part I ends as he imagines himself, in an image that is both proleptic and recapitulative, roused from death at her footsteps:

> My heart would hear her and beat,
> Were it earth in an earthy bed;
> My dust would hear her and beat,
> Had I lain for a century dead;
> Would start and tremble under her feet,
> And blossom in purple and red.
> (I.918–923)

The past that Maud represents, moreover, is also an older and more beautiful world of poetic imagination. The earliest moment that the poem recaptures, the two fathers over their wine, rises in memory as a scene from *The Arabian Nights*. Maud as an object of love is a literary object: it is in terms of art that she becomes alive, first as Marvell's dying fawn, then as a disembodied voice singing of the days of chivalry and compelling the hero to love "not her, but a voice" (I.189). Section XVIII ("I have led her home") celebrates their acknowledged love in the allusive context of *Epithalamion, Paradise Lost*, and the Bible, for his brief happiness enables him to superimpose on his own grim nineteenth-century vision of nature kinder and lovelier ones attained by great poets of the past. "Beat, happy stars, timing with things below" (I.679).[37]

In the last section of Part I the contemporary social world and the world of the poet's passionate imagination are concentrated, intensified, and juxtaposed. The Tories gather inside the hall at a "grand political dinner" (I.817), while the lover waits outside in the garden. His imagination is at its highest pitch, reaching almost to self-parody as he turns an English garden into a superb floral counterpart of the party indoors.

The red rose cries, "She is near, she is near";
And the white rose weeps, "She is late";
The larkspur listens, "I hear, I hear";
And the lily whispers, "I wait."
(I.912–915)

Maud is to link the two worlds by coming in her finery into the lyrical garden, "In gloss of satin and glimmer of pearls, / Queen lily and rose in one" (I.904–905). She does come, but her brother and the foolish suitor follow, and the two worlds meet in hatred, violence, and death.

"Come into the garden, Maud"—Part I reaches its climax in that famous and disastrously effective summons. Part II deals with its aftermath. For the hero has in effect found too many responsive auditors. His formulation in Bedlam of what went wrong is that his lyric love was overheard.

For I never whispered a private affair
Within the hearing of cat or mouse,
No, not to myself in the closet alone,
But I heard it shouted at once from the top of the house;
Everything came to be known.
Who told *him* we were there?
(II.285–290)

Overheard, it immediately and disastrously became part of the world of angry brothers, foolish lords, mercenary marriages—the world of the Victorian novel, in which the life of every individual is affected by the life of society and—as in *Bleak House*—secrets are discovered and privacy overheard.

In Part I the hero was hoping to evade this world and live in the loving, lyric solitude of recaptured innocence. In Part II private and public, lyric and social worlds merge indistinguishably: that is the significance and the horror of his madness. For he has committed the crime that had represented for him all the social evils of the times. He has not redeemed the past: he has reenacted it in the role of the aggressor. The woods are bloody again, this time with the blood he has shed, and the cry ringing in his ears now is Maud's, not his mother's. Maud comes to him in Bedlam only as an unresponsive and accusing phantom from a past he now perceives as "Stiller, not fairer" than his own world of death (II.309).

In Tennyson's earlier poems madness comes with isolation and one escapes it by rejoining the world, which presumably is sane. But what drives the mor-

TENNYSON

bid hero of *Maud* genuinely mad is entering into relations with the society he
has scorned—in his encounter with Maud's brother—and realizing that he is
morally and psychologically part of it. His Bedlam is a noisy, overpopulated
city of the dead:

> Maybe still I am but half-dead;
> Then I cannot be wholly dumb;
> I will cry to the steps above my head
> And somebody, surely, some kind heart will come
> To bury me, bury me
> Deeper, ever so little deeper.
> (II. 337–342)

But he does not cry out, and nobody comes.

His return to sanity in Part III occurs in two separate, interdependent
stages. The "old hysterical mock-disease" (III. 33) of his imagination and "the
long, long canker of peace" (the 1855 reading of III. 50) have to be cured together. First Maud appears again, as she had in the first two parts, but this
time as neither a real person nor a hostile phantom: "She seemed to divide in
a dream from a band of the blest" (III. 9), "And it was but a dream" (III. 15),
"though but in a dream" (III. 16), "And it was but a dream" (III. 18). At last he
recognizes that she has been for him a creature of his imagination, not really
part of the mortal world. She promises him "a hope for the world in the coming wars" (III. 11) and suggests that when he dies he will rejoin her: "'I tarry for
thee'" (III. 13). Then she disappears from the poem, leaving him to wait in
patience until the war begins and his cure can be completed.

The actual moment of cure is the final event of the poem, and is a close
variant of the actions that conclude the three earlier monologues.

> I stood on a giant deck and mixed my breath
> With a loyal people shouting a battle cry.
> (III. 34–35)

A battle cry calls men to death; but it is an expression of communal vision and
feeling, not simply personal ones. Since everyone is shouting at once, the
speaker's individual voice is not even heard as such: it is merged into the collective voice, just as his will and vision have merged into the collective fervor
for war. Thus he can utter his summons to death with a clear and happy
conscience.

41

Many readers then and since, however, have thought that his conscience should have been less happy. No one seems to object to the *Idylls of the King* on the grounds that they glorify violence, even though they present war not just as a symbolic battle of good against evil but also as an essential moral exercise and an outlet for energy—when the knights have no proper fighting on hand they usually get into trouble. But what remains safely symbolical or historically distant in the *Idylls* is literal and contemporary and therefore inevitably controversial in *Maud*. "It is better to fight for the good than to rail at the ill" (III.57)—this trite moral summary, which would be innocuous in the *Idylls*, is highly provocative in the context of the Crimean War. The poem not only allows us to respond in terms of our attitudes toward wars in general or the Crimean War in particular—it made such responses inevitable in 1855 and still encourages them more than a century later. The topicality is essential and emphatic: the main point, in fact, is that it *is* a real, particular war. R. J. Mann pointed out, in what might be called the official defense of the poem, that the war passages (which had been violently attacked by reviewers) were appropriately so particular because the poem had earlier been concerned with real, particular social evils.[38] The poem has set out to reconcile imagination with reality, the poet's mind and eye with contemporary social life, and so the reconciliation has to be social, contemporary, and real.

It has also, perhaps, to be violent. For while the hero is saved by his decision to participate willingly and knowingly in social reality, he cannot do so without further disaster until the society has come to share his vision of good and hatred of evil. Thus Part III, which Tennyson intended to show the return of individual and communal sanity, strikes many readers as an extension of private madness into the public sphere. But what the hero has learned is that he is a member of the society and participates in its sins. The lawless violence and destructive passion that he has seen in others and then discovered in himself is the general condition, and can be purged only in the pure, impersonal intensity of "The blood-red blossom of war with a heart of fire" (III.53). The pressure of his own imagination and the will toward death that is bound up with it demand such a solution, and since his final dream of Maud precedes by some months the actual start of the war, it seems in the post hoc, propter hoc logic of poetry to have caused it. In effect, his vision has been communicated. Such communication saved Simeon, Tiresias, and Ulysses from a life of miserable isolation, and it saves the hero of *Maud* too.

*　*　*

Percivale in "The Holy Grail" (1869) is Tennyson's last important speaker with a responsive auditor. "The Holy Grail" is not a dramatic monologue, but it very much resembles one. Ambrosius, the monk to whom Percivale tells his story, speaks pointedly and often, so that much of the poem is dialogue. Percivale's speech is not an action but a retrospective account of one: nothing happens to either Ambrosius or Percivale in the course of it or as a result of it. But the poem is largely about the communication of vision, although it does not formally enact that communication, and Ambrosius articulates the point of view of those who define the visionary's isolation by their refusal to share or appreciate his visions, and speaks for the human ties and values that the visionary typically injures or rejects.

If we follow the order of scenes as they occur in the poem rather than the fictional chronology, we find that the main outline is familiar. First we see Percivale in isolation, contemptuous of the society from which he has withdrawn, not old but ready to die. He tells how the Holy Grail appeared, both a supernatural manifestation and a symbol of the lost, sacred, heroic past, and drew him out of a corrupt and sinful society. Like the hero of *Maud* in his brief happiness, he had rejoiced then in himself and in nature: "'never yet / Had heaven appeared so blue, nor earth so green, / For all my blood danced in me'" (364–366),[39] but when he rode forth on the quest he found himself in a phantasmal world like that of Simeon or blinded Tiresias or *Maud*, Part II. He rid himself of his "'phantoms'" (444) by merging his own quest into that of Galahad (whom he had originally told about the grail), like Tiresias merging his will with that of Menoeceus, Ulysses with his mariners', and the hero of *Maud* with that of the nation at war. Then he tells how he earlier left the woman he loved and the home and duties she offered him, like Ulysses parting from Ithaca, Tiresias from his spiritual "son," and the lover from Maud's benignant spirit. The poem ends with Arthur's speech, which like the end of *Maud* presents an image of a possible reconciliation of the visionary and the social worlds.

"The Holy Grail" seems to have developed like *Maud* around a core of intense and troubled lyricism, with the ordinary human point of view represented by Ambrosius a later addition, as in "St Simeon," "Ulysses," and *Maud*, to the original conception. Tennyson said in 1859 that he had composed a very fine poem about Lancelot's quest years earlier, which he had never written down and had forgotten,[40] and Lancelot's strange and beautiful story is the longest of the few passages of verse in the prose draft of "The Holy Grail" that Tennyson wrote just before the poem itself.[41] (He had written the dreamy "Sir Galahad," a quite different treatment of the grail quest, in 1833 or 1834.) Ambrosius on the other hand, who is strikingly unresponsive to the imaginative beauty of the grail, speaks only once in the earliest draft: "And what said Arthur? did he allow your vows?"[42]—the question is brief but typically provocative, for what Arthur said was that the quest would be the destruction of the Round Table and the social order represented by it.

But the completed poem substantially enlarges Ambrosius's role and significance. His interruptions express timid affection, evoking with warm particularity the small world of simple people and showing up in contrast the cold vacancy of the quest itself and the monastic life in which, for Percivale, the quest has ended. What strikes Ambrosius most in the knight's tale is not beauty or grandeur or heroism, but loneliness. "'Came ye on none but phantoms in your quest, / No man, no woman?'" (562–563). In reply to this question Percivale tells how he sacrificed virtuous love, riches, honor, and power, making explicit the full cost exacted by the quest: "'All men, to one so bound by such a vow, / And women were as phantoms'" (564–565). Percivale's quest is Tennyson's most unambiguous statement of the destructiveness of imaginative vision. Everything Percivale touched turned to dust. At first he regretted his lost love, but finally he "'Cared not for her, nor anything upon earth'" (611). Ambrosius is saddened by the waste of life and love: "'O the pity'" (618).

Although Ambrosius is immune to the contagion of the desolating vision, Percivale's narrative is pointedly attentive to the chain of communication by which it passes from one to another and wreaks its wide destruction. It starts when Percivale's sister, whom disappointed love has made a nun, hears her confessor's innocent hope for the grail to come "'And heal the world of all their wickedness'" (94). Fasting and praying with an asceticism almost as extreme as Simeon's—though more attractive—"'till the sun / Shone, and the wind blew, through her'" (98–99), she sees the grail. She tells Percivale the story and urges him, with a faith as strong as Simeon's in the power of her own vision and example, to tell the other knights, "'That so perchance the vision may be seen / By thee and those, and all the world be healed'" (127–128). As in "St Simeon," too, while she persuades her fictional auditors of her sanctity and vision the reader is made aware of her naiveté and the motivating force of her thwarted sexuality.[43]

The medium of persuasion in this poem is not the word but the eye. To be persuaded is to be made to see, by a compulsive power like that in the essay on ghosts, with the eyes of another. Percivale sees his sister's eyes, beautiful with the vision that came to her. When he tells Galahad of it, Galahad's "'eyes

became so like her own, they seemed / Hers'" (141–142). This act of possession is confirmed when Galahad and the nun meet: "She sent the death-
less passion in her eyes / Through him, and made him hers, and laid her
mind / On him, and he believed in her belief" (163–165). Only to the selfless
Bors are the persuading eyes gentle and unaggressive: the grail appears to him
when the stars that stand for the Round Table shine into his prison "'like
bright eyes of familiar friends'" (685). Percivale himself loses his first faith in
the vision and has to be persuaded again by Galahad: "'While . . . he spake,
his eye, dwelling on mine, / Drew me, with power upon me, till I grew /
One with him, to believe as he believed'" (485–487).

The poem does not question the intrinsic value and validity of the grail any
more than *Maud* questions the hero's dark visions of nature and society, but it
does say firmly that the quest can be undertaken for bad reasons as well as
good ones, and that whatever its motives or its success, the result is to withdraw men from their social obligations and thus to injure society. The true
and right visionary experience is Arthur's, which does not interfere with his
work, comes unsummoned and unsought, and remains completely private.
Arthur says he has visions, and of course we believe him, but he does not tell
us what they are. He translates them into actions and, for a while at least, the
creation of a social order.[44]

"The Holy Grail" presents the claims of society and imaginative vision—of
auditor, that is, and speaker—as equally valid but irreconcilably opposed (except in the half-divine person of Arthur), and vision as if anything the more
potent and destructive of the two. This essentially concludes the series of explorations of form and theme that Tennyson began in 1833. Auditors are
a dimly significant presence, however, in four later monologues: "Rizpah"
(1880), "Despair" (1881), and "Happy: The Leper's Bride" and "Romney's Remorse," two very bad poems published in 1889.[45] In all of these the speakers
affirm their personal vision in opposition to the values of society, but since
they express nothing but selfless love the poems do not deal with the conflicts
enacted in Tennyson's earlier poems with auditors. The best by far is the earliest, "Rizpah," in which the dying mother's wild love and grief for the son
whose bones she buried after he was hanged pour out in answer to the lady
who has come to talk of sin and salvation. Like Simeon, Tiresias, and Ulysses, the speaker is old, isolated, a visionary and a dreamer. The outrage to her
maternal love has set her against the society that offered her son no proper
field of action and condemns him with the cold legalisms of Calvinist theol-
ogy and the punitive moralism of the law. But her speech is self-expressive in

intention, and causes nothing to happen: the visitor is not persuaded—it would be better for her if she were—and the speaker hardly cares.

> Madam, I beg your pardon! I think that you mean to be kind,
> But I cannot hear what you say for my Willy's voice in the wind—
> $$(81-82)$$

Like the poems in which Tennyson had used auditors to demonstrate the anti-social and dangerous communication of poetic vision, these four late monologues turn on the opposition between public and private worlds, communal and individual values.[46] But in all of them the private experience that is communicated is defined as pure and selfless love and the social world which tries to hinder the speaker's utterance is condemned as foolish and trivial even when its action is malign. Since there is no longer anything dangerous or even problematic for Tennyson about the act of poetic communication, the auditor element has ceased to matter very much.

TWO

Browning

BROWNING'S POEMS WITH AUDITORS encompass a much wider range of subjects, characters, and dramatic situations than Tennyson's do. Usually both speaker and auditor are highly particularized and the dramatic situation is indicated with such clarity and completeness that even the auditor's silence, a simple necessity of the form, can become a significant positive fact. But Browning is not primarily concerned in these poems either with characterization for its own sake or with the ideas or truths or values the characters represent. What interests him is why, how, and to what effect the speaker speaks, and the poems examine various ways in which speech can be exploited, perverted, and misunderstood. We implicitly acknowledge the distinctive characteristic of these poems by the question we usually find ourselves asking about them: why does the speaker speak? Browning's other dramatic monologues may lead us to wonder if the speaker is right or wrong, good or bad, self-aware or self-deceiving in what he says, but it never occurs to us to ask why he *says* it at all. But all Browning's poems with auditors before *The Ring and the Book* are concerned with the ways in which one person speaks to another. More often than not, this is what the speakers actually talk about, and they all use language self-consciously, deliberately, and purposefully. The poems fall into three groups which focus successively on three aspects of speech, as shown in the relation of the speaker to his auditor: first the power implied by the speaker's very freedom to speak as he does, then his attempts to communicate thoughts and feelings, and finally the problem of assessing the sincerity of what he says.

The first group of poems includes "My Last Duchess," "Count Gismond," "The Laboratory," and "The Bishop Orders His Tomb at Saint Praxed's Church." These appeared in *Bells and Pomegranates* (1842, 1845), at a time when Browning's literary energies were going mostly into drama. These poems turn to an advantage the essential weakness of his plays: the self-consciousness about the verbal medium of the action displayed not just by the poet (the usual weakness of poetic drama then and since) but by his characters themselves. Their obsessive concern with what they have or haven't said, will or won't say, generally retards the action and is often the center of the plot; the most extreme, but characteristic, example is A *Blot in the 'Scutcheon*, in which the idiotic, exasperating silence of the young lovers brings general ruin. Almost invariably, moreover, the hardest and most dangerous thing to say is the truth.

In 1845 and 1846 Browning was courting Elizabeth Barrett, and the same concern runs from beginning to end of their voluminous correspondence. In the early letters they discuss his reluctance to speak out in his poetry, in the later ones her insistence on concealing their meetings, engagement, and marriage. Browning always says he wants to speak out, but he usually doesn't do it. It is understood between them, of course, that what is unspoken is wholly compounded of wisdom and love, but Browning is by no means sure that others would agree. His second letter is playful but typical: "You speak out . . . I am going to try . . . yet I don't think I shall let *you* hear, after all, the savage things about Popes and imaginative religions that I must say."[1] Twice he was incautiously outspoken—when he first declared his love and when he defended dueling—and retracted his words with ignominious promptitude as soon as he realized that she was upset. (He literally retracted the declaration of love: she returned his letter and he destroyed it.)

But in the dramatic monologues with auditors that Browning published in the 1840s, people speak out. "My Last Duchess" appeared in 1842; it derives from Browning's essay on Tasso and Chatterton, written in the same year, referring to the same Duke, and explaining how poets are driven to silence and lies. In the essay Browning is passionately concerned to make two points: that Tasso usually told the truth and Chatterton wanted to, and that the world forced them to lie. The book on Tasso that Browning was ostensibly reviewing confirmed, he thought, the legend that Alfonso II of Ferrara persecuted Tasso because of the love his poems revealed; the legend had recently been questioned, and Browning is delighted to have it revived. Alfonso II, who (Browning was triumphantly sure) had punished Tasso for loving above his station and saying so in his poems, is the Duke of "My Last Duchess"; Browning's Duke hated the wife who was insufficiently impressed by his aristocratic superiority, and tells his chilling tale with impunity.[2]

His extraordinary freedom to speak is made manifest by the presence of the

auditor. The power of "My Last Duchess" has much less to do with any purpose the Duke might have for speaking so openly than with the simple fact
that he does so. This is what fascinates and appalls us. What the Duke has
done in the past is banal, the stuff of melodrama, and it is not even clear just
what he did. But what he does in the poem itself is perfectly clear: he tells,
with absolute self-command and impunity, the worst of truths. The stress
on dramatic situation, the Duke's extreme self-consciousness about his own
words, and—above all and essentially—the auditor's finely realized and gradually clarified presence continuously remind us that he is saying it all aloud.

The poem is in fact mostly about speech: what visitors dare not ask, what
Fra Pandolf said to the Duchess, how the Duchess expressed her thanks and
might have excused herself, what the Duke has said, hasn't said, and is saying. Explicit references to the spoken word appear frequently and regularly,
and the story the Duke tells is about words, spoken and unspoken. He was
offended by the way his wife "thanked men" with "approving speech"; he
would not "stoop" to correct her; he "gave commands."[3] His crime itself, that
is, like her offense, is presented as a matter of words, and while we have to
guess at their meaning, we are sure of their potency.

The Duke's license to speak derives from, reinforces, and demonstrates his
power: it *is* his power. "All *great* (conventionally great) Italians are coarse,"
Browning was later to say in defense of Caponsacchi, "showing their power in
obliging you to accept their cynicism."[4] We see the Duke's power in the envoy's silence, just as we see the weakness of the Spanish monk and Porphyria's
lover in the absence of an auditor. The monk mutters harmlessly to himself;
Porphyria's lover, passive and voiceless in her presence, socially her inferior,
murdered her in the silence and belongs in a madhouse cell. Powerless, they
speak freely but to no one. Whether they are speaking aloud, sotto voce, or
not at all is not apparent and does not matter, for their words come unself-
consciously, without premeditation, unawares; but the Duke is master of his
situation and his words.

In the Chatterton essay Browning remarks on "literary forgery in general":

> Is it worth while to mention, that the very notion of obtaining a free way
> for impulses that can find vent in no other channel (and consequently
> of a liberty conceded to an individual, and denied to the world at large),
> is implied in all literary production?

Like Tennyson in the essay on ghosts, Browning here considers the exercise of
imaginative power as a form of covert aggression that evokes responsive hostility from an audience of the poet's intimates.

And so instinctively does the Young Poet feel that his desire for this kind of self-enfranchisement will be resisted as a matter of course, that we will venture to say, in nine cases out of ten his first assumption of the licence will be made in a borrowed name. The first communication, to even the family circle or the trusted associate, is sure to be "the work of a friend"; if not, "something extracted from a magazine," or "Englished from the German." So is the way gracefully facilitated for Reader and Hearer finding themselves in a new position with respect to each other.[5]

(The suave understatement of the final sentence has the Duke's authentic note.) Since this paragraph appears in the discussion of Chatterton and is singularly inapplicable to Chatterton's first forgery (a pleasant description of a procession crossing a bridge), one may assume that Browning is thinking of himself. His own first—and anonymous—publication, *Pauline*, is the murky, half-repentant confession of a young poet who cannot "account for," "stifle," or "indulge" (596, 597, 599) his Byronically multifarious desires; nor does he succeed very well in expressing them. The Duke has the freedom, the "license," Browning thought all poets want.

The companion poem to "My Last Duchess" was "Count Gismond," which also has an auditor and also is about words and power, speech and silence. The Countess tells her story: Gauthier accused her of unchasteness, she was struck to silence, Gismond gave Gauthier the lie and killed him. The outcome seems clear and satisfactory, the antithesis of "My Last Duchess": murderous words are defeated by silent virtue. But whenever we become aware of the auditor (in the ninth, eighteenth, and last stanzas) we realize that the Countess is deliberately controlling her utterance to suit her audience; and at the end of the poem this becomes very unsettling.

> Gismond here?
> And have you brought my tercel back?
> I just was telling Adela
> How many birds it struck since May.

For a poem about the triumph of truth over falsehood, with the words "lie" and "liar" appearing five times in as many stanzas, this blatant, unnecessary prevarication makes an odd ending. It is true that if we refuse to believe the facts Browning's speakers give us there is no end to the parapoems we can construct in defiance of tradition and probability, but this is a special case. The Countess tells us that Gauthier lied, but we know *she* does, and the will to dominate and possess implied by "my tercel" and "How many birds it struck" is suggestively like the reference to the statue of Neptune taming the seahorse that concludes "My Last Duchess," and is always taken to summarize the worst aspects of the Duke's character. It appears, then, that the Countess' story is true except for one crucial detail: that Gauthier's accusation was true too. Like the Duke, she said and did nothing when her empty preeminence was challenged; Gismond acted for her, like those to whom the Duke "gave commands." Adela's silence when the Countess lies to Gismond shows, like the envoy's, the speaker's freedom and power.[6]

In "The Laboratory" and "The Bishop Orders His Tomb" (1845) the story and motive are clear—which suggests that the teasing ambiguities of "My Last Duchess" and "Count Gismond," like those of "St Simeon Stylites" and "Ulysses," may be signs that the poet has not taken account of all the peculiar difficulties of his new strategy. Here again the speakers' words exert and assert power; but sometimes they come unbidden and are primarily expressive, and the presence of the auditors lets us see the difference between the two kinds of speech. The story told and implied in "The Laboratory" is even more melodramatic, though less mysterious, than that in "My Last Duchess." And again the shock of the poem comes from the fact that the speaker says such horrible things so politely and conversationally, with so much aesthetic delectation and so little human feeling:

> That in the mortar—you call it a gum?
> Ah, the brave tree whence such gold oozings come!
> And yonder soft phial, the exquisite blue,
> Sure to taste sweetly,—is that poison too?
> (13–16)

She is relishing both her control of the moment and her imminent revenge. But when she broods on her jealousy and her rival's intolerable superiority, her voice loses its easy lilt and she seems unaware of the listening chemist:

> this never will free
> The soul from those masculine eyes,—say, "no!"
> To that pulse's magnificent come-and-go.
> (30–32)

She speaks to herself of her impotence, to the auditor of the power that her speech to him both procures and represents.

The poisoner has two voices; the bishop who orders his tomb in the best of the early monologues has three. He tries to persuade his sons to do his will; his mind wanders off into the delight in beauty and the feud with Gandolf that have dominated his conscious life; and from the depths of memory come fragments of religious language that he has never, we imagine, understood much better than he does now, but which judge the deepest meaning of his life. The decay of his mental powers lets him slide unawares from one level to another.

> Sons, all I have bequeathed you, villas, all,
> That brave Frascati villa with its bath,
> So, let the blue lump poise between my knees,
> Like God the Father's globe on both his hands
> Ye worship in the Jesu Church so gay,
> For Gandolf shall not choose but see and burst!
> Swift as a weaver's shuttle fleet our years:
> **Man goeth to the grave, and where is he?**
> (45–52)

Like the Duke and the poisoner, he speaks of his wrongdoing, but without their suave self-confidence. His deepest sins—his irreligiousness, his petty vindictiveness—he does not regard as sins at all, and what he knows to be wrong he confesses only because he has to:

> Nephews—sons mine . . . ah God, I know not!
> (3)

> And if ye find . . . Ah God, I know not, I!
> (39)

The bishop will not get his tomb; he cannot always control his utterances; but still at the end words bring him mastery. When he cannot make his sons stay any longer, he orders them to do what they are already doing in terms that assimilate their recalcitrance into his own sense of himself and his world:

> Well go! I bless ye. Fewer tapers there,
> But in a row: and, going, turn your backs
> —Ay, like departing altar-ministrants,
> And leave me in my church . . .
> (119–122)

* * *

In these four poems from *Bells and Pomegranates,* speech is a form of power and self-assertion. The auditor is there mainly to let the speaker speak aloud; all that is ultimately required from him is passive acquiescence. But the speakers in *Men and Women* (1855) try to elicit the auditor's understanding and sympathy. Almost always, they fail.

Their failures reflect Browning's concern about his own relation to his readers. He wasn't sure either that he wanted to address an audience of dullards or that anyone would listen if he did. "It seems bleak melancholy work, this talking to the wind," he wrote in 1845 of his decision to give up dramatic poetry;[7] with an auditor in the poem, the speaker has someone to talk to. Browning's theory of poetry, even more than Tennyson's and Arnold's, required responsive readers, and he was longer in finding them. He was sure that the poet must be a teacher, with designs, however impalpable, on an audience. He often addresses his readers directly, arguing, explaining, questioning, joking, exhorting, and his painters and poets usually encounter or imagine groups of onlookers. Even a dramatist, Browning says, has his eye on the audience: "an objective poet [is] one whose endeavour has been to reproduce things external . . . with an immediate reference, in every case, to the common eye and apprehension of his fellow men, assumed capable of receiving and profiting by this reproduction."[8]

To most of his fellowmen, especially after *Sordello* became a laughingstock for its obscurity, it seemed that Browning willfully refused to communicate anything intelligible to anyone. Even Elizabeth Barrett, indignant at such blindness, urged him to be more accommodating. Browning pretended not to care, but it is clear from the repeated half-angry, half-humorous promises to reform in his letters that he cared very much. When Ruskin complained that his efforts to puzzle out *Men and Women* gave him a headache, Browning vigorously defended himself: people are lazy and stupid and a poet is accountable only to God. His immediate business, however, is to communicate and instruct:

> I cannot begin writing poetry till my imaginary reader has conceded licenses to me which you demur at altogether. I *know* that I don't make out my conception by my language. . . . I try to make shift with touches and bits of outlines which *succeed* if they bear the conception from me to you. . . .
>
> Do you think poetry was ever generally understood—or can be? Is the business of it to tell people what they know already . . . ? It is all teaching, on the contrary, and the people hate to be taught.[9]

He had true and important things to say—that he never doubted—but he did worry about how to make them heard. While much of Tennyson's and Arnold's best poetry is about their search for truth, much of Browning's is about his search for a way to express it. Tennyson and Arnold struggle for light, Browning to make his light visible. He was convinced that words are inadequate to thought, "the vehicle / Never sufficient" (*Sordello*, V.653– 654), and that only an artist with little to express can express it fully: "in such songs you find alone / Completeness, judge the song and singer one" (*Sordello*, III.619–620). But the monologues with auditors in *Men and Women* that are about art or love (that is, all but "Bishop Blougram's Apology") are concerned less with the inadequacies of the vehicle than with those of the audience.

In the lovers' monologues there is little dramatic interaction, little real sense of the auditor's presence. Appropriately, all but one are about failures of communication. In "Two in the Campagna," "A Serenade at the Villa," and "Any Wife to Any Husband" the auditor is as shadowy to us as the speaker's feelings are to the auditor. In "By the Fireside" the wife sometimes is vividly present to us, as the speaker is to her, but much of the poem is silent reverie, for they understand each other without words. "I will speak now," the husband says in the twenty-third stanza, but it is hard to hear the difference. It is significant that while the wife is presumed to follow with ease the metaphorical branchings of her husband's thoughts, most readers have a lot of trouble. "By the Fireside" enacts an understanding between lovers so complete as almost to exclude the reader; the others enact failures of understanding.

The auditors in "Andrea del Sarto" and "Fra Lippo Lippi" are the audience for whom the speakers paint. An earlier poem with a similar theme, "Pictor Ignotus," has only the faintest hint of an auditor at the beginning, and at the end the unknown painter addresses someone who is not there; he talks to himself as he paints to himself, letting his words fade like his pictures. He had once aspired to show truth to the world, but "cold faces" (46) watched and frightened him, and he does not want his pictures to live among them. Andrea, on the other hand, once had a warmly responsive audience in King Francis and "All his court round him, seeing with his eyes" (159); but he preferred the cold wife who doesn't "understand / Nor care to understand" his art (54–55). Great artists care what people say:

> The sudden blood of these men! At a word—
> Praise them, it boils, or blame them, it boils too.
> (88–89)

Andrea is self-sufficient:

> I, painting from myself and to myself,
> Know what I do, am unmoved by men's blame
> Or their praise either.
> (90–92)

Instead of "Pouring his soul, with kings and popes to see" (108), he says nothing to the world in his paintings, just as he really says nothing to his wife. His paintings are ends in themselves, exercises of skill—or worse, means to get money for Lucrezia—and his words are intended to keep Lucrezia sitting with him, not to tell her anything.

Like the speakers in earlier monologues, Andrea consciously enjoys the luxury of saying the worst about himself. But it is a muted, self-enclosed pleasure—as his language shows—for Lucrezia is too amoral and indifferent to care. There is a note of querulous self-justification: "My father and my mother died of want. / Well, had I riches of my own?" (250–251). His last words, like the Bishop's, attempt to assert control over an event he cannot do anything about—"Go, my Love"—but they do not imaginatively transform the event as the Bishop's do. His words, like his paintings, make the best of a soulless, pretty reality: like his paintings, they are accurate, graceful, lifeless, self-regarding presentations of his world.

Andrea postpones Lucrezia's departure by talking to her, but since she hardly listens and does not judge, it scarcely matters what he says. The content of his utterance is fully accounted for by his melancholy self-absorption: what else would he talk about but himself? But why Fra Lippo Lippi speaks is harder to explain. The name of Cosimo di Medici settles matters with the auditors, who lose interest long before the monk stops talking. The problem itself has been taken to prove that the utterance in a dramatic monologue is gratuitous and therefore essentially lyrical;[10] but then why are the auditors there at all? The dramatic situation itself is gratuitous unless the fact that Fra Lippo Lippi is speaking—and speaking far beyond either the requirements of the opening episode or the interest and attention of the auditors—is part of the meaning of the poem.

What Fra Lippo does in the poem with words is what he does in his paintings: he tries to communicate to others his vision of the world. As in "Andrea del Sarto," verbal and pictorial expression represent each other, and the auditor is both the painter's subject and his chosen audience. In his opening banter with the guards and his reminiscences Fra Lippo tries to establish his essential kinship and equality with the watch; they can understand and even sympathize with him as a man ("your eye twinkles," 76), though not as an artist. He sees them as faces fit for his pictures; he would like to paint them, for themselves to see, instead of "bowery flowery" (349) angels for nuns or "saints and saints / And saints again" (48–49) for his patron. But they are interested only in the reveling monk, not in the artist-philosopher, and judge both merely in conventional terms. The more earnestly Fra Lippo talks of the message his art should convey to people in general, the less he manages to convey to the particular person he is talking to.

Fra Lippo Lippi knows the truth he has to tell and knows how to tell it, in paintings and in words. But the world is full of liars, like the monks who mouth piety and Latin in the intervals of self-indulgence.

> What would men have? Do they like grass or no—
> May they or mayn't they? all I want's the thing
> Settled for ever one way. As it is,
> You tell too many lies and hurt yourself:
> You don't like what you only like too much,
> You do like what, if given you at your word,
> You find abundantly detestable.
> (258–264)

How can he paint his truth—"The value and significance of flesh" (268)—for such men? And the auditor is one of them. Fra Lippo acquiesces in the auditor's judgment before he tries again to explain himself: "You understand me: I'm a beast, I know" (270).

His utterance is gratuitous in the sense that he cannot make the auditor understand it; in that sense his art is gratuitous too. But it is not wholly or even primarily expressive. He wants art to "take the Prior's pulpit-place, / Interpret God to all of you" (310–311). "Disemburdening" himself of accumulated images (144) was only the beginning; he has to find and express their meaning. A pretty face "means hope, fear, / Sorrow or joy" (210–211); the world "means intensely, and means good" (314) and "To find its meaning is my meat and drink" (315). But the "meaning," which is God's love, inheres in the audience's response. Even if beauty in a painting has no soul, "you'll find the soul you have missed, / Within yourself, when you return him thanks" (219–220). Things are "better, painted—better to us" (303) because paintings make us love them. The prior who wants art to mean "'remember matins'" (318) or "'fast next Friday'" (319), like the pious folk who scratched out the painted torturers' faces, makes aesthetic assumptions that are wrong in degree but not in kind. Like Andrea, Fra Lippo wants to reproduce the beauty of the visible world; the difference is that Fra Lippo tries to convey a meaning. Andrea paints and speaks to please himself, though he could have had the worthiest audience; Fra Lippo tries to please the only audience he has.

> I'm my own master, paint now as I please—
>
> .   .   .   .
> And yet the old schooling sticks, the old grave eyes
> Are peeping o'er my shoulder as I work.
> (226–232)

>   . . . So, I . . .
>   . . . paint
>   To please them—sometimes do and sometimes don't.
>   (242–244)

He bursts out in rage (like Browning in his letters) against uncomprehending "fools" (335), and then gives up. It was all "an idle word" (336)—really "idle" in effect though not, of course, in the sense he intends to convey. And now, instead of using words to explain his meaning directly, he uses them to paint a picture that will express it by indirection. He has tried to teach his auditor how to look at his pictures: how to find soul through sense. Now he tells him how to recognize the sensuous basis of painted manifestations of soul. Although the painting as he describes it is prettily bloodless enough to satisfy the most insipid religious taste, the earthy monk himself is at home in it, the "little lily thing" (385) in the foreground is both Saint Lucy and the Prior's niece, and the wings of the "flowery bowery" angels could be the "kirtles" (380) that hide a farcically undignified adulterer. And as he describes his own intrusion into his picture, Fra Lippo in effect rewrites the opening of the poem, making of his painted saints and angels a truly responsive audience. He comes unexpectedly into the blinding light of the picture as he had to the torches shone in his face by the watch, boldly naming himself as he had in the first line. Again he is caught, a monk in the wrong place, by those inclined to be censorious. But this time things go differently. He sees the watchmen as faces for a religious picture (though not the faces of saints); the second company recognize that they are sacred figures only because Fra Lippo made them so.

They recognize, in other words, the transforming power of art, and art alone (Saint John couldn't do it), to make manifest the latent soul. The auditor has a "proper twinkle" (42) in his eye, but the saints and angels "all smile" (377). So, instead of sitting down "hip to haunch" (44) with the auditor to begin a futile explanation, he sits hand in hand with the Prior's niece-Saint Lucy on a "safe bench" (384), and "all's saved" (388) for him. He need not speak, because his creation—Saint Lucy—has spoken for him.

The other monologues with significant auditors before *The Ring and the Book* are "Bishop Blougram's Apology" from *Men and Women* and "Mr. Sludge, 'The Medium'" and *"Dîs Aliter Visum"* from *Dramatis Personae*. These three poems are remarkably alike. They discuss modern themes of great importance to Browning: religious belief, spiritualism, romantic love (*"Dîs Aliter Visum"* is subtitled *"Le Byron de Nos Jours"*). They have contemporary settings: judgment is not disarmed by historical distance. The speakers are clever and disagreeable. The situation in each is ostensibly that of speech after long silence, when truth can be spoken at last. The speakers want to gain the auditor's good opinion and dissuade him of a previous bad one; they speak with extraordinary (even for Browning) and self-conscious ingenuity, partly for the pleasure of hearing their own clever voices, but they are aware at every moment of the auditor and never deviate like other monologuists into unrhetorical expressiveness. Though they try to ingratiate themselves with the auditor, they are predominantly hostile to him, defensive and aggressive by turns; their self-defense is largely attack. And finally, after saying much that is persuasive and true, they are revealed as disingenuous, and the reader is left with the problem of reconciling their lofty utterances to their low characters.

The movement of the three poems is toward increasing dissonance in the reader's responses.[11] Our first feeling is that the Bishop is smug and worldly, Sludge despicable, the woman almost shrewish in her anger. But then with increasing force they speak Browning's truths, often in Browning's language.

> a sunset-touch,
> A fancy from a flower-bell, some one's death,
> A chorus-ending from Euripides,—
> And that's enough for fifty hopes and fears
> As old and new at once as nature's self.
> ("Blougram," 182–186)

you fool, for all
Your lore! Who made things plain in vain?
What was the sea for? What, the grey
Sad church, that solitary day,
Crosses and graves and swallows' call?
        ("Dîs Aliter Visum," 111–115)

Religion's all or nothing; it's no mere smile
O' contentment, sigh of aspiration, sir—

    .   .   .   .

rather, stuff
O' the very stuff, life of life, and self of self.
I tell you, men won't notice; when they do,
They'll understand.
                ("Sludge," 1006–1012)

When Andrea del Sarto says, "a man's reach should exceed his grasp, / Or what's a heaven for?" (97–98) we hear his customary languor and know that this is barren knowledge with which he feeds his self-contempt. The Bishop of Saint Praxed's grave words about the vanity of life rise unconsciously from his professional memory. But the startling and uncharacteristic endings of the last group of poems make such resolutions impossible. Browning tells us that Blougram "believed, say, half he spoke" (980)—but which half? "He said true things, but called them by wrong names" (996)—which things, which names? Mr. Sludge says things that seem true, but when he recants in private he is wholly base, wholly false, and wishes he hadn't said them. The woman in "Dîs Aliter Visum" wittily, passionately, and convincingly enunciates a view of love that we know Browning shared—she even echoes "By the Fireside"—and turns out to be mean and spiteful, speaking to give pain. How are we to reconcile our revulsion at the end of the poem with our previous moments of responsiveness?

What is at issue is sincerity, and in "Bishop Blougram" and "Mr. Sludge" sincerity is the subject of the discourse as well as the question that perplexes us at the end. The Bishop argues against Gigadibs's assumption that he is a hypocrite who professes belief in what he knows to be absurd, and ends by convicting Gigadibs himself of insincerity for not acting on his professed disbelief. Mr. Sludge, caught cheating by his patron, says that he is true in his fashion and similarly convicts the auditor of insincerity. In both poems the attack on the auditor is thoroughly convincing, and the self-defenses too are at least intermittently persuasive, relying on Browning's characteristic convictions and given in his characteristic language; it takes casuistry almost equal to the speakers' own to find flaws in the arguments.[12] Both speakers confess to grave faults, but on the whole this increases our confidence in their veracity. Both define the present situation as one in which they can speak with extraordinary openness: the Bishop could never speak so to his chaplain, he says, and challenges Gigadibs to publish the conversation in full confidence that no one would believe him. Sludge's summation is even more disarming:

> I know I acted wrongly: still, I've tried
> What I could say in my excuse,—to show
> The devil's not all devil.
> (1481–1483)

But when they have convinced us that, bad as they may be, they are at least sincere, Browning tells us that they aren't.

Sincerity as a test of truth and virtue, in art and in life, became increasingly important to the Victorians as other tests seemed to fail. But sincerity itself was problematic. George Eliot explored its inadequacies as a moral test in the character of Bulstrode; Browning and Arnold worried about the fact that much of the poetry they reverenced, particularly Keats's and Shelley's, was hard to reconcile with what they knew about the poets who wrote it. For insofar as a sincere poem was defined as one that came from the true heart or soul of the poet, poems could be invalidated by biographers: by the publication of Harriet Shelley's letters, or Keats's to Fanny Brawne. (At least the Victorians were spared Annette Vallon.) If the worst charges against Shelley were substantiated, Browning says in his essay, they "would materially disturb . . . our reception and enjoyment of his works, however wonderful the artistic qualities of these."[13]

When they *were* substantiated, however, they did not in fact seem to change Browning's opinion of Shelley's poetry. In the essay Browning does what Arnold was later to do in his essay on Keats: he persuades himself that Shelley's faults were inessential, venial, and would have been outgrown (even, "had Shelley lived he would have finally ranged himself with the Christians").[14] For sincerity had another meaning too, which could rescue poems from biographers after all: it could refer to the quality of the truth told rather than to the veracity of the teller. Thus Arnold says that in Wordsworth's best poems, "Nature herself seems . . . to take the pen"—seems to do so because of "the profound sincereness with which Wordsworth feels his subject, and also . . . the profoundly sincere and natural character of his subject itself." And Carlyle describes "the eye that flashes direct into the heart of things, and *sees* the truth of them" as "sincerity of vision; the test of a sincere heart." For both Carlyle and Arnold, words (and thereby their speakers) are sincere if they seem deeply true, if they have what Arnold calls the "accent of sincerity."[15] The speakers in these three poems sometimes have this accent; by this second test they are sincere, but by the first (as the poems' endings forcefully tell us) their appearance of sincerity is shown to be a deliberate fraud.

Carlyle would not have admitted that such a problem could arise, since he believed that sincerity was the one saving virtue and the only power that could effect anything positive at all. Browning was not so sure. His plays and closet dramas, in fact, are filled with sincere liars and potent lies. The events of *The Return of the Druses*, *A Soul's Tragedy*, and *In a Balcony* are precipitated by falsehoods that are in some sense noble and true, and moreover extremely effective, told by good men to achieve good ends that truth could not effect. The lies of Jules's friends in *Pippa Passes* produce a true love that saves Phene from sin and shame and leads Jules to higher forms of art. And *A Blot in the 'Scutcheon* and *Luria* show, more obliquely, the other side of the same coin: truths that do the evil work of falsehood. *A Blot* is based on *Much Ado about Nothing*, *Luria* on *Othello*; in Browning's plays the disclosures that correspond to the central lies in Shakespeare's are true. There *is* a man in Mildred's (Hero's) bedroom; Florence (Venice, Desdemona) *is* subtly treacherous to the black champion it regards as a barbarian outsider. And although these facts are disclosed by good people for good motives, both disclosures are fatal and—as it turns out—unnecessary. Truth always triumphs in Browning's plays, of course, but not easily.

So it should not surprise us to find Bishop Blougram arguing that Gigadibs's smug notion of sincerity is cant. "If Hero means *sincere man*," says Carlyle as he approaches his discussion of Luther in *Heroes and Hero-Worship*, "why may not every one of us be a Hero? A world all sincere, a believing world" has been, will be again.[16] Blougram agrees that heroes must be sincere; he does not agree that everyone can, or even should, be so. "Enthusiasm's the best thing . . . ; / Only, we can't command it" (556–557). He can't, that is, be Luther. And he wouldn't want to be Strauss, the only sincere equivalent of Luther possible in the nineteenth century; or Napoleon, whose "crazy trust" (445) in his star led him to "blow millions up" (456) and decline into quackery and cant. If there is a God, Blougram suggests, their sincerity will not save them. And he turns the criterion itself against Shakespeare, using it as Browning and Carlyle do to judge poets: "look upon his life" (511)—which proves that Shakespeare would have preferred (if this life is all) to be Blougram.

For Carlyle, sincerity is unaware of itself, and most at home in simplest ages. Blougram prefers cultivation and consciousness. "In that dear middle-age these noodles praise" (677) men were ignorant beasts. Full belief and full disbelief are alike impossible to intelligent men, but "faith is my waking life" (245)—Gigadibs, who prefers to "recognize the night, give dreams their weight" (256), should in logic give up conscious life altogether. The mixture of plausible fancies, "amusing because new" (985), and real beliefs in Blougram's argument is a paradigm of his whole life, in which he has deliberately accepted parts of his nature as a ground on which to construct a life and a self. Browning's earlier monologuists made others into works of art; Blougram has made one of himself. At the end of his discourse he invites Gigadibs to put in writing his latest creation, the discourse itself: "'Blougram, or The Eccentric Confidence'" (962). That no one would believe it makes it all the more amusing.

Our uncertainty at the end of the poem is, then, Blougram's own. He has chosen to ignore his own inner depths, the life of sleep and dreams and the unconscious, and so he cannot in any significant way be sincere. "Certain hell-deep instincts," attributed to hell only because they are deep, he ignored "—not having in readiness / Their nomenclature and philosophy" (990, 994–995). His extraordinary control of his own discourse, his single-minded concentration on the end in view, is the measure of his self-estrangement. Mr. Sludge, too, has half-created himself, although in him fraud and reality are more confusingly mixed. Like Blougram, when he considers what he has said he ignores the hell-deep instincts that produced whatever is sincere in him, thinking of himself as a creature of argument and artifice only. He too has unwittingly cut himself off from sincerity. Both poems demonstrate what Browning feelingly says in "One Word More": that the man who has mastered an art is mastered by it (in these poems the arts of life and language and the medium's tricks), and so can never be sincere in it. And yet Blougram and Sludge can simulate sincerity; they can know and tell truths they cannot live by, or even understand.

Blougram and Sludge do not get everything they want, but they have much more effect on their auditors than earlier speakers do. "Something had struck" Gigadibs in Blougram's argument—"Another way than Blougram's purpose was" (1008–1009), but still strongly enough to send him to Australia. Hiram

Horsefalls gives Sludge "Twenty V-notes more, and outfit too" (1493), and his silence, though he won't listen to anything further. Since we are not told which parts of the speeches moved Gigadibs or Horsefalls, we have to assume that they were the parts that moved us; that they respond more or less as we would if we couldn't finally see behind the scenes. The auditor functions in these poems, then, not only to show the speakers' use of language for manipulative purposes, but to show how strangely and deceitfully they succeed. The poems demonstrate the mysterious disparity between what the speakers say and what they are, between what they intend and what they effect.

We can see the crucial significance of the auditor in these poems if we compare "Dîs Aliter Visum" to "Youth and Art," which was published at the same time. In both a woman speaks to a man of the moment of love they missed and the superficial lives they have instead. Both women imagine what the man might have said or thought. But in "Youth and Art" we do not feel an auditor's presence; the moment of speech is not particularized, and the woman seems to feel only nostalgia and mild regret. Her tone and character remain entirely consistent, even when she thinks of what might have been.

> Each life unfulfilled, you see;
>   It hangs still, patchy and scrappy:
> We have not sighed deep, laughed free,
>   Starved, feasted, despaired,—been happy.
>   (61–64)

We feel no more strain or effort in her voice than in the bouncy rhythms and easy rhymes. "Dîs Aliter Visum," on the other hand, has an elaborate rhyme scheme with an obtrusive internal rhyme in the second line of each stanza, a complicated series of quotations within quotations, exclamations and rhetorical questions, and frequent, striking caesurae. We are extraordinarily aware of the voice that is just keeping in control an immensely complicated set of verbal elements. But the auditor is unpersuaded and the speaker turns nasty and spiteful:

> You knew not? That I well believe;
> Or you had saved two souls: nay, four.
>
> For Stephanie sprained last night her wrist,
>   Ankle or something. "Pooh," cry you?
> At any rate she danced, all say,

63

Vilely; her vogue has had its day.
Here comes my husband from his whist.
(144–150)

And we realize just how deliberate and manipulative, and therefore insincere, her words have been.[17]

Browning has used auditors first to create situations in which significant speech is possible; then to show how hard it is to communicate one's deepest thoughts and feelings to another person; and finally to explore abuses of speech and show that persuasive utterance may be an inaccurate index of character and character a bad criterion of truth. In *The Ring and the Book* (Browning's next work after *Dramatis Personae*) these concerns recur in one monologue or another, but neither the form nor the meaning of the poem rests upon them. The auditors are rarely present to us; the monologues are designed to characterize the speakers and elaborate the pattern and meaning of the poem, and the fact that most of them are spoken aloud is relatively unimportant. Judgment is made easy: Browning tells us what to think of the characters before they say a word, and they are never allowed to mislead or confuse us.

At the end of the twelfth book Browning explicates the "one lesson" he wants the British public to learn from the poem—a lesson that applies at least as strongly to the dramatic monologues with auditors that preceded it:

> This lesson, that our human speech is naught,
> Our human testimony false, our fame
> And human estimation words and wind.
> (XII.834–836)

Only the artist can interpret truly, only art can speak truly. For, as the dramatic monologues in *Men and Women* and *Dramatis Personae* demonstrated,

> How look a brother in the face and say
> "Thy right is wrong . . ."
> .   .   .   .
> Which truth, by when it reaches him, looks false,
> .   .   .   .
> While falsehood would have done the work of truth.
> (XII.841–853)

But the artist looks no one in the face, addresses no one directly.

Art,—wherein man nowise speaks to men,
Only to mankind,—Art may tell a truth
Obliquely, do the thing shall breed the thought,
Nor wrong the thought, missing the mediate word.
(XII.854–857)

This seems a satisfactory conclusion to Browning's long exploration of the nature of speech; insofar as it underlies the success of *The Ring and the Book* it obviously *is* satisfactory. But Browning does in fact speak directly to the reader, *in propria persona* and at enormous length, in the first and last books, and the characters' monologues still have the problematic qualities of speech defined by the earlier poems. The utterances are gratuitous in the sense that they are in excess of their ostensible purposes; insofar as they give "vent" to "impulses" (in the words of the Chatterton essay) they are outlets for energy rather than moral acts. But they are all (except the Pope's, which is not spoken aloud, and possibly Pompilia's) purposeful, manipulative; and the better the speaker controls his words to fit his purpose, the more deceitful he is and the more estranged from himself. Of the main characters Guido, who is the most subtle and false and can speak truly only to express evil, is the most consistently aware of his auditors. The lawyers and the representatives of Roman society demonstrate a variety of lesser ways in which language perverts or misuses truth for private motives. Caponsacchi tells his story with furious vividness and absolute candor, but not to persuade—his audience is prepared, now that it is too late, to believe him, and their belief can do him no good. Pompilia, who has never been able to make words help her, is even more candid, even more powerless. But for the Pope, the only speaker in the poem who has real power, interior dialogue with imaginary auditors will suffice. Browning tries to circumvent what he sees as the inherent unsatisfactoriness of direct speech by composing his poem of several juxtaposed speeches made in different circumstances;[18] but the urgency with which he explicates the genesis and meaning of his poem suggests that if he does not trust direct speech to communicate truly, he does not really trust obliquity either. And so his later poems will be more oblique, more convoluted, and more radical in their analysis than his earlier ones, for the problems have not been solved.

After the publication of *The Ring and the Book* in 1868 and 1869, Browning paused for a few years and then produced four very long poems in rapid succession: *Balaustion's Adventure* and *Prince Hohenstiel-Schwangau* in 1871,

Fifine at the Fair in 1872, and *Red Cotton Night-Cap Country* in 1873. All of these are fundamentally concerned with poetry as speech and with the effect art has on its audience. They all make some use of auditors. In three of the four the auditors function chiefly to focus our attention on the communicative aspect of speech and to define the poem—however improbably—as being spoken aloud, but no responses are recorded or expected and they have no effect on the development of the speakers' discourse. Balaustion recites her own history and a translation, with commentary, of Euripides' *Alcestis*. Prince Hohenstiel-Schwangau tries to define the meaning of his career to an auditor whom he turns out to have been just imagining. *Red Cotton Night-Cap Country* is a narrative poem in which the narrator keeps calling attention to himself as storyteller and purports to be talking to a friend. But *Fifine at the Fair*, the best, most interesting, and widest ranging in subject matter and mood, is from start to finish a dramatic monologue with a responsive auditor that reenacts the concerns of all Browning's earlier poems in that form.

Balaustion's Adventure opens the series in a mood of blithe holiday innocence, asserting that all art can be assimilated to the model of powerful speaker and responsive auditor. Art in one medium may evoke a response from the audience in another: defending the inclusion in her narrative version of the *Alcestis* of much that a spectator could not have seen, Balaustion explains that art "speaking to one sense, inspires the rest" (319). "Who hears the poem, therefore, sees the play" (335)—"Hear the play itself!" (336). Her main point, however, is that "poetry is power" (236): power enormous, creative, and benign. She felt the power of Euripides' play so deeply that her retelling of it won safe harbor for the ship she rode on and a husband for herself. For Balaustion is a paragon of intelligence and virtue, a sort of Pippa, Pompilia, and Elizabeth Barrett in one, and her power, like Pippa's and Pompilia's, is a function of her selfless innocence. Although she certainly spoke in order to gain something from her auditors, her object was to save herself and many others, and her individual gain (the lover) was unforeseen and unintended. Moreover, the poem itself presents not that fruitful telling but a disinterested retelling, later, to a few friends whose responses are not recorded.

Balaustion takes no credit for her words: "'Tis the poet speaks" (343). She regards herself as just an audience, a translator or interpreter, and is quite unaware that she is translating Euripides' play onto a higher moral and spiritual plane. She has sometimes been seen as a figure of the ideal poet, but her own modest self-valuation is more nearly accurate.[19] The poet who could imagine her could hardly think to emulate her: her power is a function of the interplay between her unself-conscious innocence and the wider awareness of poet and reader that encompasses her. Nor is she interpreting myth pure and simple, but rather responding to Euripides' highly intellectualized literary version of it. Her crystalline vision depends for its value, meaning, and even existence on the flawed and darker minds of Euripides and Browning. Like Pippa, she says more than she knows, and she shares neither the pains nor the guilt of artistic creation. Correspondingly, she describes an ideal relationship between a poet and a responsive audience—one that saves rather than threatens life— but she does not enact that relationship in the poem itself.

With *Prince Hohenstiel-Schwangau*, however, Browning returns abruptly to the present time and to his doubts about the value and power of his art. Balaustion's character has the deep clarity and transparency with which Browning always portrays innocence, but the Prince is corrupt and opaque. He represents a controversial contemporary figure (Napoleon III), and his ingenious self-defense, like that of Blougram and Sludge, involves issues of immediate general interest and is suddenly and surprisingly undercut at the end of the poem. This time, however, the ending casts in doubt not just the particular speaker's sincerity or our ability to assess it, but the very possibility of self-knowledge and therefore of any sincere self-revelation at all. Such doubt was latent in the earlier poems, and is now explicit and central. Like Blougram, the Prince defends himself as a man of ordinary capacities who makes the best of the existing world and of himself as God made him. But while Blougram ignores "certain [unspecified] hell-deep instincts" (990) beneath the temporalities he manipulates so purposefully and well, Hohenstiel-Schwangau's reverie ends with a glance into a dark underworld of murder (as exemplified by the ancient priests of Nemi) and adultery (as practised in the great families of modern Europe) by which power is acquired and transmitted. This glimpse of the depths suggests that as long as we remain, as the rest of the poem does, on the level of moral analysis and evaluation of character, character will be unknowable and thus, of course, incommunicable.

The speaker himself discovers how words deceive. In the first half of the poem he learns that his "confession" to a woman who herself has great pretentions to virtue is in fact self-praise: "I condescend to figure in your eyes / As biggest heart and best of Europe's friends, / And hence my failure" (1210–1212). In the second half he tries to describe himself as a censorious historian would and concludes that all words lie: "words deflect / As the best cannon ever rifled will" (2133–2134). The imagery says that speech is a weapon that misses its mark, aggression but not power.

But deeds lie too. Hohenstiel-Schwangau argues persuasively at the beginning of the poem that any one act, properly understood, will give the key to a man's character and to everything else he has done. The way he doodles with inkblots explains "certain things he did of old, / Which puzzled Europe" (61–62). Thus encouraged to watch and analyze the speaker's behavior, we observe him exiled in England explaining himself to a woman of the streets— only to learn at the end that we have been witnessing a silent reverie at a different time and in another place. It has been noted that most readers evidently feel not only confused but cheated by this unexpected conclusion,[20] and this typical reaction is a significant fact about the poem's meaning. For what we are cheated of is the comfortable assurance that we can assess the speaker's sincerity—his purpose, meaning, and character—by reference to his behavior in a particular dramatic situation. Our sense of moral and intellectual superiority is shattered by the double realization that we have wholly mistaken the situation, and that the speaker's attempt at self-analysis was not motivated by circumstances or designed to impress an auditor, and so was probably (it is just such things that we cannot be sure of) disinterested.

The surprise at the end does not deepen or illuminate the situation presented before; it just cancels it. The Prince imagined an auditor to assure himself of his own reality ("we must co-operate," 23, "Lend me your mind," 76), and when the pretended auditor and situation disappear the self that is left doubts its own sincerity and truth even more than we have done.[21] We thought we saw round him; we were wrong. Critics who confidently locate ironical undercutting of the speaker in almost every Browning monologue hesitate at this one. Browning's own numerous and varied comments on Napoleon III hardly clarify his own attitude, let alone his intention in the poem—which seems to be both an analysis and a demonstration of the opacity of deeds and words alike.[22]

Unlike the two poems that preceded it, *Fifine at the Fair* does not just discuss or imagine auditors; it is really a dramatic monologue with an auditor, recapitulating in its movement Browning's evolution of the form and including in its scope both Balaustion's ideal vision of the relation between speakers and auditors and the Prince's tricky demonstration of the futility of speech. Don Juan first uses speech to exercise power and assert control; then he tries to communicate his deepest feelings and most profound vision to an unresponsive and effectively absent auditor; finally, after he has impressed us with the earnestness of his yearning for truth, he suddenly reverts to the fickleness that his name and the dramatic situation imply. The poem as a whole demonstrates the impossibility of speaking sincerely when one cannot find a real self to speak from; it is a quintessentially Victorian reinterpretation of the Don Juan story, in which the famous seducer and defier of the heavens becomes a seeker after truth who pursues love as a means of self-discovery, deceives women because he does not trust his own feelings from one minute to the next, and is appalled by his fear that the only enduring realities are those the Prince saw in the dark legend of Nemi: change, sexuality, and death.

Don Juan is called "Don" (545) and he once bought a Raphael from a prince. In all other respects, however, he is less an aristocrat than a bourgeois gentleman and very much of the mid-nineteenth century. His feelings find expression in the music of Schumann. Intellectually he has accepted skepticism and relativism, which emotionally he finds deeply unsatisfying.[23] He despairs of finding an absolute, permanent manifestation of divine truth, but he does not on that account cease to desire it. His quest for knowledge and self-knowledge, moreover, is carried on in the stifling context of what is in effect the social world of the Victorian novel. Fifine's primary appeal to him is that she is outside that society, and thus the antithesis of Elvire, who stands for a life of rigid, self-protective bourgeois cosiness and privacy in an "honest civic house" (2326) in the middle of the town with its door bolted fast. He has been married to Elvire for a long time—they bought their Raphael "years ago" (512), and although he has long since tired of her, they are still very much married.[24]

No hero of a Victorian novel, in fact, is more trapped psychologically in society and its basic and representative institution, marriage, or more obsessed by moral pressure to be respectable. His frantic beating at the bars of his cage just proves his imprisonment. He despises Fifine as much as Elvire herself could, and finds it necessary to keep justifying his attention to her on abstract, philosophical, and therefore morally respectable grounds. Her blatant sexuality attracts him just to the degree that it disgusts and appalls him. Even so, he does not seduce her; she seduces him—literally, it has been pointed out, "*behind his own back.*"[25] He does not even, like Molière's or Mozart's hero, try to flee Elvire; he drags her about with him, endlessly demanding that she acknowledge his virtue and approve his behavior. What really amazes and bewilders him about Fifine and her troupe is that they seem genuinely not to care about approbation, to be free of the psychological trammels in which society has enmeshed him; they look like outcasts, but actually, he thinks, they deliberately "gave society the slip" (65) and wouldn't return if they could. They seem positively indifferent to respectability: to what people will think, what the neighbors will say, their "own good fame and family's to boot" (105). Eight sections of the poem (VI–XIII) barely suffice to express his wonder at such freedom.

The secret, he thinks, must be that they have an inner self, an inner life and reality, independent of social forms and inaccessible to view: neighbors cannot see it, nor can their words touch it. This inner life appears to be entirely independent of the usual forms and ties of the family itself: the man who exhibits wife and daughter to prurient eyes for five sous does not care about "hearth and home" (131) and would not want to cover his "womankind" (131), as respectable men do, in "as multiplied a coating as protects / An onion from the eye" (131–133) From Fifine's shamelessly naked self-display, however, Don Juan infers the existence of a central self that he can never see. Fifine shows herself as she is—she speaks truth, as he puts it—because there is another, quite different self unrevealed:

> To me, that silent pose and prayer proclaimed aloud
> "Know all of me outside, the rest be emptiness
> For such as you!"
>   (397–398)

He imagines Fifine comparing herself to her tambourine that men put money into:

> "I'm just my instrument,—sound hollow: mere smooth skin
> Stretched o'er gilt framework, I: rub-dub, nought else within—
> Always, for such as you!—if I have use elsewhere,—
> If certain bells, now mute, can jingle, need you care?"
>   (404–407)

Don Juan's own impelling fear is that he himself *has* no inner self, no buried life, no "use elsewhere." /

It is characteristic of the essentially novelistic quality of this poem that although Don Juan takes for granted that only the socially outcast and morally reprobate are in touch with their inner lives, he still expects to find himself, if at all, only through other people. In his dream he delights in watching a crowd:

Just so I glut
My hunger both to be and know the thing I am,
By contrast with the thing I am not.
(1814–1816)

But since he values others only as instruments for his own self-discovery, he cannot maintain even the illusion of disinterested affection and all his relationships are factitious. Like a character in a Victorian novel, he defines himself by others' vision of him. For this purpose, just about anyone will do. He is like a visitor to hell, reassured that he is alive by the response of "male enemy or friend, / Or merely stranger-shade" (1158–1159)—someone, anyone. Perhaps this inherent paradox—looking to those one regards as dead for proof of one's own life—accounts for the impatient cruelty with which Don Juan treats Elvire: he seems to be trying to force from her a reaction strong enough to jolt him into a sense of both her reality and his own. As much as any of Tennyson's visionary speakers, Don Juan needs a responsive auditor.

Much of what the speaker says, and particularly the manner in which he says it, can only be explained by his desire to get a strong response from his wife; whether he wounds, exasperates, or placates her hardly matters.[26] Thus he insists that she attend to his most highly colored, lingeringly lascivious description of Fifine (XV). She first sighs and turns pale (XIV) and afterward counterattacks. "Words urged in vain, Elvire!" (169). Browning pointedly reminds us by such interjections that the praise of Fifine is addressed to Elvire. With elaborate cruelty, Don Juan imagines Fifine speaking Elvire's complaints about her own lost youth and beauty and her husband's indifference. Elvire evidently tries to break away at this point, for he interjects: "Your husband holds you fast, / Will have you listen, learn your character at last" (462–463). He compares his wife to his Raphael, which he wanted badly till he got it and afterward ignored (XXXV)—but he would certainly save it or burn with it, he says, if the house caught fire (XXXVI). This placates her—"I get the eye, the hand, the heart, the whole / O' the wondrous wife again" (578–579)—but mere possession, which has been the dominant theme of his images so far, is not enough. Immediately he is off again, demanding that she see herself precisely as he sees her and admit that she is the creation of his perceiving eye. She is to watch her phantom vie with those of Helen, Cleopatra, and Fifine: "I want you, there, to make you, here, confess you wage / Successful warfare" (581–582). Furthermore, since "in the seeing soul, all worth lies" (824), her beauty depends entirely on his vision. He wants not just to

71

control but to form, even create, other people: to people his world with his own creations. Setting out to establish a sense of her independent reality, he in fact does just the reverse.

For his lust to dominate and possess is, he explains, only a substitute for his more fundamental desire to "teach" mankind—that is, to remake the world with his own vision of truth. He deals with women rather than men only because they yield themselves to be remade: "Women grow you, while men depend on you at best" (1179). Browning had bitterly told Ruskin years earlier that people "hate to be taught," and Don Juan angrily complains that to "master men" (1229) one must deny one's true self, dissimulate, descend to their brute level. (The elaboration and violence of this complaint seem to show that it is not itself a dissimulation.) He uses images of hunter and hunted, captor and beast, and his tone is as contemptuous as his imagery.

> To make, you must be marred,—
> To raise your race, must stoop,—to teach them aught, must learn
> Ignorance . . .
> Change yourself, dissimulate the thought
> And vulgarize the word, and see the deed be brought
> To look like nothing done with any such intent
> As teach men . . .
> So may you master men.
> (1222–1229)

So, he says, he turns in disgust from mankind to show his "best self revealed at uttermost" (1254) to a sympathetic woman.

But he finds nothing to show her except his vision that the world is "All false, all fleeting too!" (1469). He concludes the first part of the poem with praise of actors, "the honest cheating" (1517) that, because it does not pretend to be true, affirms the value of truth by pointing to its absence. He repeats the first lines of the poem:

> trip and skip, link arm in arm with me,
> Like husband and like wife, and so together see
> The tumbling-troop arrayed, the strollers on their stage.
> (1519–1521)

"Like" husband and "like" wife—the first time round the word may have suggested to us the sham marriages of an earlier, less respectable Don Juan, but by now it is clear that Browning's couple is really married. And yet they have to play at being so. They are actors like the troop they scorn, but without the saving grace of fully acknowledging it. In the next part of the poem, Don Juan transforms Fifine's fair into Venice's carnival and concludes that the carnival represents "the state / Of mankind, masquerade in life-long permanence / For all time" (1858–1860).

He reaches this more inclusive generalization through a different kind of speech. "Weary words" (961), despite his extraordinary verbal resourcefulness, got him to nothing but negation and empty, half-cynical paradoxes: silence speaks, lies tell the truth, the worst art like the worst woman is the best. Now he tries to communicate a feeling and a vision rather than to provoke or over-power or persuade. He no longer addresses himself directly to Elvire (in the central part of the poem she has effectively vanished) or to his own particular situation or problems. He describes sense experience, then music, then a dream, trying to circumvent language, logic, and his own limiting individu-ality. That morning, he says, his mind "kept open house" for sensations, fan-cies, memories—even perhaps of the "antenatal prime experience" (1561). Then, since "Thought hankers after speech, while no speech may evince / Feeling like music" (1566–1567), he played Schumann's "Carnaval." The music in turn gave place to a visual dream. He was in Venice, where he saw a crowd "dumb as death" (1724) whom he understood "by sight,—the vulgar speech / Might be dispensed with" (1727–1728). People spoke to each other,

> but all seemed out of joint
> I' the vocal medium 'twixt the world and me. I gained
> Knowledge by notice, not by giving ear,—attained
> To truth by what men seemed, not said: to me one glance
> Was worth whole histories of noisy utterance,
> —At least, to me in dream.
> (1760–1765)

So he came to see that the fair is an image of life, and that the only perma-nence is the ceaselessness of change.

Finally, he says, the diverse images of his dream resolved into the Druid monument that he and Elvire have just arrived at in their walk. The dream image is now present and actual, visible to speaker and auditor alike, a dark text that resists interpretation, baffles commentary, and yet cannot be misun-derstood. At the heart of the main stone structure is an image that means death:

a cold dread shape,—shape whereon Learning spends
Labour, and leaves the text obscurer for the gloss,
While Ignorance reads right—recoiling from that Cross!
(2057–2059)

There is also a huge stone pillar, fallen and half-buried in vegetation; the Curé earnestly tries to impose an edifying interpretation on its traditional phallic significance, but the people obstinately go on believing

that, what once a thing
Meant and had right to mean, it still must mean. So cling
Folk somehow to the prime authoritative speech,
And so distrust report, it seems as they could reach
Far better the arch-word, whereon their fate depends,
Through rude charactery, than all the grace it lends,
That lettering of your scribes! who flourish pen apace
And ornament the text, they say—we say, efface.
(2126–2133)

Indeed, as all the images of his dream fell into this primeval monument Don Juan did hear one single "arch-word" that both included and transcended the message of the stones. It whispered of permanence in change, of truth the soul finds when it reaches up and finds "an outer soul" (2186) beyond the senses, and finally of a new, true language that "leaves, in the singer's stead, / The indubitable song" (2202–2203) and sets forth instead of "speech, act, time, place" the naked "principle of things" (2205–2206).

Such a word cannot be spoken, only imagined or heard by the inner ear. A poem can be at best an approximation, or translation, of it. And the function of art as Don Juan sets it forth is to provoke the audience to recreate the work of art—to merge his own approximation of the original unspoken word with the artist's. Don Juan prizes, even more than his painting by Raphael, a block of stone that Michelangelo (he thinks) began to carve, for he can imaginatively complete the statue himself. When he wanted to express his feeling, he played Schumann's music. Such cooperative expression by its very nature asserts both the reality and the central unity of the experience, moving toward the reconciliation of partial points of view in a shared impersonal vision, and thus toward transcending irony.

The verbal equivalent of this recreative process is translation. The poem itself is in a sense an ironic translation of a traditional story. Unlike Browning's usual monologuists—imaginary people, obscure foreigners, puzzling and

74

controversial public figures—Don Juan is known and familiar, brilliantly defined in art. The epigraph is from Molière, but for Browning, who was passionately fond of music, Mozart's *Don Giovanni* would have been the more
significant, as it would probably have been the more intimately familiar, of
the two.[27] Browning's version is a diminution of the earlier ones and his characters are smaller versions of their predecessors. His anxiety-ridden intellectual hero is neither an insouciant skeptic nor even a seducer; Fifine and her
pimp-husband are not pretty peasants or robust comic rustics; Elvire has neither grandeur nor passion. The strange title seems to have been chosen as a
sort of comic rhyme to Molière's subtitle as an Englishman might pronounce
it: "*Le Festin de Pierre*." The statue of the murdered commendatore that
comes to dinner in the climactic episode (to which Molière's subtitle refers) of
the traditional story becomes the shapeless stones of the Druid monument.
The monument, like the statue, images forth the connection between sex and
violence and death, but whereas the statue speaks and acts with spectacular if
comic grandeur, asserting and executing the decree of divine justice, the
monument is grimly silent and Don Juan is its interpreter, not its victim.

His interpretation ends by focusing precisely and emphatically on the act of
verbal translation. The highest point that Don Juan's imagination reaches,
the "outer soul" that produces "the indubitable song," he describes in a phrase
from *Prometheus Bound*: "'God, man, or both together mixed'" (2188). The
phrase hints at the incarnation, the word made flesh, suggesting that the im-
mortality of love and the soul is the true meaning of the "arch-word" of the
Druid monument to the permanence of sexuality and death. The phrase first
turns up in the poem much earlier, in Greek, when Don Juan in a passage of
violently mixed allusions and tonal contrasts defines "love's law" (899) as a
sort of heavenly hide-and-seek with a giantess:

> each soul lives, longs and works
> For itself, by itself,—because a lodestar lurks,
> An other than itself,—in whatsoe'er the niche
> Of mistiest heaven it hide, whoe'er the Glumdalclich
> May grasp the Gulliver: or it, or he, or she—
> *Theosutos e broteios eper kekramene,*—
> (For fun's sake, where the phrase has fastened, leave it fixed!
> So soft it says,—"God, man, or both together mixed"!)
> (900–907)

Here it arrives in joking translingual rhyme to relieve the sudden grotesque
horror of a heaven that has turned without warning into a Brobdingnag

peopled by beings of enormous size and indeterminate gender. The English phrase evokes the Greek, which by the time it has been translated into English has effectively purged the image of both joking and horror. When it reappears it is part of a similar revision of the Druid stones, this time straightforward and serious. Don Juan repeats the phrase in English (2188) and then in Greek (2210), as the closest he can come to the word of truth itself.

But then he questions the accuracy of his translation, asking himself whether he is using the words to express what Aeschylus intended:

> As I mean, did he mean,
> The poet whose bird-phrase sits, singing in my ear
> A mystery not unlike? What through the dark and drear
> Brought comfort to the Titan?
> (2212–2215)

And right here, directly in answer to this question, Don Juan's tone suddenly and decisively changes. He remembers Fifine, of whom we have heard nothing for a very long time, and as he does the vision he had just attained disappears for good. The change occurs as a deliberate misreading of the next lines of *Prometheus Bound*. The "'God, man, or mixture'" that Prometheus heard coming to bring comfort was a chorus of sea nymphs; Don Juan translates their words when they arrive, with an interpolated commentary in tones of sneering irony that apply them to his encounter with Fifine.

> "God, man, or mixture" proved only to be a nymph:
> "From whom the clink on clink of metal" (money, judged
> Abundant in my purse) "struck" (bumped at, till it budged)
> "The modesty . . ."
> (2216–2219)

He goes on like that through the rest of the speech from Aeschylus, annihilating distinctions of value by aggressive verbal play, leveling what had seemed tender and sublime to the clever and nasty.

As in many of Browning's earlier poems, the speaker's self-conscious mastery of language is the mark of his self-estrangement. "As I mean, did he mean?" The viciousness of his parody is directed against himself: his scorn is not for Aeschylus's lofty music, but for his own inability to repeat it except to debase it, to "mean" something less by it, to mistranslate it. When Balaustion in her innocence tells the story of Euripides' *Alcestis*, she translates the staged play into a narrative faithfully, she thinks, yet she raises it to a higher spiritual plane: her simplicity makes something greater than the text, whereas Don Juan with his sophisticated intelligence makes something less. Balaustion thinks that, on the whole, Euripides is speaking through her (*Balaustion's Adventure*, 343); Don Juan is not so innocent as to imagine that such a thing is possible. And as soon as he asks himself whether his meaning is the same as Aeschylus's, he is bound to become aware of a difference. For a moment he seemed to himself to have shared the wider, higher vision of the Greek poet, but when he recognizes—as he has to—the separateness of his own point of view, the illusion of unitary truth gives way to the conscious duplicity of irony.

As Don Juan puts it, "poetry turns prose" (2227) and "dreaming disappoints" (2230). "We end where we began" (2242)—at home, with nothing communicated, nothing accomplished, nothing resolved. Instead of affirming immortal love, they have confronted death and sex as the sole realities of human life and seen that the two are really one:

> wherever we were nursed
> To life, we bosom us on death, find last is first
> And henceforth final too.
> (2243–2245)

The completed circle of their walk has become an image of human life as a circuit from death to death, with a terrifying suggestion of a dead or murderous mother, the womb as the grave. Instead of using Elvire to prove and augment his own living reality, Don Juan has diminished hers.

> How pallidly you pause o' the threshold! . . .
> .   .   .   .
> Suppose you are a ghost! A memory, a hope,
> A fear, a conscience!
> (2306–2311)

He describes the life they will lead locked up at home together if she will be "but flesh and blood" (2338)—and then at the last minute, on the very doorstep, he turns from that sad imprisonment to follow Fifine round the endless circle once again. If Elvire wants him back, she will also have to reenter the unreal world of experience, like the ghost of Helen that went to Troy while the real woman stayed quietly at home:

I go, and in a trice
Return; five minutes past, expect me! If in vain—
Why, slip from flesh and blood, and play the ghost again!
(2353–2355)

These are Don Juan's final words. They announce his own flight from reality in the overt irony—the verbal equivalent of the "honest cheating" he had admired in the gypsies—with which he inverts the usual sense of "ghost" and promises to come right back without either meaning it or intending to be believed. He has been brought to a halt by the same grim facts beneath the surface of society, morality, and consciousness that Prince Hohenstiel-Schwangau found at the end of his not dissimilar meditations, and he rebounds like the Prince into the more cheerful realm of random and meaningless action.

Behind Don Juan's failure of vision and will there seems to lie something of Browning's own self-reproach both as a lover and as a poet who was often (as in "One Word More") uneasy about writing just dramatic monologues, ironic refractions of the pure white light into representations of highly particularized points of view. And since his wife, too, had urged him to drop his masks and express his own vision of truth, so ironic and brutally sexual a poem could itself be seen as a kind of infidelity to her memory. *Fifine at the Fair* is a disturbing and rather disagreeable poem: its energy and inventiveness seem constantly to turn against themselves, and there is an excessiveness in the speaker's contempt for himself and others and in the poet's implied contempt for him that neither the ideas he articulates nor the dramatic situation seem fully to account for. The poem may reflect Browning's bitterness after his quarrel about marriage with Lady Ashburton, as well as the state of mind that would have led to that ill-conceived proposal in the first place.[28] It is sometimes even said that Elvire stands for Elizabeth Barrett Browning, but it seems nearly inconceivable that Browning would represent his wife as the sullen, conventional, and passive object of his own contemptuous bullying. What the poem does reflect is her absence: life without love, the choice between the prison of Elvire's respectability and the antisocial, impersonal lewdness of Fifine.[29]

But the fact that the turning point of the poem comes as a question of translating *Prometheus Bound* is the single most significant allusion to Elizabeth Barrett Browning. She had actually published two translations of that play, one in 1833 and another in 1850. When Browning met her in 1843 she was working on the second version; in some of her earliest letters she consulted him on the interpretation of particular passages, and their later letters contain several references to other Aeschylean projects that she had in mind.[30] In *Fifine*, Browning does not use her renditions of the crucial phrase ("god or man, or half divine / Being" in 1833, "a god, or a mortal, or nature between" in 1850)[31] or of the chorus Don Juan cynically misinterprets. Part of the point would be the difference in their translations. He had reason, furthermore, to associate that chorus in particular with his wife, for whom it seems to have had some special significance. She drew attention to it in 1833 with a rather pointless note, wondering whether the nymphs were "shoonless" for sorrow or haste and concluding that "it may be more poetical" to think it was both. And then in one of her early letters to Browning she applied the lines to herself.

> Yet when you tell me that I ought to know some things, tho' untold, you are wrong, & speak what is impossible. My imagination sits by the roadside . . . like the startled sea nymph in Aeschylus, but never dares to put one unsandalled foot, unbidden, on a certain tract of ground— never takes a step there unled![32]

She is telling Browning that she will not anticipate his wooing, even in imagination; if he wants to be understood, he must speak out plainly. The behavior of the seductress Fifine is precisely the opposite, in Browning's version of the same line: "'Impulsively she rushed, no slippers to her heels'" (2222), drawn by the sound of money to seek her prey.

Fifine is the only nymph who comes to Don Juan. But outside the closed circle of restlessness and fragmentation that the poem describes there is the frame, comprised of the prologue and the epilogue, in which Browning speaks in what sounds very much like his own voice and imagines a solution to the problem that Don Juan in the poem never solves.[33] The speaker of the prologue, "Amphibian," cheerfully wonders how the dead woman whom he loved would look, from her inaccessible superiority, on his earthly weakness. In the epilogue, "The Householder," he has found out. He was tired, angry, and alone—and suddenly she came.

> just a knock, call, cry,
> Half a pang and all a rapture, there again were we!—
> "What, and is it really you again?" quoth I:
> "I again, what else did you expect?" quoth She.
> (5–8)

The energies that are thwarted and deflected in the poem itself find relief and release here. Instead of monologue, there is dialogue—and in every stanza the wife gets the last word. She fits none of the female stereotypes set up in the poem itself, and her voice strikes an entirely new note; tart, terse, and loving. The speaker's voice is filled with a responsively happy, reckless energy of immense relief. They end the poem together by dismissing the problem of language. They collaborate in composing an announcement of his death; they do it as fast as they can, using the tritest, most comical country-churchyard formulas—words carved by simple folk on tombstones, a more cheerful counterpart to the stones of the Druid monument—which will serve as well as anything.

> "What i' the way of final flourish? Prose, verse? Try!
> *Affliction sore long time he bore*, or, what is it to be?
> *Till God did please to grant him ease.* Do end!" quoth I:
> "I end with—Love is all and Death is naught!" quoth She.
>   (29–32)

The final words are splendidly sweeping, lighthearted, and absolute: what would be a grandiose and empty conclusion if Don Juan managed to reach and utter it becomes inoffensive and even persuasive by its air of casual exuberance. Nor does the speaker represent himself as saying the words, but only as hearing and reporting them. Without love, the epilogue seems to be saying, no words will find truth—the speaker had been alternately "Tongue-tied" and "blaspheming" (4) just the minute before; with love, any old words (the older, the better) will do. But such an affirmation, pleasing though it may be to the sentimental reader, turns its back on more than Don Juan's endlessly proliferating arguments, speculations, and images. It is like the word that Don Juan heard in his dream but could only try to describe, not repeat; it turns away from readers and from poetry, into privacy and silence.

When the crazed, self-mutilated protagonist of *Red Cotton Night-Cap Country* has climbed his tower and is about to jump to his death, the narrator pauses, as he often does, to reflect on his own narration.

> He thought . . .
>   (Suppose I should prefer "He said"?
> Along with every act—and speech is act—

There go, a multitude impalpable
To ordinary human faculty,
The thoughts which give the act significance.
Who is a poet needs must apprehend
Alike both speech and thoughts which prompt to speak.
Part these, and thought withdraws to poetry:
Speech is reported in the newspaper.)

He said, then, probably no word at all,
But thought as follows—in a minute's space—
One particle of ore beats out such leaf!
(3276–3287)

The minute's thought is then reported in a little over two hundred lines of poetry.

The whole poem can be read as an attempt to unite speech with both thought and action. In Browning's monologues with auditors, "speech is act" and examined as such. From "Bishop Blougram's Apology" on, however, he shows an increasing interest in the ways in which speech can hide the thoughts that "give the act significance," even from the speaker himself. The monstrous narrative machinery of *Red Cotton Night-Cap Country* works almost entirely to push into the forefront of the poem our awareness of the double nature of words, as thought and as action. Thus the frame insists that the story is being told aloud, to an auditor, while at the same time it ostentatiously refuses to help us forget that the poem cannot possibly have been spoken aloud at the time and place it claims to have been. (For one thing, it is too long: Browning wrote when he had finished it, "I am going to read the poem, or as much of it as proves digestible at a sitting, to Miss Thackeray [the auditor in the poem] this morning.")[34] We are not encouraged to distinguish between the poet and the narrator, or to regard the poem as a fiction in which we should suspend disbelief. The narrator insistently reminds us that he actually knows only the barest facts of the story—little more than the speech reported in the newspapers; he reminds us not only that we cannot know what Miranda thought in that final minute but that we don't even know that he didn't in fact speak ("probably" he didn't), and that in any case a minute is too short a time for the thoughts the narrator ascribes to him. The whole point appears to be the immense gap between words and deeds and their meaning: the action of the poem, played out in its grotesquely elaborate formal machinery, is not what Miranda did but the narrator's efforts to explain it. Thus while he gives us Miranda's thoughts instead of his speech, he presents his own thought—with blatant implausibility—as spoken aloud. What the poem enacts is the process of interpretation: it is a lesson in reading the newspaper, understanding speech.[35]

After *Red Cotton Night-Cap Country*, Browning's examination of speech as action, aggression, deception, self-betrayal, truth telling, teaching, and communication of whatever sort becomes if anything even more wide-ranging and inconclusive. Instead of being concentrated in monologues with auditors, it is diffused throughout his later work. In a few of the shorter poems, however, we see him returning to the form and elaborating the concerns of his earliest short monologues. "Martin Relph" (1879) records the annual public confession of a man who failed to speak when his speech would have saved the life of the woman he was in love with (the man whom she herself loved had run out of breath); the confession is both an attempt to determine whether his motive was jealousy or fear, and an act of atonement. "Pheidippides" (also 1879) balances "Martin Relph" with the tale of a runner who gasped out good news and died. Pheidippides spoke out, as Browning had long ago promised Elizabeth Barrett he would try to do, though at the cost of his life. (This covert association of outspokenness and death recalls the image in "One Word More" of the camel that opens its breast and dies.) At the end of the poem Browning praises his fate:

> He saw the land saved he had helped to save, and was suffered to tell
> Such tidings, yet never decline, but, gloriously as he began,
> So to end gloriously—once to shout, thereafter be mute:
> "Athens is saved!"—Pheidippides dies in the shout for his meed.
>   (117–120)

And finally, there is "Christina and Mondaleschi" (1883), which brings us back full circle to the world of "My Last Duchess" and "The Laboratory." Christina teases her auditor, terrifies him, and finally has him killed.

·e§ THREE ҙ·

Arnold

THE QUESTION OF HOW he can speak to his audience, and how (if at all) the audience will respond is even more urgent and difficult for Arnold than it is for Tennyson or Browning. But there is no fear of aggression or danger in Arnold's enactments of speech: instead of imagining that his poetry could be effective enough to hurt, he wonders whether it will be possible to speak and be heard at all. Each of his first three volumes of poetry contains one poem with an auditor—"Resignation" in 1849, "The Buried Life" in 1852, and "Philomela" in 1853—that both demonstrates and more or less explicitly sets forth the vision of the world and the theory of how poetic vision is communicated that dominate the volume in which it appears. In "Resignation" the speaker confronts and tries to argue away his auditor's emotional resistance to his ideas on God, on nature, and on human life. The auditor in "The Buried Life" seems willing enough to listen sympathetically, but the speaker discovers that it is almost impossible for him to speak sincerely, and therefore with any significance or truth, even when the depths of his being are stirred by love and his fears allayed by trust. "Philomela" exemplifies the assertion of the 1853 Preface that what art should communicate is emotion, and that it does so best when it does it obliquely, through an action proved efficacious for the purpose by its survival through time. And finally, there is "Dover Beach," first published in the *New Poems* of 1867 but almost certainly written in the early 1850s. "Dover Beach" uses the same poetic form not to talk about problems of communication, but to solve them.

In all four of these poems the auditor is a woman. In all but "Philomela" the relationship between speaker and auditor is explicitly one of easy, reciprocal affection, and in "Philomela" the setting and situation—a man talking to

a woman of nightingales and passion in the moonlight—are those of courtship. All four poems are set in the ordinary, pleasant here and now. None
makes any effort to suggest that the speaker is not the poet himself, or that the
poet's attitude toward him is ironical or even particularly detached. The fiction of all four poems (except "Philomela," where the personal relationship
matters least) is that the speaker is talking, with no deliberate self-concealment
and little premeditation, to someone he loves and trusts, and who loves and
trusts him. If ever a man could be both sincere and persuasive, Arnold clearly
thinks, it would be under these circumstances.[1] But it turns out, in the first
three poems at any rate, not to be so easy.

The four poems together are paradigmatic of Arnold's relationship with his
audience at its best, both as he imagined it and as it actually turned out to be.
He never really expected—though he certainly hoped—that his poems would
reach any other audience than the fit and very few (his prose, most of it written to be popular, was another matter). Their artistry seemed frigid and aca-
demic even to those who could perceive it, and many could not. The personality they revealed was too distant, erudite, weary, or subdued to please. In
1869 Arnold ascribed whatever popularity they had had to their representative
truthfulness.

> My poems represent, on the whole, the main movement of mind of the
> last quarter of a century. . . . I have less poetical sentiment than Tenny-
> son, and less intellectual vigour and abundance than Browning; yet, be-
> cause I have perhaps more of a fusion of the two than either of them,
> and have more regularly applied that fusion to the main line of modern
> development, I am likely enough to have my turn.[2]

This assessment seems accurate. Readers who were not offended by his pessimism and could appreciate more than the accessible pathos of "The Forsaken
Merman" were won by the significance of what he said to appreciate the
charm with which he said it. George Eliot wrote in 1855 that one read
Arnold's poems first for the sake of "converse" with the mind behind them,
and came gradually to perceive their "poetic beauties."[3] But there were not
many George Eliots, and even in 1869 Arnold does not think his "turn" has
come yet.

For the most part, moreover, Arnold's matter was even less likely to please
than his manner, as he perfectly well knew. Few readers were willingly to acknowledge that his chart of "the main movement of mind" was an accurate

one. Fewer still—not even that notorious doubter, Clough—wanted to hear that God is absent, nature dead, love illusory or destructive, and man blind and thwarted at every turn. In "The World and the Quietist" (1849) Arnold accurately forecast his readers' objections to his "'mournful rhymes / Learned in more languid climes'" (what Clough later called "the dismal cycle of his rehabilitated Hindoo-Greek theosophy").[4] His assertion in the same poem that "With no ungrateful sound / Do adverse voices fall on the world's ear" was less accurate, and he no doubt knew that too. *The Strayed Reveller, and Other Poems* is full of adverse voices, although they usually present their bleak visions (in the longer poems especially) with dramatic or semidramatic obliquity. When Arnold speaks without a visible mask, he generally shows his uncertainty about whom he is addressing, how he should speak to them, and how—if at all—they might respond.[5]

Uncertain about his audience, he has trouble finding his voice. He stutters and clears his throat: "Who prop, thou ask'st, in these bad days, my mind?" He stumbles: "Artist, whose hand, with horror winged, hath torn." He explodes in pointlessly derivative bluster: "'O monstrous, dead, unprofitable world.'" He finds it easier to begin when the addressee is clearly identified, whether as Shakespeare, a Republican Friend, or an Independent Preacher, and easier still when imaginary characters speak in clearly defined dramatic settings. But such characters generally get no answer to their words at all, or, like the Sick King in Bokhara, not the answer they want. Mycerinus addresses his people as from a high platform, expecting and receiving no response; the New Sirens go silently away when the speaker questions them; and the fact that Margaret does not hear the merman generates the most penetrating pathos in all of Arnold's works. Shorter poems are filled with questions that there is no one to answer ("To a Gipsy Child by the Sea-shore," "A Question") and prayers to the deaf or dumb or absent ("Stagirius," "Quiet Work," "Written in Emerson's Essays"). Even Shakespeare tells Arnold everything except what he most wants to know (and so "We ask and ask").

For despite its surface confidence, *The Strayed Reveller, and Other Poems* is a book of doubts, contradictions, and uncertainties. Just about every assertion about God or nature or human life is balanced by an opposing assertion, or undercut by the speaker's emotional resistance, or both. Not only do "In Harmony with Nature" and "Quiet Work," for instance, contradict each other— each contains within itself an emotional undercurrent that goes against the surface statement. "In Harmony with Nature" exudes a horrified admiration of the brute strength it deplores, and "Quiet Work" offers nature as a moral exemplar but concludes quite cheerfully that though man dies the forces of nature endure, "Still working, blaming still our vain turmoil, / Labourers that shall not fail, when man is gone." Cold comfort, surely. "*In Utrumque Paratus*" presents an idealistic metaphysics in the first half and a materialistic one in the second, and cries out sadly at the end against the hypothesis it has just so confidently asserted. "The Strayed Reveller," "The Forsaken Merman," "The New Sirens," "The Sick King in Bokhara," and "Mycerinus" all express feeling's rebellion against the moral conditions of human life; the only resolution these poems offer is the tentative stoicism ("It may be") of Mycerinus, and the Sick King's fancy entombment of the man he could not save.

But in "Resignation" emotional resistance is embodied in Fausta; by directly confronting her hostility or indifference, the speaker integrates them into his idea of the world. The problems that loom so menacingly in *The Strayed Reveller, and Other Poems*—problems of audience, of tone, of an uningratiating subject matter, of truths that contradict each other or against which the heart rebels—are the structural basis of "Resignation," the last poem in the volume and the one in which Arnold sets forth unambiguously, and to all intents and purposes in his own voice, his most serious ideas about life. The first two-thirds of the poem (1–198) consists of three parallel sections, each of which describes first people who are in bondage to time and then those who stand still watching the movement of life and expect nothing for themselves. The speaker is trying to persuade Fausta, his sister, that action and passion are futile; he offers her the first scene in each section as an illustration of this futility, the second as an example of proper resignation and detachment. At the end of each section, he turns his attention—and therefore ours—directly to her, but each time she is less sympathetic, and so each time he tries a new tack.

This stopping and starting, this repetition of the same theme and structure in different keys, gives an effect of discontinuity, or of a series of inconclusive conclusions that lead only to new beginnings from the same point. Unlike the sort of Romantic poem that it superficially resembles, "Resignation" does not follow the impulse of the speaker's mind as it discovers itself through confrontation with the landscape; the speaker does not even appear to notice the actual, present scene until he is well along into the poem (line 90).[6] He knows from the start what he is going to say; all that is to be explored is the way of saying it, so that from one point of view the poem is just a set of discoveries that underlie the poem's structure and determine its movement: he discovers his auditor's responses to what he says, and his own responses to hers.

He begins with elaborately contrived, blatantly literary sketches of pilgrims,

Crusaders, Goths, Huns, and allegorical Hours, which don't seem to interest Fausta at all. She cares about what is personal and immediate: "We left, just ten years since, you say, / That wayside inn we left today" (40–41). So he translates the pilgrimages of the formal, impersonal first section into a parallel description of that walk ten years ago and the scenery about them now, and draws the same moral again. But Fausta rejects his mood and his moral alike, breaking the gathering momentum of his speech when his eye focuses on her restless presence in the scene he is dreamily evoking: "On this mild bank above the stream, / (You crush them!) the blue gentians gleam" (102–103). Finally, after a more meditative and generalizing description of gypsies' wanderings and poets' visions that proves his third failure, he has to come to terms with her vivid indifference. "You listen—but that wandering smile, / Fausta, betrays you cold the while" (199–200).

For that smile calls into question not merely the persuasiveness of the speaker's words at that moment, but the value of Arnold's entire post-Wordsworthian vision. Immersion in the "general life . . . / Whose secret is not joy, but peace" (191–192) might well satisfy poets, the speaker understands her to be thinking, but the poet's wide-ranging visionary experience is simply useless, not even interesting, to her. Wordsworth assumes that what the poet sees and feels and says is of potentially universal application, but Fausta flatly denies that this is so:

> In the day's life, whose iron round
> Hems us all in, he is not bound;
>
> .   .   .   .
>
> He escapes thence, but we abide—
> Not deep the poet sees, but wide.
> (209–214)

Arnold gives Fausta's challenge serious expression and full and serious rebuttal: the speaker agrees with everything he imagines her saying and then brings her argument round to a different conclusion. Fausta, in this patently autobiographical poem, has traditionally been held to represent Arnold's sister Jane, who was the closest to him of his brothers and sisters, the one most likely to sympathize and to comprehend him, and also one of the very few whose opinion of his poetry mattered most to him.

> You—Froude—Shairp—I believe the list of those whose reading of me
> I anticipate with any pleasure stops there or thereabouts.

87

You and Clough are, I believe, the two people I in my heart care most to please by what I write.

You were my first hearer . . . and such a sympathising, dear—animating hearer, too.[7]

While we need not take any of this too seriously—much of it is affectionate compliment, much is affected disdain of reviewers, and the list of preferred readers is by no means immutable—these letters and the many others like them demonstrate a real anxiety to please his sister. If she would not like his poems, who would?

In fact, Fausta's lines are prophetic. They accurately forecast, if not Jane Arnold's reception of her brother's poems, that of many friends and reviewers: the charge that Arnold's poetry is remote, superior, out of touch with the hearts and lives of ordinary people. One friend whose opinion mattered to Arnold, James Anthony Froude, complained to Clough in 1849 about this very poem: "I don't see what business [Matt] has to parade his calmness and lecture us on resignation when he has never known what a storm is and doesn't know what he has to resign himself to."[8] The speaker in "Resignation" explicitly defines himself as one whose "natural insight can discern / What through experience others learn" (233–234), and asks Fausta not to "blame" him for it—anticipating objections, that is, did not avert them. Clough too, foremost among both friends and reviewers, was soon publicly to condemn Arnold's poems on the very grounds suggested in "Resignation." In his 1853 review Clough compares the tone and matter of Arnold's 1852 poems unfavorably to Alexander Smith's, and contemporary poetry in general to the contemporary novel. He backhandedly praises Arnold's "refined" and "highly educated sensibilities,—too delicate, are they, for common service?" The central thesis of Clough's review is an extrapolation of Fausta's objection: that people want poetry to deal with "general wants, ordinary feelings, the obvious rather than the rare facts of human nature . . . every-day life . . . business and weary task-work . . . our grievously narrow and limited spheres of action."[9] Two lines Arnold added to the poem in 1881 make the similarity, clear enough already, even clearer: "*He leaves his kind, o'erleaps their pen, / And flees the common life of men*" (211–212).

The rest of the poem is an earnest, carefully argued response to Fausta's crucial and representative assertion that no one is interested in hearing the things that Arnold wants to say. The speaker replies, quite simply, that he can't help it: people should be interested. The "general life . . . of plants, and stones, and rain" (191, 195) is real; the world of passions that attracts Fausta ("aversion . . . love, / . . . effort, interest, hope, / Remorse, grief, joy," 216–218) is not. She may not like what he says, but it is true.

Fausta loses the argument, but she wins the poem. Although we hear no more of her responses, from this point on we feel her presence with accumulating intensity. The tender, almost anxious pleading, the tentative but insistent self-justification ("Blame thou not . . . blame not," 231, 238) keep us continuously aware of her. More than this, while the speaker insists still, and increasingly, on the truth of his vision, he also accepts the truth of her feelings, which gradually come to dominate in his tone. In the first part of the poem (1–39) his voice is impersonally authoritative, his allusions stiffly literary, his syntax obtrusively formal and elaborate. He grandly condescends: "These, Fausta, ask not this; nor thou, / Time's chafing prisoner, ask it now!" (38–39). But her expression of more personal concerns leads him into reminiscences (40–107) in which the images of journey and struggle that he has just used for exhortation return saturated in nostalgia and regret.

> Once more we tread this self-same road,
> Fausta, which ten years since we trod;
> Alone we tread it, you and I,
> Ghosts of that boisterous company.
> (86–89)

He answers her impatient assertion that nothing has changed with a comparison of gypsies' obliviousness to change and poets' detached vision of process. He begins with renewed, confident didacticism, but the "cold" (200) inattentiveness that he notes in her when he finishes reflects, and perhaps has helped to produce, the gradual dissipation of his confidence and vigor. For his vision has darkened:

> The life of plants, and stones, and rain,
> The life he craves—if not in vain
> Fate gave, what chance shall not control,
> His sad lucidity of soul.
> (195–198)

By the end of the poem he shares her feeling:

89

Enough, we live! and if a life,
With large results so little rife,
Though bearable, seem hardly worth
This pomp of worlds, this pain of birth.
(261–264)

These lines and those that follow to the end of the poem are the ones that R. H. Hutton chooses to represent Arnold's characteristic "'lyrical cry.'" This is a particularly significant judgment because Hutton, applying contemporary critical standards with his usual vigor, thoroughness, and penetration, says that Arnold's poetry tends to be rhetorical rather than truly poetic: interested in persuasion rather than disinterestedly expressive. Hutton finds "a didactic keenness with the languor, an eagerness of purpose with the despondency, which give half the individual flavour to his lyrics." [10] Now this is precisely descriptive of "Resignation," though Hutton does not say so; Hutton is acutely sensitive to, and not pleased by, Arnold's didacticism (he disapproves of Arnold's gloomy non-Christian world view); and so it is particularly interesting that he finds Arnold's purest lyric voice at the end of "Resignation." For in "Resignation" didacticism has become part of the subject matter of the poem, not a separable strategy or tone. The "didactic keenness" and "eagerness of purpose" are the speaker's, not the poet's. The speaker's endeavor to persuade is half the poem, and the auditor's refusal to be persuaded is the other half; as they fuse they become (using the terms as the Victorians do) not rhetoric, but lyric.

It is striking and suggestive, furthermore, that the lyrical cry is approached here by what is essentially the method of irony. In "Resignation" more than any other Victorian poem, the presence of the auditor serves the essential function of irony: to incorporate into the poem an awareness of other possible points of view than the speaker's own. And it does so without falling into an inconclusive "dialogue of the mind with itself" (which to the early Victorians would seem morbid); without adopting an ironical tone (which would sound unpoetical); and without setting the poem loose to welter in moral uncertainties (which would seem an evasion of the poet's moral responsibilities). There are only two points of view in the poem, they are clearly defined, and they eventually merge. The auditor's presence is felt, richly and increasingly, as a resistance that the speaker must incorporate—not just overcome—to make his statement work. Once we have become aware of her resistant presence, we hear in the speaker's every word his effort to persuade her, and thus we feel the presence of her opposition even when she is silent. The flat assertion of bleak certitude at the end of the poem carries absolute conviction because it has recognized intellectually, and incorporated emotionally, Fausta's point of view. In the last line—"The something that infects the world"—the speaker's ideas have been infected by Fausta's feelings. This is the world as perceived by the speaker, as felt by Fausta.

And why "Fausta"? She is Faustian insofar as she wants more scope than life offers for experience, development, and change. But the poem is an anti-*Faust*: she is not its protagonist. "Resignation" insists by both its form and its content on the separate and equally valid lives of speaker and auditor; it is a protest against the kind of poetry—*Faust* or "Tintern Abbey" alike—that tries to absorb everything into one voracious central consciousness. In "Resignation" the ultimate voracity is not the poetic consciousness at all, much less any Romantic or Faustian craving for experience; it is rather the unconscious, grimly inhuman "general life." But by the very fact of being self-conscious both of its own individuality and of the separate individualities of others, consciousness resists the undifferentiated general life, even while it accepts it intellectually and morally. Such a self-defining withdrawal of the self from the world of merely personal experience into the world of impersonal poetic vision and discourse is the anti-Romantic, anti-Faustian lesson of "Resignation."

But there is a palinode. When the 1849 poems were published, Arnold advised his sister to "resign nothing" after all.

> The true reason why parts suit you while others do not is that my poems are fragments—*i.e.* that I am fragments, while you are a whole . . . a person who has any inward completeness can at best only like parts of them; in fact such a person stands firmly and knows what he is about while the poems stagger weakly & are at their wits end. I shall do better some day I hope—meanwhile change nothing, resign nothing that you have in deference to me or my oracles.[11]

By attributing his poems' collective weakness to their maker's lack of inner integrity rather than to any faults in themselves or in the world they portray, Arnold seems to accept Fausta's view of poetry as expressing a merely personal idea of life. A similar view informs the analysis of poetic truth as a function of personal sincerity in "The Buried Life."

Trying very hard to say something nice about Clough's poems in 1848, Arnold praises them for a single and dubious virtue: sincerity.

The good feature in all your poems is the sincerity that is evident in
them: which always produces a powerful effect on the reader. . . . The
spectacle of a writer striving evidently to get breast to breast with reality
is always full of instruction and very invigorating—and here I always
feel you have the advantage of me.

This is mock humility and faint praise, for Arnold regarded Clough's "line" as
one that "most of the promising English verse-writers" were currently following, one that necessarily neglects the real virtues of poetry: beauty and form.
Clough is not "an *artist*": his poems excel in "direct communication, insight,
and report," but they are deficient in beauty. Because Clough is "a mere
d——d depth hunter in poetry," he will not make the sacrifices form requires.
And "absolute propriety—of form," not "wealth and depth of matter" is "the
sole *necessary* of Poetry as such." So when Arnold quotes "Resignation" at
Clough—"'Not deep the Poet sees, but wide'"—the preceding correspondence amplifies and enforces the meaning of the line: intensity of insight
and "propriety" of form—that is, sincerity and "Poetry"—are opposite and
incompatible.[12]

Less than a decade later, however, we find Arnold remarking on the temptation (which should be resisted) to write in "a region where form is everything. . . . It is only in the best poetical epochs . . . that you can descend into
yourself and produce the best of your thought and feeling naturally, and without an overwhelming and in some degree morbid effort."[13] Although he still
opposes form and surface on the one hand to sincerity and depth on the other,
now he would like to have them all. We can see the shift taking place as we
move from "Resignation" to "The Buried Life," in which Arnold tries to
plumb the depths, and then to the attempted synthesis of width and depth,
order and intensity, surface and sincerity, in "Philomela."

"The Buried Life" considers the possibility of using romantic love to produce poetic speech. The poem opens with an image of ambiguous feelings
and aggressive words channeled and formalized into play: a "war of mocking
words" (1) that for a moment recalls the relations between speakers and auditors in Tennyson and Browning. But suddenly from the depths comes a wave
of sadness, unsummoned and irresistible, nameless and formless (and, alas,
bathetic): "Behold, with tears mine eyes are wet! / I feel a nameless sadness
o'er me roll" (2–3). Like Tennyson with his similarly idle tears, the speaker
knows not what they mean; he only knows that words do not placate or even
identify "a something" (6) in him. ("Something" is not, like the preceding

lines, mere ineptitude; it suggests both the "something far more deeply inter-fused" of "Tintern Abbey" and the "something that infects the world" in "Res-ignation.") Perhaps if they stop talking he will see a wordless solution in her eyes: "let me read there, love! thy inmost soul" (11). But (not surprisingly), her inmost soul is as mysterious as his own.

> Alas! is even love too weak
> To unlock the heart, and let it speak?
> Are even lovers powerless to reveal
> To one another what indeed they feel?
> (12–15)

Yes; because they don't know what they feel. When the speaker has accepted this as a fact, the auditor's function is complete and she disappears from the poem. The speaker forgets about her, and so do we, as he meditates on the meaning of the episode.

What it seems to mean is that poetic meaning has become impossible. "Resignation" says that personal passion is irrelevant to poetry because it is unreal. Now it is real, and it is the source of poetry, even of the impersonal vision of 1849; unfortunately, however, it is inaccessible. We cannot speak truly because we cannot reach our genuine selves. We need to understand

> the mystery of this heart which beats
> So wild, so deep in us—to know
> Whence our lives come and where they go.
> (52–54)

Without such knowledge, we are worse than speechless. We have "an un-speakable desire" (47) to know our buried self, "to utter one of all / The nameless feelings that course through our breast" (61–62). But those true feelings are "for ever unexpressed" (63), and meanwhile "what we say and do / Is eloquent, is well—but 'tis not true!" (65–66).

When we try to be sincere, that is, we are only eloquent; we try to make love and make mocking war instead; we try to write poems and are only rhe-torical. We are back to Mill's dislike of self-consciousness and Browning's fear of fluency, to the twin paradoxes that the harder one tries to be sincere the less one can be, and that the more one masters speech, the less one speaks the truth. It is curiously appropriate, in the light of this surprisingly conventional theorizing, that "The Buried Life" defines the true voice of feeling in the images and accents of Arnold's most popular (most conventionally pleasing) poem, "The Forsaken Merman."

> Yet still, from time to time, vague and forlorn,
> From the soul's subterranean depth upborne
> As from an infinitely distant land,
> Come airs, and floating echoes, and convey
> A melancholy into all our day.
>   (72–76)

The poem begins with the wish for a true expression of feeling in the ideal candor of love. As we read on we realize that feeling itself is instrumental. We want to be loved so that we can feel, to feel so that we can speak: we want to know our feelings so that we can know ourselves, and to know ourselves so that we will understand life in general, the general life, and be able to say something of more than private importance. When we feel that we are loved we can feel more deeply, and then "The eye sinks inward, and the heart lies plain, / And what we mean, we say, and what we would, we know" (86–87). Man seeks his buried self so that he can know, ultimately, "The hills where his life rose, / And the sea where it goes" (97–98).

The speaker in "The Buried Life" does not find the knowledge he seeks, and his baffled introspectiveness is the key to the 1852 poems and what chiefly differentiates them from those of 1849. The 1849 poems are not self-conscious or introspective. Most of them examine ideas and make pronouncements about life, and the ones that present experience and feeling are usually narrative and dramatic. The poems that exhort to stoic self-sufficiency do not move on to self-examination. "Live by thy light," Arnold says in "Religious Isolation," but he never says what his own light shows us. He seems generally to be using poetry as a prelude to self-discovery, but not for self-analysis: the poems state or enact different views of life and the world and try to work out their consequences. Such poetry is in effect a deliberate rejection of the sincerity, self-expression, and direct communication of feeling that, Arnold knew, poets were expected to provide. "More and more I feel bent against the modern English habit (too much encouraged by Wordsworth) of using poetry as a channel for thinking aloud, instead of making anything." Thus in 1849 Arnold defends *The Strayed Reveller, and Other Poems*; writing to Clough on the same subject he says, "Shairp urges me to speak more from myself: which I less and less have the inclination to do: or even the power." [14]

94

But the 1852 poems contain many attempts, at least, at speaking from the poet's self, and fewer satisfactorily made "things" than the 1849 ones. With the significant exception of the three best poems in the book ("Tristram and Iseult," "Empedocles on Etna," and "To Marguerite—Continued"), there is less dramatization, use of personae, or objectification in images, and much more direct use of the poet's own experience than in 1849. But again and again these poems discover the impossibility of communication. Even in the dramatic parts of "Tristram" and "Empedocles" the characters seldom really address or understand each other and when they do seem to be communicating they speak awkwardly or in a declamatory falsetto. Tristram's speeches are the worst part of his poem; Empedocles speaks only half his mind to Pausanias, and responds to Callicles' offstage songs in ways that Callicles does not at all intend.

In a remarkably large number of the nondramatic poems, however, the speaker imagines some kind of verbal response. The volume reverberates with spectral voices that say what the poet already knows or wants to hear. In "Longing" the speaker imagines the words his beloved does not say; in "Meeting" "a God's tremendous voice" urges him away from love; in "Stanzas in Memory of the Author of 'Obermann'" and "Memorial Verses" he restates the words of dead poets; "Nature" speaks in "The Youth of Nature" and "Morality"; voices come from heaven in "Self-Dependence," "A Summer Night," and "Progress," from within in "Youth and Calm." The moral or metaphysical statements from without, however, are ventriloqual projections of the speaker's own voice. In "Self-Dependence" his heart echoes the heavenly counsel, and in "The Second Best" inner and outer are fused (perhaps just by the exigencies of rhyme) as "an impulse, from the distance / Of his deepest, best existence" (21–22), with "distance" suggesting outer rather than inner space. But in the 1852 poems, more than in earlier or later ones, we feel that Arnold desperately wants his poetry to speak out and to be heard.

Empedocles on Etna, and Other Poems (1852) falls into four parts: the title poem itself; a series of lyrics, mostly about love; "Tristram and Iseult"; another series of lyrics, mostly longer than the first ones and mostly on large, general subjects: poetry, nature, life. "The Buried Life," which is in the last group, recapitulates the main themes and situations of the love poems and considers their implications for the writer of poetry. If we read the love lyrics as they appeared in 1852, before they were regrouped as "Faded Leaves" and "Switzerland" (with a few dropped and a few separated from the others) their movement is essentially that of "The Buried Life." First the lover wants the woman to soften her smiles and let him speak and weep; then he realizes that the fault is in his weakness, rather than her disdain; increasingly he generalizes his immediate failure into an assertion that men are isolated from each other, from themselves, and from the source of life and reality.

Thus in the first of the love lyrics, "The River," the second and third stanzas of the poem as it appeared in 1852 strikingly resemble the opening of "The Buried Life."

> Let those arch eyes now softly shine,
> That mocking mouth grow sweetly bland;
> Ah, let them rest, those eyes, on mine!
> On mine let rest that lovely hand!
>
> My pent-up tears oppress my brain,
> My heart is swollen with love unsaid.
>   (29–34)

Next comes "Excuse" (later "Urania"), which describes a woman who smiles and mocks; the "excuse" is: "She is not cold, she is not light; / But our ignoble souls lack might" (3–4). Next, in "Indifference" (later "Euphrosyne"), she is said to be aloof because she is complete in herself and does not need love. The vicissitudes of courtship continue through three more of the poems later to be grouped as "Faded Leaves" ("Too Late," "On the Rhine," "Longing") and then four that later form part of "Switzerland" (and with them "Destiny"). Since the "Faded Leaves" poems were almost certainly written later than the "Switzerland" ones, this ordering represents a reversal of chronology; psychologically the movement of the series in 1852, like that of "The Buried Life," is downward and inward. For in the "Switzerland" poems the failure of love is increasingly seen as the speaker's own, and moreover as inevitable. "What heart knows another? / Ah! who knows his own?" ("Parting," 73–74). The love poems proper end with the definitively final last line of "To Marguerite—Continued": "The unplumbed, salt, estranging sea"; the group as a whole tapers off with five sad poems about life and death. "The Buried Life" recapitulates this story, considering it primarily from the point of view of language: language as self-knowledge, self-expression, and communication. As in "Resignation," the situation the poem establishes is the best possible one for the communication it wishes to achieve; even more than in "Resignation," communication fails. The problem now is not that the auditor won't listen, but that the speaker can't speak.

"'Resolve to be thyself'" ("Self-Dependence," 31) is both the great moral imperative of the 1852 poems, and the great impossibility. It is impossible because the self is so well buried that it is very hard to find; and because of the poet's suspicion—his near-certainty, in fact—that if he does manage to exhume it, it will prove a disappointment. Two sad quatrains entitled "Destiny" sum it up:

> Why each is striving, from of old,
> To love more deeply than he can?
> Still would be true, yet still grows cold?
> —Ask of the Powers that sport with man!
>
> They yoked in him, for endless strife,
> A heart of ice, a soul of fire;
> And hurled him on the Field of Life,
> An aimless unallayed Desire.

What kind of sincerity is possible to such a being? We feel the speaker in "The Buried Life" to be sincere in the sense that he is not acting a part or trying to persuade. The auditor's presence at the beginning makes the speaker's later unawareness of her, and thus of any audience at all (ourselves included), a positive fact about the poem. By the end he seems to have forgotten her completely. She is there just long enough to define the situation as one in which the speaker can speak absolutely freely, and to define his unselfconsciousness in doing so; but what he will say is simply that he cannot really speak the truth at all. All he can sincerely say is that he would like to be sincere. This is only the sincerity of self-doubt, weakness, and failure: what Arnold so often and so ambiguously celebrates in Senancour and others. It is the sort of thing Clough achieves, though without Clough's energy; it is not what Arnold thinks is really poetry. It is moral, not visionary: not the sincerity that sees into the self which makes us "one with the whole world" ("Empedocles on Etna," II.372) and into the "heart [that] beats in every human breast" ("The Buried Life," 23), and thus into the heart of nature, the life of things.

"Not deep the poet sees, but wide" ("Resignation," 214)—but though the speaker in "The Buried Life" wants a very wide view indeed, a landscape stretching from the origins of human life to its end, he says that one must see "deep" first if one is to see at all. He does not succeed in doing either. Empedocles has to die to find his deep-buried self, and the gloom of all the 1852 poems on this theme, their disheartened and unsuccessful search for an inner certitude that corresponds to an external reality, their lurking fear (expressed most vividly in "The Future") that life is buried in the dark recesses of prehistory—suggests finally that the self has not been buried to further the darkly benevolent schemes of "Fate" or "God," but because, like other things when they are buried, it is dead. The title is either an oxymoron or a nightmare.

The Preface to *Poems* (1853) expounds a theory of poetic communication that can best be understood as the next stage in Arnold's consideration of the problems he explored in "Resignation" and "The Buried Life." For once the poet has said that he has no certain access to his buried life, it follows from the assumptions of the poem that he has nothing further to say. He becomes subject to the "terrible sentence" that Arnold applied in the 1853 Preface to most modern poets: "*Il dit tout ce qu'il veut, mais malheureusement il n'a rien à dire.*" [15] One of the great virtues of old stories for a modern writer is quite simply that they provide him with something to say. In the 1853 Preface Arnold argues for classicism and objectivity and against romanticism, subjectivity, and the merely contemporary. Although his tone is that of a man gallantly defying a unanimous multitude, however, the single point on which the Preface irreconcilably differs from the critical consensus is its recommendation that modern poets use ancient subjects. [16] For the Preface invokes classicism to serve romantic ends, objectivity to make subjective poems possible. It turns to old stories, and to drama rather than lyric, in order to escape the impasse of "The Buried Life" but still attain the end set forth in that poem: to find something to say.

When Arnold's Empedocles could no longer write poetry, he jumped into the volcano to become reunited with his deep-buried self and thus with the whole world. That self is not mind or thought: it is reached through fire, and if it is any one thing, it is passion. The Preface suggests that the other way round might work better: instead of going into one's own self to find the general self of the race, one could begin by rearticulating some already existing expression of the general self, and through that find one's own. There are stories that offer access to the real self. Thus Arnold defines "the most excellent" actions:

> Those, certainly, which most powerfully appeal to the great primary human affections: to those elementary feelings which subsist permanently in the race, and which are independent of time. These feelings are per-

manent and the same; that which interests them is permanent and the same also. . . . To the elementary part of our nature, to our passions, that which is great and passionate is eternally interesting; and interesting solely in proportion to its greatness and to its passion.[17]

Thus his examples of great actions are stories of passion asserting its primacy by defying the gods and moral laws: Achilles, Prometheus, Clytemnestra, Dido, not decent Hector, competent Agamemnon, civic-minded Aeneas.

The sources of art are so primitive, lawless, and antisocial that civilized poets can only reach them by indirection, but the validation of art comes directly from the responses of ordinary people, ancient and modern alike. An audience should have the experience sought by the speaker in "The Buried Life." Art makes people happy, the Preface announces: "the more tragic the situation, the deeper becomes the enjoyment; and the situation is more tragic in proportion as it becomes more terrible."[18] That is to say, feeling is both the source and end of art: the happiness described here is that of feeling, of knowing oneself to have felt, of being one with one's buried life. "I am past thirty, and three parts iced over,"[19] Arnold told Clough sadly in 1853—but one can get below the ice. Since the "primary" and "elementary" passions are "permanent and the same," a poet can feel them not just in his own frozen heart but in the depths of human history. Arnold's insistent and redundant nondefinition implies, furthermore, that we know them to be primary and elementary by the only test he can think of, the pragmatic one: they have survived in literature that moved people long ago, and moves them now.

Thus when Arnold offers classical writers, and especially Greek dramatists, as models for emulation, it is not just because of their proximity to a prehistorical golden age of noble action and feeling, but also because of their distance from it. "On the Modern Element in Literature" defines Periclean Athens as "modern"; Arnold's Greeks, who are never Dionysian, never brutal or irrational, resemble idealized nineteenth-century liberal humanists. The great virtue of the Greek dramatists in the light of the Preface is that they were able to exploit their distance from the mythic past. This is what moderns can emulate. Arnold knows that the story of Oedipus is a myth, and that Sophocles' *Oedipus Rex* is not. What fascinates him, what the Preface attempts to explicate and presents for imitation, is the way in which a highly intellectual "modern" poet like Sophocles availed himself of the passionate, primitive powers of myth. One might almost say, in fact, that Empedocles had to jump into the volcano, and was then ejected from *Poems* (1853), because he had lost the power to respond to myth except by either corrosively intellectual, or debilitatingly sentimental, analysis. The only parts of "Empedocles on Etna" that Arnold reprinted in 1853 and 1855 were a few pieces of Callicles' mythmaking.

The most richly imagined and elaborately wrought lines in the Preface—the lines that are at its imaginative center—are those in which Arnold describes the experience of the original spectators at a Greek tragedy.

> The terrible old mythic story on which the drama was founded stood, before he entered the theatre, traced in its bare outlines upon the spectator's mind; it stood in his memory, as a group of statuary, faintly seen, at the end of a long and dark vista: then came the poet, embodying outlines, developing situations . . . stroke upon stroke, the drama proceeded: the light deepened upon the group; more and more it revealed itself to the riveted gaze of the spectator: until at last, when the final words were spoken, it stood before him in broad sunlight, a model of immortal beauty.[20]

The poet has power over his audience because he shows them what is within them; he articulates what they know. The story is "terrible," "old," "mythic": the terms seem interchangeable, and both the antiquity of the story and the fidelity with which it is reembodied are essential to its effectiveness. Facts being what they are, Arnold can say only that the Greeks did not *prefer* contemporary subjects to older ones; but we gather from this passage that he would have preferred them to have used no contemporary subjects at all. For he describes here a dramatist who clarifies and articulates what already exists in the spectator's memory—in his buried self and in the memory of the race—in the collective buried self. Mythic discourse undoes the separateness of speaker and audience, the poet and the world. The interest in myth of the early Victorians, like their interest in philology and particularly in etymology (which emerges very strongly in Arnold's religious books) was part of a search both for origins and for primal unity.[21] The one primeval language, the key to all mythologies—the assumption underlying quests for such unitary origins is that "once . . . we were / Parts of a single continent" ("To Marguerite—Continued," 15–16). At the source of life, from which all true selves flow, we were all one. Thus "The Buried Life" speaks of

> an unspeakable desire
> After the knowledge of our buried life;

A thirst to spend our fire and restless force
In tracking out our true, original course;

A longing to inquire
Into the mystery of this heart which beats
So wild, so deep in us—to know
Whence our lives come and where they go.
(47–54)

The "mythic" past of the Preface is the Edenic world in which speech and poetry were one, when feeling expressed itself spontaneously and hearts lay open to be read. In "The Future," the last poem in the 1852 collection and the last in the category of lyrics in later editions, Arnold laments the Old Testament days of unworn green fields and "vigorous, primitive" tribes (33), of deep, pellucid, and tranquil feeling and clear visions "Of God, of the world, of the soul" (43). "The Future" is merely nostalgic for that irrecoverable world, but the Preface says it is still indirectly available to us, in myth.

But poets are easily distracted, Arnold thinks, from the really modern and classic: if not by the love of contemporaneity, then by the lure of language—what he calls in the Preface "expression." In his desire to expose the potential destructiveness of language, he pushes the contrast between poetry and rhetoric almost to the point of trying to get rid of words entirely. The poetical, as he implicitly defines it in the Preface, is subverbal, preverbal, though it needs words to body it forth. Thus Menander said his comedy was finished before he had written a line, and Shakespeare's expression is faulty whenever it distracts attention from the action;[22] it is a great virtue of Greek tragedy, one gathers, that it can be described as a group of statues in the sunlight: an arrangement of motionless, clearly seen forms.

This attempt to do away with language is, of course, not an attack on critical orthodoxy but an exaggeration of a critical commonplace, and the same is true of the exceedingly pragmatic view that the Preface takes of poetry. Not opposition, but the extreme lengths to which the argument is carried, accounts for most of the belligerence and self-defensiveness of the Preface. Poetry is defined almost exclusively in terms of its effect on the audience. It must "inspirit and rejoice the reader . . . convey a charm, and infuse delight." The unity and coherence Arnold desires is expressed in similar terms: a poem should make a "total impression." The modern poet will realize "that it is this effect, unity and profoundness of moral impression, at which the ancient poets aimed; that it is this which constitutes the grandeur of their works, and which makes them immortal. He will desire to direct his own efforts toward producing the same effect." The criterion for an excellent action turns out to be simply that it be an effective one: that it move the reader. There are not good and bad or better and worse effects imagined in the Preface, just stronger and weaker ones. "The more tragic the situation, the deeper becomes the enjoyment."[23]

The poetic of the Preface is pragmatic insofar as it considers poems almost exclusively in terms of their effect on the reader. It is objective insofar as it imagines the center of a good poem to be an action, and a good action to be a "grand, detached, and self-subsistent object."[24] But it is expressive and romantic insofar as feeling is the implied source and object of communication and action alike, feeling for its own sake, valued for intensity alone. Its very objectivity is subjectivity upside down (or inside out); the poem should be cut free from its creator, formed and shaped, not because form is valuable and beautiful, but so that it will make a stronger impression.

In other words, the Preface is an attempt to find a nonlyric form for the lyric's expressive power: a form as capacious and "interesting"[25] (Arnold's repeated use of the word is itself interesting) as the novel, but without the novel's bondage to the trivial, superficial, and transient. The Preface shows Arnold looking for an alternative both to the novelistic with its immersion in the local and temporal, its entanglement in detail, and to the lyrical, which—so it seems to Arnold in 1853—is both likely to seem merely personal and to require access to personal sources of feeling that are no longer available. Arnold sees two dangers: the welter of mere objective detail on the one hand, the swamp of mere subjectivity on the other. But the Preface attacks a poetry and a poetic that manage to choose both these evils simultaneously, both the ephemera of modern life, and the "allegory of the state of one's own mind."[26] This is what Arnold derides in the Preface: it is what he saw as the poetic of Alexander Smith's *A Life Drama*, Clough's *The Bothie of Tober-na-Vuolich* and *Amours de Voyage*, and later of *Maud*. (If Arnold wanted poetry to be poetry, he wanted prose to be prose, social, sociable, and dispassionate: he preferred Bulwer's *My Novel* to the "hunger, rebellion, and rage" of *Villette*[27]—another example, clearly, of the wrong sort of compromise, the poeticizing equivalent in fiction of the novelizing poems he disapproved.)

Arnold thinks, then, that both lyric and novelistic poetry—the only kinds that seemed in 1853 to have any life left in them—are radically and about equally unsatisfactory. This goes far toward explaining his concentration in the Preface on epic and tragedy. For we should not forget how patently absurd it was to offer the forms and plots of Greek tragedies as models for poets writing in 1853. It was considerably more absurd then, even, than it would have been a century later, when Joyce and Eliot had shown how myth could be used as a structural principle, enabling writers to organize their perceptions of the fragmented contemporary world, and how the use of myth, and not just the content of a particular myth in itself, could become part of the work's meaning. Arnold's own long poems on ancient subjects are quite simply imitations of the antique (in intention, at least), and the fact of imitation is not part of the poems' structure or of their content. "Sohrab and Rustum" is contemporary—that is, Romantic—despite its author's evident and expressed intention: its modernity of feeling, like that of *Merope*, is its saving but unintended grace, and its similes are as obtrusively decorative as anything Arnold could reprehend in Keats.

The self-evident (one would think) fatuity of the enterprise helps, too, to explain Arnold's attacks on "expression." "Expression" does not just distract from the whole; it presents subordinate "objects"—as in Keats's "vivid and picturesque turns of expression, by which the object is made to flash upon the eye of the mind"[28]—and most nonnatural objects belong to a particular time and place. The poet's business is not with the "outward man of Oedipus or of Macbeth, the houses in which they lived, the ceremonies of their courts," which "he cannot accurately figure to himself";[29] these (though Arnold does not quite carry the logic this way) he had better leave alone. Sophocles' austerity of expression has an additional, not-quite-stated value as a model: it is least likely to betray that the poet is unfamiliar with the surface of the world he is writing of. And we may guess that the Preface says more of drama than of epic, and of the epic more of the most dramatic episodes, because these demand relatively little temporal detail. When Arnold says that the time and setting of an action do not matter, he seems to want us to forget that the poet must place it somewhere, at some time; though he thinks that the less of an alien and antiquarian background the poet gives us, the safer he will be. The crucial fallacy of the Preface is that it argues too simply from effects to causes: it prescribes a poetry that not only turns out to be, but deliberately sets out to become, independent of any particular time or place, and speaks not to one particular auditor but to all mankind.

* * *

The dominant theme of the 1853 poems is that of the Preface: the association of pain and beauty, suffering and art, and the difficulty of finding any of these with adequate intensity in the modern world. Only "Philomela," however, exemplifies, although hardly in the form the Preface envisions, the use of ancient stories to discover and express the permanent passions and to communicate them to an auditor. But while it is the nature of their being that auditors in dramatic monologues lack substantiality, even in that company of shadows the auditor in "Philomela" is noticeably unnoticeable. Her only attribute is a name, Eugenia, and her nullity makes her presence particularly call for explanation. Unlike "Resignation," this is not a poem with an argument or idea about life to impose, and Eugenia unlike Fausta is not there to resist persuasion. Nor is it a love poem, except insofar as the setting and the fact that the auditor is a woman with a romantic name make it so; unlike the woman in "The Buried Life," Eugenia does not fade permanently from the poem as the speaker finds his voice and subject and turns his eye inward. Just the opposite, in fact; although he begins with an address to her—"Hark!"—for most of the poem the speaker addresses the nightingale, and Eugenia is noted again and named only five lines from the end. But her presence makes the poem into a paradigm of the sort of poetic communication imagined in the Preface, set in the homely context of two people speaking to each other. Whether Eugenia responds positively or not, or responds at all, the poem does not bother to tell us (like the audience at a play, she is not invited to participate); but we know from the beginning that she is there, we do not doubt that she is listening, and we feel the speaker's consciousness of her attentive presence in the ease and confidence with which he superimposes the ancient story on the present scene.

A man and a woman stand outdoors on a moonlit spring night, listening to the nightingale. It is the setting that in "To Marguerite—Continued" represents hopeless romantic yearning, but in "Philomela" the speaker bridges the estranging sea by making the song of the nightingale into a myth that asserts the permanence, and thus the reality, of passion: "That wild, unquenched, deep-sunken, old-world pain" (8). The language insists both on the immediate particularity of the present scene and moment ("that moonlit cedar," 3; "this fragrant lawn," 10; "to-night," 16; "Here . . . on this English grass," 17) and on the immense temporal and geographical distance from which Philomela comes and in which she still imaginatively lives.

> And can this fragrant lawn
> With its cool trees, and night,

And the sweet, tranquil Thames,
And moonshine, and the dew,
To thy racked heart and brain
Afford no balm?
(10–15)

The answer, of course, is no. The question itself points forward to the assertion in "Thyrsis" that myth does not operate now in England, and moreover never did; poetry cannot charm Proserpine into giving back a buried life, for "ah, of our poor Thames she never heard" (98). But whereas in "Thyrsis" this distance from mythic power is an aspect of the poet's loss, in "Philomela" it is both the vehicle and the proof of the poet's power. (The speaker can hardly mean by his question that he would like the nightingale's pain to be assuaged and the song thus silenced.) For in contrast to the speaker in "The Buried Life," who could not dig beneath the conventional surface of language, the speaker in "Philomela" exploits in what appears to be a similar situation the theories of the Preface: he reaches by the indirection of myth to the impersonal (or subpersonal) depths where life is buried and alive.

Keats's nightingale shifts, alters, and fades away under the varying pressures of the poet's imagination. Arnold's, on the contrary, is an increasingly substantial objectification of just such a "terrible old mythic story" as the Preface imagines coming into light and solidity on the Greek stage. Except for a few brief, rather bald exhortations to Eugenia to attend to the nightingale ("Hark . . . Listen"), which serve in turn to make us attend to her, the speaker's eye is on the object—first the tawny bird, then the story. He does not even really tell the story: rather, by a series of allusions to some of its chief incidents, he asks it to tell itself; he reminds us of it. The story, like that of a Greek tragedy as Arnold describes it in the Preface, already exists in the auditor's memory, as it does in ours. Her experience is a reexperiencing, a recognition. So is the experience attributed to Philomela herself: "Dost thou again peruse . . . The too clear web?" (19–22). And so, of course, is ours.

The address to the bird, furthermore, consists entirely of a series of questions that direct our attention to the aspect of the myth that Arnold wants to emphasize: its endurance. Each question is the same: are you still reliving your past? does your passion still endure? Since that past and that passion exist only as myth, and since the song awakens the speaker's memory of the myth just as his words awaken the auditor's and our own, the answer has to be reassuringly positive. The stress on memory was even more emphatic in *Poems* (1853), where "Philomela" is paired with Callicles' song about metamorphosis and memory. Cadmus and Harmonia, in contrast to Philomela, forget and are silent; they

> Wholly forget their first sad life, and home,
> And all that Theban woe, and stray
> For ever through the glens, placid and dumb.
> ("Empedocles," I.ii.458–460)

Is it all happening over again, the speaker in "Philomela" asks the bird, just as it did before? Yes; but the poem is saved by the fact that it asks the question. In his classicizing essays of the 1850s Arnold envisions a modern literature that would function as a sort of collective memory, reconstructing the past as literally as possible rather than reinterpreting it or exploiting the distance between the present and the past. In the preface to *Merope* (1858) he explains that it is usually best to keep to the traditional details of a story: "The tradition is a great matter to a poet; it is an unspeakable support; it gives him the feeling that he is treading on solid ground." [30] *Merope* itself is a lifeless reconstruction—except for the character of Polyphontes, whom Arnold found inadequately presented in the older versions and therefore felt free to reinvent; Arnold could not bring back the mastodon or make the antique past live again. But he could imagine himself doing so, and imagine an audience attentive and moved as he did; and so "Philomela" is alive.

Before his desperate classicizing of 1853, however, Arnold had already written "Dover Beach," the one poem in which he shows communication from speaker to auditor as open, direct, complete, and wholly unproblematic. As in "Philomela," the situation and the auditor are sketched in so lightly that the poem seems poised on the borderline between dramatic monologue and a more conventional lyric form. A man and a woman are in a room at Dover; presumably they are a married couple spending the night at a hotel on their way to or from the continent. [31] The speaker talks mostly on impersonal topics, turning near the end (as Wordsworth so often does) in an impassioned address to his companion. But the auditor's dramatic presence is established from the very beginning—the speaker describes what he sees from the window and asks her to join him there, and we assume that she does—and her presence is felt sufficiently clearly to exclude both soliloquy and all other possible auditors, ourselves included. The speaker is speaking out loud to someone in the poem, not to us, and we overhear the unself-conscious intimacy that culminates in his direct appeal in the last paragraph: "Ah, love, let us be true / To one another" (29–30).

If there is a secret to the extraordinary charm of "Dover Beach," it lies in the contrast between the absolute bleakness of its statement about life in general and the pleasantly affectionate intimacy of the particular moment in which we hear the statement being made. [32] The poem plainly enunciates Arnold's darkest view: beauty is an illusory glimmer on the surface of things, faith was an aberration that history has left behind, and nothing—in descending order from joy to help for pain—is left. But the peace and love that have vanished from the darkling plain are still present in the room that looks out on it. The poem takes a long view of human history, and the images implicitly submerge the inner life of the individual in a historical process as inevitable as the ebb of the tide. Simultaneously, however, the poem enacts the retreat into private, domestic life and personal affections that is the usual alternative in Victorian fiction to the evils of the social world. "And we are here as on a darkling plain" (35)—"we" means simultaneously everyone and the two lovers alone.

The interplay of public and private, social and personal, prophetic and domestic elements appears primarily as a matter of the relation of content to form. The oracular, visionary statement about the spiritual desolation of the modern world is in the tradition of Carlyle and Ruskin, but the speaker does not preach or declaim, he talks. (In other poems that make similar statements Arnold's voice tends to be shrill or stagy.) Since he has an auditor whom he knows to be interested and sympathetic, he does not try to persuade anyone or to defend himself against hostility or indifference. The syntax is often artfully elaborate and the diction is sometimes discreetly elevated, but the pace is reflective and unhurried. If the ideas seem the product of long meditation, their expression seems extemporaneous, determined by the accidents of a particular scene and moment. The sea seems to draw forth words and images that follow the sound and rhythm of the waves until they transform the crash of the sea on the shore into the clash of human armies in a dark world from which the sea has finally withdrawn. The characteristic movement of Arnold's best poems ("The Scholar-Gipsy" and "Thyrsis" as well as "Resignation" and "The Buried Life") is that of exploration and discovery, testing ideas and images in a quest toward an unforeseen conclusion. But in "Dover Beach" the speaker finds a perfect vehicle for the expression of his ideas, and his thought unfolds steadily and certainly, with no equivocations, no revulsions of feeling, no second thoughts.

"Dover Beach" is probably the most widely popular short poem of the Victorian period. It is certainly one of the best. It is generally taken, moreover, as the representative statement of the Victorian malaise, the definitive assertion of the pessimism that the twentieth century has found the most "modern" and congenial aspect of Victorian art. And except for that pessimism it meets the criteria of the early Victorian reviewers too. It presents one person talking to another about his inmost thoughts and feelings. The dramatic situation defines his speech as sincere and spontaneous, produced naturally by the occasion, not manipulative or rhetorical, and unaware of the reader listening in. The subject is contemporary and the setting suggests an ordinary episode in an ordinary life. The poem is Arnold's clearest and most complete statement of the dark side of his vision of human life, the statement he knew no one wanted to hear. But in "Dover Beach" he imagined a situation in which he could speak out without worrying about how others might respond. The perfect confidence and felicity with which the speaker addresses his companion provide perhaps the single best demonstration of the usefulness of auditors.

~§ FOUR §~
Clough and Meredith

ARNOLD'S "SWITZERLAND" MIMICS some of the gestures of auditor poems and the longer works that are related to them, but the gestures remain only mimicry. Although the sequence is full of apostrophes, many are to shadowy gods or natural forces, and we can hardly imagine that Marguerite is listening when the speaker says to her, for instance: "To the lips, ah! of others / Those lips have been pressed, / And others, ere I was, / Were strained to that breast" ("Parting," 67–70); we are not surprised to find him just five lines later addressing the winds instead. Neither any individual poem nor the sequence as a whole is ever deflected from its set course by the speaker's awareness of another person. We do not feel the presence, responsive or resistant, of the social world as we do in *Maud*. Nothing happens except within the speaker's mind; no human voice reaches him from without. Marguerite remains the object of his distant reverie: he makes no attempt to approach or persuade her and responds to no movement on her part. Although he attributes some specific attitudes and behavior (mostly foolish and frivolous) to her, there is no awareness of another possible point of view and therefore no irony—indeed, if one tries to read some of the poems through Marguerite's eyes or ears they become quite strikingly unpleasant. The speaker says that the modern social world has made love impossible, but that world is not a presence within the poem either as a point of view or as an attitude toward language.

Maud, Fifine at the Fair, Amours de Voyage, and *Modern Love,* in contrast, develop the auditor element in two clear ways: as the social world in which the speakers' utterances take place, and as the attention given to the speakers' use of language as an essential part of their engagement with that world. All four poems suggest that literary convention in general and poetic speech in particular can be agents of morbidity or self-deception or violence, and at the very beginning they establish heightened language, and particularly imagery, as an object for our continued attention as we proceed. *Maud* begins with characteristic emphasis on the speaker's violently imaginative speech:

> I hate the dreadful hollow behind the little wood,
> Its lips in the field above are dabbled with blood-red heath,
> The red-ribbed ledges drip with a silent horror of blood.
>   (I. 1–3)

Tennyson added some lines in the second edition that point to the deliberate excessiveness of the opening: "What! am I raging alone as my father raged in his mood?" (I.53). *Fifine* moves from the easy, flexible short-lined stanzas of the prologue into a glaringly awkward singsong bounciness and foolishly simple diction that makes us excruciatingly aware of the long, long rhymed lines.

> Does she look, pity, wonder
>   At one who mimics flight,
> Swims—heaven above, sea under,
>   Yet always earth in sight?
> ("Amphibian," 73–76)

> O trip and skip, Elvire! Link arm in arm with me!
> Like husband and like wife, together let us see.
>   (1–2)

Don Juan, who is always very aware of the limitations and power of his language, uses it most aggressively in his early lurid descriptions of Fifine. *Modern Love* opens with the most violent of many contrasts between acute observations expressed in simple, supple language and opaque, elaborate, self-admiringly literary images:

> By this he knew she wept with waking eyes:
> .   .   .   .
>   Then, as midnight makes
> Her giant heart of Memory and Tears
> Drink the pale drug of silence.
>   (1)

Amours de Voyage begins with the poetical voice of the narrator:

Over the great windy waters, and over the clear crested summits,
  Unto the sun and the sky, and unto the perfecter earth,
Come, let us go.
  (I. 1–3)

And then we hear Claude at his most self-conscious and ironical, recording his first impressions of Rome and drawing attention to his diction, his tone, and the fact that he is writing at all:

Dear Eustatio, I write that you may write me an answer,
Or at the least to put us again *en rapport* with each other.

. . . .

Rubbishy seems the word that most exactly would suit it.[1]
  (I. 11–12, 20)

But Claude cannot find his appropriate voice without defining his relations with the social world of his English friends, the art of Rome, and the potentially heroic politics of the risorgimento.

Clough's poems like Arnold's impress us by the literalness, sincerity, and accuracy with which they seem to represent the spiritual and intellectual malaise of their times. On the whole the two agreed about what was wrong, but they had very different ideas about what the appropriate poetic response should be. Arnold disliked Clough's poems for being immersed in the time stream, too concerned with content and not enough with form, and not beautiful; he found them, in short, unpoetical.[2] In 1853 Clough responded to these criticisms (expressed fairly tactfully but very firmly in their correspondence) by asserting in an essay in the *North American Review* that Arnold's poetry, with all its charm, was too remote from life and action to be salutary or really please. Readers prefer novels to poems, he said, because novels address themselves to the concerns of the everyday world in which people actually live. "To be widely popular, to gain the ear of multitudes, to shake the hearts of men," poetry must do likewise.[3] Arnold in his turn said in the 1853 Preface that to do all this poetry should, on the contrary, resolutely avoid the trappings of modernity and peculiarly modern concerns. In *Amours de Voyage* (which Arnold seems to have particularly disliked)[4] Clough examines the rival claims of poetry and prose fiction, the lyrical impulse and the unpoetical world, and attempts to reconcile them. The poem experiments with ways of speaking of, in, and to the modern world.

Amours de Voyage is often referred to as a novel (or even a novelette) in verse. Clough himself called it "my 5 act epistolary tragi-comedy or comi-tragedy."[5] To this hodgepodge of generic descriptions we can add another: an extended dramatic monologue or sequence of monologues. Although Claude writes rather than speaks and often seems more interested in self-analysis than in communication, his words almost always arise from a particular situation, are genuinely addressed to one particular person whose response he cares about, and exhibit a pervasive self-consciousness about his statements and modes of speech. In the intervals between letters, his feelings and attitudes are tested and modified by experience. The poem is mostly made up of Claude's letters, though we see some from Mary and her trivial-minded sister Georgina too; and since these three do not write to each other, their parallel monologues never converge into dialogue. Mary's one note to Claude is mislaid before he or the reader ever gets to see it. The letters from Mary and Georgina give a context to his successive monologues without being heard by him or directly affecting what he says. They characterize the two women, show us how Claude appears to others, and provide some information inaccessible to him; above all, they establish the social world as a firm and recalcitrant reality that will test the congruence and power of Claude's utterance. He must speak in this world if he wants to speak at all.

The novelistic aspects of the poem are the most readily apparent: a fairly elaborate plot, subtle and convincing characterization, a richly detailed and precisely contemporary setting, and minute attentiveness to manners, grada-tions of class, and the trivia of everyday life. Like many fictional heroes of the 1840s, Claude is addicted to thinking, about both topical matters and his own inner life.[6] But the poem is less concerned with characterization than with the idea of character, less with presenting an action than with considering the na-ture and meaning of action. It begins by accepting the essentially novelistic assumption that one's self is significantly defined by one's social role, and proceeds to test and explore the consequences for lyric poetry of such self-definition. Almost the first thing Claude discovers (not to his surprise) when he gets to Rome is that he can't escape from his social self. He rejoices to be free of friends and relations, "All the *assujettissement* of having been what one has been, / What one thinks one is, or thinks that others suppose one" (I.30–31). But the affectation of his language immediately defines his aware-ness that this is just another familiar, conventional role, and prepares us for his admission in the next line that "in despite of all, we turn like fools to the English" (I.32). The poem records both Claude's struggle to evade his merely social self and behavior, and his discovery that his real self is deeply engaged in what he rather despises as merely conventional modes of thought and feeling.

His disengaged awareness of such engagement typically and appropriately expresses itself in irony. "Do I look like that? you think me that: then I am that" (I.86). He is most crudely ironical about his snobbery and his shyness, the two complementary forms in which he acknowledges his lack of psychological ease and freedom. Mrs. Trevellyn "Greatly, I fear me, looks down on my bookish and maladroit manners" (I.207)—Claude is simultaneously mocking her vulgar refinement, his own awkwardness, and above all his humiliating sensitivity to what others think of him. When he complains that she "Grates the fastidious ear with the slightly mercantile accent" (I.212), he is registering distaste less for the offending accent itself than for the snobbery (comically reified and distanced as "the fastidious ear") that attends to such gradations and is so easily offended. Highly conscious and critical of his own social behavior, he is too sensible to imagine that he could live in the social world and be untouched by its values. He is just awkward enough in company to be perpetually uncomfortable, but not nearly enough of an outsider to enjoy any romantic self-satisfaction in the role. Clough with fine tact canceled a letter in which Claude complains, rather in the vein of "Locksley Hall," that there is no place for him in England: "What can a poor devil do who would honestly earn him his victuals?"—England has given up fighting wars, commerce is ignoble, the church is contentious, begging is shameful, and to learn to dig one must go abroad.[7] The Bothie of Tober-na-Vuolich, which as its subtitle says is a pastoral (more accurately, perhaps, a romance), had ended happily with the last of these alternatives: the hero transcends the problems of class and class-bound English accents by marrying a poor but very well educated Scottish girl, and finds their place in the world on a farm in New Zealand. Amours de Voyage is neither pastoral nor romance, and will not allow such evasive solutions. Philip Hewson finds a new and better world, first in the Highlands and then in the Antipodes, but Claude discovers England waiting for him when he gets to Rome.

Claude's letter writing itself is both an act of social engagement and, since in the letters he reflects (generally unfavorably) on himself and the world around him, an act of withdrawal. His correspondent, Eustace, is more easygoing and conventional than Claude is, encouraging him to stop thinking and doubting and act, marry, be happy. As an intelligent and sympathetic representative of the wider society, Eustace would make the poem's ideal reader; he responds to Claude (in letters Clough omitted from the final version) with the same affectionate exasperation that most sympathetic readers probably feel. But when Clough showed the poem to a few of his own friends soon after he wrote it, they did not like it.[8]

The epistolary form itself, which was frequently used in eighteenth-century fiction and poetry but is very rare in Victorian literature, was a serious affront to his friends' notions of poetry. Matthew Arnold criticized and tried to praise Clough's *Ambarvalia* poems in much the same terms he was later to use about the literature of the eighteenth century: they have the virtues of good prose, but they are not beautiful, not poetry.[9] Francis Palgrave said in the memoir he published with Clough's poems not only that their spirit and matter were finer than their manner of expression, but that "one feels a doubt whether in verse he chose the right vehicle, the truly natural mode of utterance."[10] Clough did not mean his poems to be objects fit to put away in Palgrave's golden treasury, but he shared to a large degree his friends' conceptions. He recommended that Victorian poets study eighteenth-century writers even though "there is but little inspiration in the compositions of the last century," for "English was really best and most naturally written, when there was, perhaps, least to write about."[11] To our ears, Clough's poetry sounds subtle, supple, and "natural," his prose undistinguished and rather stiff. But in 1849 a voice that could be distinguished from that of an eighteenth-century epistle chiefly by its greater flexibility and informality sounded highly unnatural in a poem.

In 1895 John Morley noted the decline in popularity of the epistolary novel and offered an explanation for it: "Even the lurking thought in anticipation of an audience destroys true epistolary charm. This is one reason why stories told in that form, or portions of stories so told . . . have fallen out of vogue, give but inferior pleasure, and are even found thoroughly tiresome." Letters, Morley continues, should be spontaneous: "intimate effusions," "the genuine outpouring of the writer's own feelings."[12] Such debased and redundant Wordsworthianism, which was very much in the air in 1849 too, almost forces the user of epistolary literary forms to make sincerity an ideal or at least an issue. In *Amours de Voyage* it is both. Letter writing allows Claude to exercise the subtle self-scrutiny that genuinely accompanies or follows his thought or the expression of his feelings and impedes his emotional freedom and momentum. Since the significant events in Claude's emotional career do not directly involve Eustace, and are only reported to him after the fact, we never see Claude acting or immediately reacting to things. So his feelings strike us as not quite spontaneous. The epistolary form inhibits spontaneity and intensity, encourages polite self-deprecation, and enforces self-consciousness.

It enforces, that is, an ironical point of view. Clough's seriousness, like Claude's sincerity, expresses itself most interestingly and accurately in irony. The most characteristic shading of Claude's epistolary tone, lingering on the edge where seriousness just shades into self-mockery, is both explicated and exemplified in an 1853 essay in which Clough presents (with rather heavy jocularity and some nice parody of Carlyle) a theory of art as excretion. "Most true, indeed, by writing we relieve ourselves, we unlearn." Perhaps, he says, this is true even of the most sublime of the ancient writers. "In the divine eloquence of Plato there are intonations in which I hear him saying to me— 'You know I don't quite *mean* all this.'" At any rate, it is true of the moderns:

Each striking new novel does but reveal a theory of life and action which its writer is anxious to be rid of; each enthusiastic address or oration is but that which its speaker is just beginning to feel disgusted with. Oh! happy and happy again, and thrice happy relief to the writer; but to the reader—?[13]

This is an interesting view of the spontaneity of artistic creation, and suggests a nicely literal idea of catharsis. But no doubt the essay is its own illustration.

Clough's use of hexameters tends, like the epistolary form, to enforce self-consciousness and ironic disavowals of seriousness and to call attention to the poem's verbal surface. As an unusually sympathetic reviewer acutely says:

Clough's line is, and is meant to be, conscious of being a hexameter: it is always suggestive of and allusive to the ancient serious hexameters, with a faint but a deliberate air of burlesque, a wink implying that the bard is singing academically to an academical audience, and catering for their artificial tastes in versification.[14]

While this is most obviously true of *the Bothie*, it applies to *Amours de Voyage* as well. The hexameter as Claude uses it looks two ways: both to the heroic standards by which he judges himself and life and art, and to his awareness that it is pretentious pedantry to do so. We feel that Claude is mocking himself, not being mocked by the poet: he almost seems to be aware that he is using hexameters. It is just the sort of thing he *would* do. Mary and Georgina do not give at all the same impression, though they use the same meter: the language and rhythms of Mary's letters are straightforward and unaffected, while Georgina's have their own quite different affectations. Claude is most blatantly affected, even mock-heroic, when he is nervously trying to give precisely the right expression to his romantic impulses. "Am I prepared to lay down my life for the British female?" (II.66)—he thinks he probably is, but he can't do so without self-mockery. He would like to be on the barricades, but he has to struggle for language in which to say so:

> Should I incarnadine ever this inky pacifical finger,
> Sooner far should it be for this vapour of Italy's freedom,
> Sooner far by the side of the d——d and dirty plebeians.
> Ah, for a child in the street I could strike; for the full-blown lady—
> Somehow, Eustace, alas! I have not felt the vocation.
>   (II.72–76)

The monosyllabic simplicity of positive assertion ("for a child in the street I could strike") is reached by way of a self-belittling allusion to Lady Macbeth and a denial of any sort of political idealism, and is quickly followed by Claude's typically parodic elaboration of qualifying syntax and comically inflated terminology ("vocation").[15]

Much of Claude's defensive self-consciousness comes from his anxiety to avoid falling into conventional attitudes or simply doing in Rome as other literary travelers have done. He is not in much danger from what Clough in 1845 called "the Corrine high beauty-beatification line, Italy and Art and love a l'Asthetique."[16] The formidable precedent is Goethe's. *The Bothie* reminded Clough's contemporaries of *Hermann and Dorothea* (though he himself blamed Longfellow's *Evangeline* for his outbreak of hexameters); *Dipsychus* is clearly related to *Faust*; and in the background of *Amours de Voyage* stand both Goethe's *Roman Elegies* and his *Italian Journey*.[17] Like the *Italian Journey*, Clough's poem is a series of letters to friends, organized into sections with separate passages of explanation and commentary. Like the *Roman Elegies*, it is a sequence of poems in a classical meter that tell the love story of a tourist in Rome, meditate on love, life, nature, and art, and encompass a rich variety of subjects and tones. Even Claude's distinctive note of self-mockery has a precedent in the first of the *Elegies*, in which the speaker devotes himself to the tourist's proper business of sightseeing while he waits for love. In a manuscript version of the first canto, Claude justifies his dispraise of Rome as an attempt to find his own way, even if it proves to be along an already well trodden path:

> Flippant all this and absurd, and doubtless your host of exclaimants,
> Goethe included, are right, but till I admire, I shall cavil.
> Admiration I doubt not is due . . .[18]

He does eventually come to admire, though not with Goethe's enthusiasm. Goethe speaks again and again in his letters of the rebirth he felt himself to have experienced in Rome; Claude distrusts his own hope of a similar renewal. Goethe tried, not entirely successfully, to avoid German social circles in Rome, and the speaker of the *Elegies* quickly acquires an Italian mistress and celebrates the unifying and transcendent force of love. The difference between these experiences and Claude's is self-evident. And yet Claude eventually manages to separate himself from the society of his countrymen, discovers the power of love, and comes to a new understanding of himself and a new self-dependence. The poem does not set up a simple ironic contrast between heroic past and insipid present, or between genius and dilettantism. Nor do Claude's hesitancies and self-consciousness make him merely unheroic; instead, they help to ensure that the positions he arrives at and the certainties he attains will be—however well precedented—genuinely his own.

For the whole poem is a tribute to a simple and unattainable ideal of absolute sincerity. Claude dreams of a sudden moment of freedom, feeling, and vision that will be what Arnold describes in "The Buried Life": the source of life, certitude, and lyrical power.

> Shall we come out of it all, some day, as one does from a tunnel?
> Will it be all at once, without our doing or asking,
> We shall behold clear day, the trees and meadows about us,
> And the faces of friends, and the eyes we loved looking at us?
> Who knows? Who can say? It will not do to suppose it.
> (V.181–185)

The wish and the image are Arnoldian, but the colloquial accent of blank common sense in the last line dismisses them as daydreams. Arnold hoped to find his buried life through love, but Claude (as the epigraph has it) "*doutait de tout, même de l'amour.*" When he is actually surprised by spontaneous feeling, he inspects it with ingenious suspicion. He likes Mary—but it's only "Juxtaposition, in short; and what is juxtaposition?" (I.226). He wants neither to will love nor to love against his will, and enters relations with the Trevellyns as if armed with moly to protect him against Circe and a rope to get him out of the Labyrinth (I.234–252). Writing of Mary in terms that show he loves her, he ends with the assertion that he does not, "exactly" (II.263), and in the next letter he defines his characteristic self-doubt: "I tremble for something factitious, / Some malpractice of heart and illegitimate process" (II. 271–272).

He wants to look, watch, wait, "unhurried, unprompted!" (II.274)—and offers an image of unwilled emotional certainty that points up the folly of the very idea:

> Shall not a voice, if a voice there must be, from the airs that environ,
> Yea, from the conscious heavens, without our knowledge or effort,
> Break into audible words? and love be its own inspiration?
> (II.279–281)

These are rhetorical questions that expect the answer no.

Later, however, the mere fact that he has experienced real feelings does not make him trust the genuineness of their source.

> After all perhaps there was something factitious about it:
> I have had pain, it is true; I have wept; and so have the actors.
> (V.164–165)

As he says in a canceled passage, he knows how easily "Make belief changes to fact; and acting converts into action." [19] And even if, as he admits, his feelings had once been a genuine response to Mary's presence, in her absence they seem less certain and spontaneous. Arnold had recently written of a similar situation: "Ere the parting hour go by, / Quick, thy tablets, Memory!" ("A Memory Picture"); but Claude says, "I will let myself go, forget, not try to remember" (V.53). To nurture memory would be to falsify feeling; moreover, to love in memory would be to love an unreality; for even if love could remain the same, its object could not. "Is she not changing, herself?—the old image would only delude me" (V.57).

And yet Claude does love and suffer, as we have seen and he admits. That Mary was the right woman for him to marry, he, she, and the reader would agree. In fact, he very nearly does marry her. What went wrong, then? The only thing that consistently thwarts Claude, impeding and confusing first his feelings and then his pursuit, is the necessity of discerning and expressing his feelings within the terms set by the expectations, interpretations, and language of the social world. He cannot bear to have his burgeoning love touched by convention and conventional language, or indeed by any forms at all—any touch would deform it. He is afraid to woo, for expressive words once uttered become commitments. He cannot bear that his behavior have normal social consequences, for that would turn freedom into everything summed up in the "Terrible word, Obligation" (III.190). He loves Mary because she allows him freedom from consequences, holds him to nothing, lets him draw back every day from the implied commitments of the day before (III.197–206). When at last he is clumsily asked about his "intentions," he realizes that the privacy and freedom in which his love seemed to be finding its own dimensions were illusory. "Great Heaven! to conduct a permitted flirtation / Under those vulgar eyes, the observed of such observers!" (III.278–279). Conscious of being seen, he could not be sincere.

In his *North American Review* essay on Arnold and Alexander Smith, Clough says that poetry should try to irradiate the real world with its own light: to build as the novel does "a real house to be lived in" and still "prove to us, that though we are what we are, we may yet, in some way, even in our abasement, even by and through our daily work, be related to the purer existence."[20] Claude struggles to do in life what Clough wants to do in art: to reach toward the purer existence through the everyday world of social trivia, conventional politeness, pretentious mothers, silly match-making sisters, and the rest. His love begins from "juxtaposition" and is defeated by an accumulation of small accidents: bumbling interventions, lost letters, ill governesses, plans changed at the very last minute. No single decisive event terminates it: Claude dashes about Italy from city to city and hotel to hotel for quite a while, writing, seeking, and calling on other English travelers, and in general behaving like a mad parody of the tourist as romantic lover. But he begins to feel foolish, as well he might. "I weary of making inquiries; / I am ashamed, I declare, of asking people about it" (V.28–29). Under the repetitiousness and triviality of the search his original impulse finally wears away.

The ending is for many readers both a disappointment and an affront, violating our expectations very much in the manner of Browning. Emerson spoke for many readers then and since when he complained of "this veracity of much preparation to no result" and said that "tis bad enough in life, and inadmissible in poetry."[21] But the whole poem asserts the claims of such veracity against the spurious finalities of "poetry." In a draft of the envoi, Clough tells his poem to defend itself against those who will call for a happy or at least conclusive ending by saying that it is only a mirror to "the vile dirty face" of the world.[22] We are not even offered the comfortably sentimental cynicism with which Thackeray had ended *Vanity Fair* a few years earlier; for we admire Mary and regret her disappointment even more than we do Claude's.

The natural and expected ending, particularly since the love story gradually but firmly displaces the themes of art and war in Claude's mind and in the poem, is of course marriage. (Clough could not very well alter the course of the siege of Rome to provide a satisfying conclusion.) But Clough's unsentimentality about marriage is notorious. He wrote to his fiancée: "What was the true apple? do you know? I believe its true name was 'Love is everything.' Women will believe so, and try and make men act as if *they* believed so." And again: "We are companions—fellow-labourers—to the end of our journey here, and then it will not have been in vain; we shall still be something, I think, to each other. But as for everlasting unions, and ties that no change can modify, do not dream of them." [23] At first Claude is mildly contemptuous of his friend Vernon's "perfect delight in the general tender-domestic" (I.117), and later even in the depths of depression he keeps a painfully acute sense of proportion:

Rome is fallen; and fallen, or falling, heroical Venice.
I, meanwhile, for the loss of a single small chit of a girl, sit
Moping and mourning here,—for her, and myself much smaller.
(V.115–117)

The fact that he cares more for Mary than for Rome does not alter his sense of their relative importance. And in a discarded version of her final letter Mary suggests that she has caught something of Claude's point of view on "the old family ties, the quiet and simple affections":

I am quite certain within that they are quite true and sufficient,
Though I have something at times that appears a new light upon them. [24]

Claude's experiences of Rome and the war follow a similar curve of weariness, emotional engagement, self-doubt, withdrawal, and lingering regret. His aesthetic responses to the city are more predictable and less interesting. At first he is violently disappointed, as tourists often are, at the muddle and jumble of Rome. His crudely contemptuous dismissals of Jesuit worship and decoration recall the outraged and disgusted letters Thomas Arnold had written from Rome two decades earlier, but he does not share the old headmaster's automatic enthusiasm for ruins and views untainted by popery. [25] Slowly he finds forms of pure beauty that he can really admire; but art proves unable to engage him fully and he puts it aside for further consideration later.

The war is another matter. Claude opens the second canto by asserting that he has never wished to concern himself with politics and expressing with awkward embarrassment his sympathy with the "poor little Roman republic"

(II.22). He makes similarly embarrassed jokes about heroism in the next letter—"*Dulce* it is, and *decorum*, no doubt, for the country to fall,—to / Offer one's blood an oblation to Freedom" (II.30–31). This letter expresses his uneasiness about what he will or should do, concluding comfortably that the Romans won't die for Rome, nor will he. But when he realizes that there actually will be a battle, his skepticism dissolves immediately into daydreams about his own heroic participation (II.58–62). Skepticism immediately reappears, however, when he reflects that the only heroic chance likely to be allotted to him would be "to lay down my life for the British female" (II.66); the prospect does not inspire him, but he admits that he probably will do just what is expected. He would like, as in his love, to "attend for the ripe and indubious instinct" (II.84). But again actuality is an unexpected and unsettling mixture of the prosaic and the genuinely dramatic. Even murder turns out not to be indubious:

> So, I have seen a man killed! An experience that, among others!
> Yes, I suppose I have; although I can hardly be certain.
> (II.162–163)

Claude does feel a strong though brief enthusiasm for Rome and Mazzini (II.235–249). If he were part of their heroic struggle, he thinks, he could let himself speak in the poetical voice that he continually stifles because he feels he has no right to use it. But since he cannot fight, and is disgusted at himself for merely talking (III.60–78), he drops the subject for quite a while. When he picks it up again in the last canto, it is to lament the fall of Rome and Rome's heroes and then reject his lament as "declamation" (V.125). The point is not that heroism and freedom are illusory, or that Claude is too weak or too skeptical to applaud them, but that it is just about impossible for a well-bred, pacific young Englishman to either join a foreign battle or abandon the British female. Claude's experience of the siege is necessarily discontinuous and contingent; the moment to be a hero never arrives, and whatever he is prepared for is not what happens. He does not think of himself as a poet either, who would be entitled as such to stand aloof and sing of the passing fray; the rhetoric that is appropriate to the events themselves strikes him as absurd and factitious when it comes from his own pen. "Whither depart the brave?—God knows; I certainly do not" (V.128).

Claude would have a much easier time of it if he could regard his own desires and dreams and emotions as valid and important in their own right, whether or not they correspond to anything outside himself. But this is just what he can't do. Generalizing to religious experience, he cherishes the comfort that came to him from a barrel organ playing an English psalm tune (V.86–94), but rejects any greater comfort springing merely from "trusting myself, and seeking support from within me" (V.95). Instead,

> I will look straight out, see things, not try to evade them;
> Fact shall be fact for me; and the Truth the Truth as ever,
> Flexible, changeable, vague, and multiform, and doubtful.
>
> (V.100–102)

He will not try to impose his will any more than his imagination on the world: "I will go where I am led, and will not dictate to the chances" (V.179). What is real finally is what is outside oneself, what happens to one—though he can't quite call it providence (V.176–178)—and what one knows. Arnold finds life and truth in Philomela's eternal passion and eternal pain; but Claude says only that "Knowledge abideth" (V.198).

This bears directly on Clough's argument with Arnold about the proper nature of poetry. He objects that Arnold does not really look at things and depict what he sees; he has similar reservations about Wordsworth:

> instead of looking directly at an object and considering it as a thing in itself, and allowing it to operate upon him as a fact in itself,—he takes the sentiment produced by it in his own mind as the thing; as the important and really real fact.—The Real things cease to be real; the world no longer exists; all that exists is the feeling somehow generated in the poet[']s sensibility. [26]

The distinctive note of Clough's poems, as of Claude's letters, is their refusal of romantic transcendence and of the transformations by which the imagination possesses the world. In his poems Clough tries to leave the world as he found it, with only clarity added.

Such an attitude would seem to work against irony; and in fact Claude's acceptance of the primacy of knowledge is part of his movement away from irony. Moreover, the poem as a whole is by no means as intensely or conclusively ironical as it seems when we focus our attention on Claude alone. For Claude's voice comes to us mediated by a narrator who opens and closes each canto and, seeming sometimes to be identified with the hero, sometimes with the poet, forms a link between the two and a guide for our judgment and sympathies. Claude and the narrator never contradict each other, and often say the same things: but they say them very differently. The narrator's voice is generally lyrical, and (except very slightly, near the end) it is not ironical. The effect is to validate both Claude's enthusiasms and his withdrawals, since the narrator shares them both and can express them without self-denigration or self-doubt. The narrator opens the poem by celebrating Rome as "*the perfecter earth*" (I.2) where the golden age can still be found, even though he hears and records a voice that says travel is pointless, the world "*the same narrow crib*" (I.6) everywhere; the two voices remain separate and the lyrical one of the narrator predominates. This opening passage sets forth, plainly and without any effect of irony, the two incompatible attitudes which in Claude's mind and voice continually undercut each other and produce his characteristically self-denigrating tone. At the end of the first canto and the beginning of the second the narrator expresses Claude's fear that his growing responsiveness to Rome is submission to illusion, and defines, again without irony, Claude's endlessly reflexive self-consciousness: "*Reverent so I accept, doubtful because I revere*" (I.284). His next several passages celebrate love with a lyric intensity that we know Claude feels—it is the motive power of his action when he does act, the source of his energies while they last—but that he cannot himself express. There is some confusing pronomial drift which reflects the shifting distance between the two speakers but (particularly at the end of Canto II) marks the narrator's voice as essentially an intensification of Claude's. The two voices are sometimes comically juxtaposed—at the beginning of the fourth canto the narrator sings (in the first person singular) of the pursuit of Mary, concluding:

> *Weariness welcome, and labour, wherever it be, if at last it*
> *Bring me in mountain or plain into the sight of my love.*
> (IV.9–10)

Immediately we hear Claude: "Gone from Florence; indeed; and that is truly provoking" (IV.11). But the two voices complement without undercutting each other. Claude could not speak as the narrator does—it is not a plausible tone in which to write to a friend, nor is it suited to the exasperations of a real journey—though he feels what the narrator's tone and words express.

The two speakers come closest together in Canto IV, the shortest canto in the poem and entirely taken up with Claude's whole-hearted, frantic quest for Mary. The narrator begins it on a high note:

Eastward, or Northward, or West? I wander and ask as I wander,
Weary, yet eager and sure, Where shall I come to my love?
(IV.1–2)

Claude acts out this sentiment in the muddle and jumble of real places and feelings and events:

Gone to Como, they said; and I have posted to Como.
There was a letter left; but the *cameriere* had lost it.
Could it have been for me? They came, however, to Como,
And from Como went by the boat,—perhaps to the Splügen,—
Or to the Stelvio, say, and the Tyrol; also it might be
By Porlezza across to Lugano, and so to the Simplon
Possibly, or the St. Gothard,—or possibly, too, to Baveno,
Orta, Turin, and elsewhere. Indeed, I am greatly bewildered.
(IV.19–26)

And yet as he dashes about in farcical bewilderment he speaks with unusually direct feeling and solemn imagery of "the marriage-morn and the orange-flowers and the altar, / And the long lawful line of crowned joys to crowned joys succeeding" (IV.35–36). He unrestrainedly uses such love language to speak of what he renounces or thinks he has lost. The mountains beckon him northward:

Somewhere among those heights she haply calls me to seek her.
Ah, could I hear her call! could I catch the glimpse of her raiment!
(IV.49–50)

He resolves to do the sensible thing, however, and return to Florence where he can make inquiries. But his intuitive reluctance is vindicated by the event, for nothing works out sensibly. His only clue was a false one, the note Mary left him got lost, and no news awaits him in Florence.

The thwarting of love by circumstances affects the narrator's voice, which at the end of the fourth canto and the beginning of the fifth modulates into a comically self-conscious awkwardness rather like Claude's own.

Hither, recovered the clew, shall not the traveller haste?
(IV.83)

> *or are we to turn to*
> *England, which may after all be for its children the best?*
> (V.7–8)

The narrator is withdrawing from Claude. He knows what Claude does not: that Mary is in Lucerne (IV.76–83); he wonders but does not know what Claude will do next (V.1–8). Finally in the envoi—"*Go, little book*" (V.218)—he moves out of the fiction and becomes the man who wrote the poem.

This final distancing does not imply disapprobation: on the contrary, it is as if the narrator had shared Claude's hopes and is withdrawing from his own disappointment. As in *Maud, Modern Love,* and *Fifine at the Fair,* the relation between the poet and his hero is both close and distinctly ambiguous, a matter less of biographical situation than of tone, style, and basic attitudes. It would be as foolish to deny the similarity between Clough and Claude as to assert their identity. The poet defended the "unfortunate fool of a hero"[27] whose self-consciousness, scruples, and antisentimental common sense are very like his own. Claude's Roman experiences draw on Clough's, the fictional letters on real ones; Claude's awkward, excited detachment from the Italian cause reflects Clough's own tempered sympathy, though Clough does not provide him with the experience of Paris in 1848 or the conversations with Mazzini during the siege of Rome that underlay his own attitude.[28] Clough's letters are full of his sense of the fatuity of being a tourist in a besieged city; and of the fatuity too of getting excited about a struggle one can share only through such tourists' gestures as withdrawing from cafes. But what really matters is the pervasive similarity of rhythm, tone, and diction between Clough's letters and Claude's. Here, for instance, is Clough writing to Tom Arnold in 1849, just before his trip to Rome:

> Alea jacta est. I stay for the present here. I have accepted the Stinco-malean position [at University Hall, London]. I commence there in October. With a good deal of misgiving, it must be confessed; but on the whole I believe myself not wrong. . . . Anyway so it is, and so it must rest, for the present. . . . You know too, I am not, my dear Tom, so clear as you are of the rottenness of the poor old ship here—Something I think we rash young men may learn from the failure and discomfiture of our friends in the new Republic. The millennium, as Matt says, won't come this bout.[29]

We recognize the mixed diction, inverted syntax, elaborately precise qualifications, and self-deflating irony as Claude's too; and also the energy, directness, vividness, and good humor. *Amours de Voyage* uses for poetry the voice in which Clough speaks to his best friends: a voice warm, casual, flexible, capable of seriousness without solemnity, and able to accommodate a wide range of shifting tones, feelings, and topics.

That voice asserts its rights as poetry largely by demonstrating that the romantic, lyrical tradition it intends to displace cannot be sustained in the everyday world. But this demonstration is not cynical, or even particularly sad. For at the end the poem offers us, unambiguously if rather quietly, the assurance that the modern world affords high and serious subjects for a new poetry. It affirms the value of Mary's intelligent love and Claude's resolute integrity, and the last two lines remind us that the political events recorded in the poem were real ones, part of a long-continuing struggle between freedom and tyranny.

> "But," so finish the word, "I was writ in a Roman chamber,
> When from Janiculan heights thundered the cannon of France."

Amours de Voyage is brought to a conclusion, like *Maud* (the last part of which was written, Tennyson said, when cannon were booming in the Solent), by the sound of real guns.

Modern Love is composed, like *Amours de Voyage*, of a series of poems very much like dramatic monologues, framed and interrupted by a highly problematic third-person narrator, that tell a contemporary tale of the failure of love between two highly intelligent, introspective, analytical, and scrupulously honest people. But *Modern Love* is both more obtrusively "poetical" (in a derogatory sense) and more intricately novelistic than *Amours de Voyage*. Despite the rich, dense imagery, the self-sufficiency of many of the individual stanzas (which stand well by themselves, as Clough's do not, in anthologies), and the paucity and obliquity of narration (the latter a characteristic of Meredith's fiction too), the poem's narrative structure continually tests and often repudiates its poetry. It treats a theme that produced some of the richest and strangest poems of the nineteenth century—the fatal woman, *la belle dame sans merci*—in terms of the psychological realism, the awareness of social context, and above all the temporal development of personal relationships that characterize the Victorian novel in general and Meredith's novels in particular. It tells its story in heightened poetic language as a sequence of intense emotions, but its intensity is undercut by ironic self-awareness and its extreme subjectivity is sharply responsive to the reality of others. The husband's monologue is usually internal and silent, but it is continually being altered or deflected, within a single poem or between poems, by others' responses to his moods, visions, and self-projections. The narrator, meanwhile, who at the beginning is nearly indistinguishable from the maddened husband, has become by the end the wise, aloof, omniscient narrator who presides over the great mid-Victorian novels.

Modern Love is one of the most significant points of intersection between Victorian poetry and the Victorian novel, and definitively marks Meredith's transition from poet to novelist. Meredith's first book was *Poems* (1851). During the 1850s he wrote poetry, two odd works of prose fiction—*The Shaving of Shagpat* (1856) and *Farina* (1857)—and then his first novels, *The Ordeal of Richard Feverel* (1859) and *Evan Harrington* (1860). After *Modern Love and Poems of the English Roadside*, published in 1862 but containing much that had been written in the preceding decade, he wrote mostly novels. The shift was no doubt ultimately determined by his talents and influenced by his need for money, but it seems to have been precipitated by an experience that shed new and disagreeable light on two recurrent subjects of the poetry and fiction he had written so far: innocent nature and love, and fatal or fallen women. In 1849 he had married Mary Nicolls, the widowed daughter of Thomas Love Peacock; a son was born in 1853; in 1856 or 1857 she went off with the Pre-Raphaelite painter Henry Wallis, to whom she bore a child in 1858; she died in 1861, still estranged from her husband. Meredith's first literary response to her infidelity was his first real novel, *The Ordeal of Richard Feverel*, which tests against this experience both the poetic dream of innocence and various ways of responding to its loss, and vents his rage in the angry, satirical, and dismissive characterizations of Lady Feverel and Bella Mount. *Modern Love*, written soon after Mary Meredith's death, brings the theme of the fatal or fallen woman to a similar test.[30]

"Why did I write it?—Who can account for pressure?"[31] We may speculate: to analyze, to exorcise, to find emotional release; but much of this he had done in *Feverel*. More significant, probably, for the genesis of *Modern Love* was the fact that the experience he had just lived through was precisely the sort he had liked to write about. Mysterious women defying morality, convention, or husbands had been the subjects of much of his most original and powerful—though not always his best—poetry and prose. When the woman daring all for illicit love was his own wife, his life became, in effect, a grotesque parody of his art, and in *Modern Love* he reexamines his earlier poetic vision from the unfamiliar point of view of the betrayed and humiliated husband.

Meredith had written of good and beautiful women masked by ugliness, such as Noorna in *The Shaving of Shagpat* and the hag in "The Song of Courtesy"; of evil and hideous ones masked by beauty, such as Rabesqrat and the aging Bhanavar in *Shagpat*. (The education of Shibli Bagarag, the hero of *Shagpat*, consists essentially of learning to tell the two kinds apart.) The wife in *Modern Love* is a masked mystery too, but of greater complexity, hiding sin beneath beauty and virtue beneath the appearances of sin. She is also one of the fabulously serpentine women, good or evil, who turn up so often in Meredith's early writing: Bhanavar, for instance, innocently lethal queen of serpents, or the wicked Rabesqrat whose touch thrills like "little snakes twisting and darting up, biting poison-bites of irritating blissfulness"[32]—a description that foreshadows much in *Modern Love*. "I, the serpent, golden-eyed, / Twine round thee," says the (presumably) harmless speaker in "Song: Come to me in any shape"; Bhanavar wears the serpent jewel in her hair to enhance her beauty; the husband in *Modern Love*, his mind teeming with such ambiguous images, is helplessly fascinated by "The gold-eyed serpent dwelling in rich hair" (7).

Meredith had written about women seduced, betrayed, "fallen," but like the wife in *Modern Love* brave, powerful, and essentially pure. Most of these poems remained unpublished or incomplete—they tend to be verbose and shapeless, alternately flat and shrill, and many would have offended Mrs. Grundy. But they are interesting failures, for they show Meredith trying to present fallen women seriously and sympathetically, with neither the pathos that attaches to weakness nor a haze of romantic evil. Two of the most curious and instructive are "Marian," spoken by a woman who waits at the grave of her child for the lover who will not come back, and "Josepha," which is about a pregnant woman who killed her lover and is lynched by American gold miners. Marian is mad, Josepha a murderer, but Meredith evidently wants us to admire their courage and the purity of their love as well as their sanctifying motherhood; the poems are aesthetically deplorable, but in their mixture of innocence and perversity, in subject and language both, we can discern the dim beginnings of the more sophisticated vision of *Modern Love*.[33]

 The most interesting single precursor of *Modern Love*, however, is "Shem-selnihar," published in 1862 but substantially written earlier. Shemselnihar, favorite concubine of Haroun al Raschid, speaks to her lover in words surprisingly like those of *Modern Love*:

that accurst scimitàr
In thought even cuts thee from Shemselnihar.
("Shem.," 35–36)

Each wishing for the sword that severs all.
(*ML*, 1)

The life that here fawns to give warmth to thy feet.
("Shem.," 22)

I dreamed a banished angel to me crept:
My feet were nourished on her breasts all night.
(*ML*, 23)

And he [the caliph] came, whose I am . . .
. . . .
I shrivelled to dust from him, haggard and dry.
("Shem.," 7–10)

She took his hand, and walked with him, and seemed
The wife he sought, though shadow-like and dry.
(*ML*, 49)

In the second of these quotations from *Modern Love* the husband dreams, in effect, that he is Shemselnihar's lover, while the third shows him in waking reality as her unloved master. But he is not the withdrawn and magnanimous caliph of the *Arabian Nights* tale, for he sees his wife with the acuteness and intensity with which Meredith examines Shemselnihar. Meredith is interested in Shemselnihar not just as a vehicle for erotic lyricism (although that certainly predominates), as the final stanza in particular shows:

> Yes, I would that, less generous, he would oppress,
>   He would chain me, upbraid me, burn deep brands for hate,
> Than with this mask of freedom and gorgeousness,

Bespangle my slavery, mock my strange fate.
Would, would, would, O my lover, he knew—dared debar
Thy coming, and earn curse of Shemselnihar!
(37–42)

The husband's awareness that his wife has similar feelings—suitably toned down, of course—both exacerbates his torments and instructs his cruelty: he sees her need for dramatic self-justification, and rebuffs with ironical politeness her attempts to parley or confess.

When Meredith turned his marital disaster into poetic fiction, then, he had cruelly appropriate models available in his own earlier work. The disaster, moreover, fit precisely that part of his love poetry that was most alive, most capable of growth. His celebrations of innocent love and marriage, chivalric, pastoral, or autobiographical, his ghastly sentimentalities about mothers and children (much of this, fortunately, he did not publish) were on the whole the thinnest, most derivative part of his work. But in his poems on women seductive or seduced, blatant and inept as many of these poems are, he had begun to develop not just his feminist bias but his peculiar subtlety in psychological and social analysis. When his wife imitated his art he could not, despite his initial outburst of rage in *Feverel*, simply mourn and denounce, for his own writings both glamorized and exculpated his wife and proclaimed his own moral ignominy.

Most critics who consider *Modern Love* as an autobiographical document are impressed by Meredith's willingness to share the blame, his endeavor to be fair, which is all the more striking in contrast to the angry cruelty in *Feverel*. Within the poem, the husband's struggle to be just makes him seem generous, and both his and the narrator's attitudes are strikingly out of keeping with Meredith's behavior to Mary Meredith and his few recorded references to her after her death. He was neither understanding nor forgiving; only when she was dying did he reluctantly let her see their son again; she was nearly mad, he later said.[34] Like Sir Austin Feverel he seems to have tried to obliterate her memory and comforted himself for a while with bleak misogyny. But *Modern Love* generously deviates not only from such feelings but from the actual events: there are no children to provide sentimental complications in the popular vein of *East Lynne*, the wife does not go off with her lover, she is not even technically adulterous. She is perfectly sane. The husband's affair with the Lady, which rights the moral balance, is almost certainly invented. The husband recognizes his own mean, self-serving impulses, and scorns the easy comfort—in which Meredith himself appears to have indulged—of conventional moral outrage:

> what's the name?
> The name, the name, the new name thou hast won?
> Behold me striking the world's coward stroke!
> (6)

The point is that *Modern Love* is true neither to events themselves nor, so far as we can tell, to what Meredith felt about them. Many Victorian writers recreated their own lives as fiction, whether they called the result a novel, an autobiography, or *Sartor Resartus*. In *Modern Love* Meredith recreated in poetry his own poetic and fictional world in terms of lived experience, and destroyed that world as he did so. To a reader who knows Meredith's earlier writings the wife seems at first a new Bhanavar or Shemselnihar, dropped from the *Arabian Nights* into the conjugal bed, a dream come true as a nightmare. For while *Modern Love* must have drawn its subject and self-tormenting energy from Meredith's experience, that experience is immediately subsumed into a preexisting literary pattern; and the pattern itself, not distanced by fantasy, allegory, or exotic setting and seen from the new point of view of the betrayed husband, reveals itself as arbitrary and illusory. The pattern fit the experience so well, moreover, just because it contained the seed of its own destruction: an analytic curiosity about erotic stereotypes. Meredith's interest in the moral complexity of women who act immorally leads directly to the husband's struggle against facile judgments, and his acute, tormented scrutiny dissolves the wife's glamour and with it love itself.

Two sets of images, snakes and devils, show how preexisting categories and attitudes proliferate into self-destroying complexity as they are modified by experience. [35] First the wife is a snake-woman who like Bhanavar cannot suppress her lethal power:

> The strange low sobs that shook their common bed,
> Were called into her with a sharp surprise,
> And strangled mute, like little gaping snakes,
> Dreadfully venomous to him.
> (1)

(Bhanavar is horrified to learn that the serpents who sustain her beauty feed yearly on one of her lovers.) The lover is the serpent in Eden:

> If he comes beneath a heel,
> He shall be crushed until he cannot feel,
> Or, being callous, haply till he can.
> (3)

Proud and shameless, she has the "gold-eyed serpent" in her hair (7). When the husband perceives her inner struggle, however, she diminishes: "Poor twisting worm, so queenly beautiful" (8). The very subtlety of his observation, furthermore, makes him a serpent himself, a venomous one:

> A subtle serpent then has Love become.
>
> .   .   .   .
>
> Henceforward with the serpent I am cursed.
> I can interpret where the mouth is dumb.
>
> .   .   .   .
>
> you that made Love bleed,
> You must bear all the venom of his tooth!
> (26)

The eyes of both husband and wife "dart scrutinizing snakes" (34) and even the commonsensical Lady becomes an asp (32); all four actors turn out to be snakes alike. And in a final blurring of the simplistic use of the image with which the poem began, the wife crushes "under heel" (45)—the fate earlier promised to the lover—the rose that is emblematic of the Lady. For in life (as opposed to art) character is not fixed and autonomous:

> "In Paris, at the Louvre, there have I seen
> The sumptuously-feathered angel pierce
> Prone Lucifer, descending. Looked he fierce,
> Showing the fight a fair one? Too serene!
>
> .   .   .   .
>
> Oh, Raphael! when men the Fiend do fight,
> They conquer not upon such easy terms.
> Half serpent in the struggle grow these worms.
> And does he grow half human, all is right."
> (33)

And as opposites come together they lose both their moral and their pictorial clarity. Vivid description gives way to an unvisualizable image of grossness and shapelessness: "*While mind is mastering clay, / Gross clay invades it*" (33).

The devil images proliferate and cancel out in a similar way. First the wife seems genuinely satanic (2, 7); the husband tries to emulate, with indifferent success, her pride and evil glory (27, 28); snake and devil images merge and together change their meaning in the comments on Raphael's painting (which shows Lucifer with a serpent's tail) and in the trodden snake and rose. Finally the wife is both Eve and the biblical serpent, but without glamour, venom, or sting:

> Their sense is with their senses all mixed in,
> Destroyed by subtleties these women are!
> More brain, O Lord, more brain! or we shall mar
> Utterly this fair garden we might win.
>
> (48)

The demonic is no longer sin, pride, or clay, but "subtlety": that is, the impressionable, observant, mixed natures that make husband and wife human and humanly responsive to each other. "A subtle serpent then has Love become," the husband has said: "I can interpret where the mouth is dumb" (26). Sense and senses may be wrongly mixed, subtlety may lead to sin or error, but an unmixed nature is inhuman and impossible.

Observation and responsiveness eventually show the husband that the love that had defined his life is an illusion, just as analysis had undercut the erotic stereotypes in Meredith's earlier writings, and he wants more than anything else to ward off this bleak knowledge. Snake, devil, poison flower: in the first half of the poem he sees his wife as the Pre-Raphaelite fatal woman who draws men to blissful misery. As such, she inflicts pain, but the image clearly defines her, locates her in a well-mapped world of art, and invites the eye to gaze but not to be seen or deeply see. He lingers as long as he can in this ready-made world, where the atmosphere is appropriately sultry and "languid" and an evil glamour plays about the profanation of sacred mysteries and casts on the wife a demonic glory. "Poor twisting worm, so queenly beautiful" (8) recalls the "passionate twisting" of Morris's Queen Guenevere holding her accusers at bay with praise of her own beauty. The wife is like Rossetti's Lilith, "subtly of herself contemplative"; her mirrored image draws the husband but "Eyes nurtured to be looked at" do not see him (5).[36] It is all so conventional, in fact, that we may well become suspicious. In *The Shaving of Shagpat* Meredith had laughed at the enchantress Rabesqurat and her mirror, a trayful of human eyes; when the husband bitterly remarks that the barber's "art can take the eyes from out my head, / Until I see with eyes of other men" (7), he is mocking without mirth his susceptibility to illusion, the corruption by "art" (in a wider sense) of his humane vision. And the echo of *Shagpat* reminds us that for Meredith this is the very stuff of comedy, which feasts on rigid and self-serving illusions.

Thus she attracts him most when she is most brazenly pretending, helping him to sustain the illusion while taking the responsibility for it herself.

> Once: "Have you no fear?"
> He said: 'twas dusk; she in his grasp; none near.
> She laughed: "No, surely; am I not with you?"
> And uttering that soft starry "you," she leaned
> Her gentle body near him, looking up;
> And from her eyes, as from a poison-cup,
> He drank . . .
> (9)

When she tries to stop pretending she loses her beauty, even her substantiality, and he draws back:

> For she turns . . . , and tossed
> Irresolute, steals shadow-like to where
> I stand; and wavering pale before me there,
> Her tears fall still as oak-leaves after frost.
> She will not speak. I will not ask.
> (22)

He invokes "Shame . . . , and Pride, and Pain" to protect himself from such appeals to his humanity, but she invades his dreams (23), and when she reaches her apotheosis as a Pre-Raphaelite heroine it is the last time he lets her appear in that role, for the role has lost its comforting simplicity. She has not sinned in the flesh, she is not simply "fallen":

> The less can I forgive, though I adore
> That cruel lovely pallor which surrounds
> Her footsteps; and the low vibrating sounds
> That come on me, as from a magic shore.
> Low are they, but most subtle to find out
> The shrinking soul.
> (24)

In diction and conception this is quintessentially Pre-Raphaelite, but the emphasis is on real moral ambiguity, not easy paradox; on human responsiveness, not magic spells. The conventional language may seem gratuitous and inadequate, but that is Meredith's point: this is the husband's last, desperate use of the convention. "The less can I forgive"—she is more dangerous, more hateful, because more, and more touchingly, real. "I do but wait a sign!"— but he repels her: "Go thy ways!" (24).

He defends himself first by trying to believe that she is still deliberately acting ("play[ing] upon [her] womanhood," 24), although we know better and he probably does too; and then by undertaking some serious acting himself. If she will not be a simple Pre-Raphaelite heroine, he evidently decides, then he will be a Byronic hero. With this new fiction, this new attempt to fit life into the forms of art, the second movement of the poem begins.

He has already briefly played many roles, though mostly internally: Epicurean, cynic, Byronic sinner, Othello, aspiring devil. The main problem has been finding an audience. While his wife is triumphantly engrossed in her own role she will not look at him and he can create a spectator only through rhetorical sleight of hand: "Lord God,"

See that I am drawn to her even now!
(3)

All other joys of life he strove to warm
. . . .
But they had suffered shipwreck with the ship,
And gazed upon him sallow from the storm.
(4)

Behold me striking the world's coward stroke!
(6)

. . . you still had seen me go . . .
(10)

But his one constant spectator is himself, distanced from the performing self sometimes by analysis ("What's my drift?," 31), more often by the irony that gives the poem its pervasive ambiguity and bitter flavor. Like his fascination and rage when his wife enacts the fatal woman, the irony reflects a double impulse: to dispel illusion and to create it. As earnest self-analyst he takes himself seriously (as in 19 and 40) and ultimately will reach self-knowledge. As ironist, on the other hand, he disavows his feelings in the very act of describing them. He wears the mask of irony to mitigate his lust and rage: cheerful descriptions of his demonic impulses make them seem harmless (20, 27, 28). When he furiously thrusts before his wife her letter to her lover, he simultaneously recognizes and disavows the implicit violence of his behavior by the ironical acknowledgment that he is only pretending to be Othello (15). And irony itself—a mask of indifference meant to be perceived as a mask—is his best weapon against his wife, expressing his fury while allowing him to pretend that he isn't angry at all (25, 34). For the essential function of the irony, like the blatancy of the fictional images he imposes on his wife and himself, is to make desperate matters—his wife's sin, vacillation, and sorrow, his own aggression and hungry pride—tolerable and manageable: literature, a play, play. Thus he can give life the pleasing shapes of fantasy without succumbing to illusion himself.

At best, when two actors perform consciously and harmoniously together, the tragedy they play becomes a game. The four appearances of the word "game" in the poem clearly delineate its significance: with both the wife and the Lady there is one game the husband plays and one he refuses to play, drawing back when it seems that pretense is being taken for reality. His favorite is "Hiding the Skeleton," "a most contagious game":

> At dinner, she is hostess, I am host.
> Went the feast ever cheerfuller? She keeps
> The Topic over intellectual deeps
> In buoyancy afloat. They see no ghost.
> With sparkling surface-eyes we ply the ball.
>
> .   .   .   .
>
> But here's the greater wonder; in that we
> Enamoured of an acting nought can tire,
> Each other, like true hypocrites, admire.
>   (17)

This has the characteristics of a true game: it is highly conventional, the players are having fun, they disinterestedly admire each other's skill, the excitement of the play carries them buoyantly on and on, the ostensible purpose (to hide the truth) becomes almost incidental; above all, both are fully aware that they are pretending.

But "Such play as this, the devils might appal!" (17)—they are really imposing an illusion on others. Still worse, however, is for the player to delude himself. When his wife's love for him first seems to have been revived by jeal-

136

ousy he rebuffs her: "The game you play at is not to my mind" (14). It is a game because it is conventional ("I open an old book, and there I find, / That 'Women still may love whom they deceive,'" 14), and because it consists of pointless repetitions ("another veering fit," 14). It is a bad game because she takes it seriously.

His games with the Lady parallel those with his wife, except that now he is in danger of taking them too seriously himself. He is "content / To play with [her] the game of Sentiment" (28) if it will make him an object of envy; the game fails when he tries to delude himself too (29). And worst of all is "that hideous human game" he asks her to save him from: "Imagination urging appetite" (38)—the game in which the player actually lusts after an illusion he has himself created.

But play that is completely detached from reality is wearisome and pointless.

> At Forfeits during snow we played, and I
> Must kiss her. "Well performed!" I said: then she:
> "'Tis hardly worth the money, you agree?"
> Save her? What for? To act this wedded lie!
> (35)

The game is now empty form, the drama running down. "Our tragedy, is it alive or dead?" (37). About to reconsummate their marriage, they cannot even keep up the appearances of love: "O, look we like a pair / Who for fresh nuptials joyfully yield all else?" (41). For the last time she arouses his desire by what he sees as deliberate role playing (42); but as Huizinga says, copulation cannot be a game,[37] and in the morning self-disgust teaches him that one cannot turn one's life into a play.

> In tragic life, God wot,
> No villain need be! Passions spin the plot:
> We are betrayed by what is false within.
> (43)

The next stanza begins with a little allegory; there are no more dramatic metaphors in the poem.

The end of acting is the beginning of self-discovery, which is what the poem is all about; but acting makes it possible by allowing husband and wife to test and dismiss possible selves. It is worth noting that before *Modern Love* the fatal woman comes into Meredith's novels as an actress, a comic counterpart of the enchantresses (themselves often rather funny) in *Shagpat*—Bella Mount in *Feverel*, the Countess of Salazar in *Evan Harrington*—who entangles the hero in her snaky coils; but in all Meredith's novels acting is essential to the social game. For women it is a legitimate and often courageous mode of self-defense and self-assertion; for both men and women it is a way to self-discovery.[38] In Victorian novels characters are defined and come to self-knowledge through their relationships with others, and the husband in *Modern Love* discovers his true feelings through the interactions with his wife and the Lady that the assumption of roles makes possible. The roles themselves are often conceived in the pervasively social context of Victorian fiction, adopted to deceive one's friends, to awaken envy, to fulfill the "spurious desire" aroused by the desire of others (41). But both husband and wife secretly desire the kind of absolute self-knowledge that poets suggest is the true fruit of love: a self-realization such as Arnold imagines in "The Buried Life" that effaces not only society but even personality. *Modern Love* expresses the ideal of love as transcendent union through a series of images of eating, drinking, and sucking, and these, like the images of snakes and devils associated with fallen love, are modified by experience until they lose their original meaning.

These images are intimately related to those of snakes and devils, but since they express the husband's deepest desires they are more richly developed. The snakes are poisonous, they bite, and from beginning to end the poem is dense with images of eating, drinking, tasting, sucking. First these connote secrecy, deception, and death. Midnight drinks "the pale drug of silence" (1), "Each sucked a secret" (2), the wife's beauty has a "bitter taste" and affects him like the "breath of poison-flowers" (2), her lying eyes are "a poison-cup" (9). Such imagery often mingles desire and aggression: he has the teeth and hunger of a "wild beast" and could "squeeze" her "like an intoxicating grape" (9). It often represents escape from consciousness: one can "drink oblivion" (12), "taste forgetfulness" (27), find happy ignorance in beer (28). It also represents escape from time: he wants "a taste of that old time" (8) that haunts him as the salt taste of her tears (16). By tasting forgetfulness he hopes (ironically) to "rise new made" (27). But more and more clearly it comes to represent union and communion, first made explicit in the creepy inversions of a dream:

> I dreamed a banished angel to me crept:
> My feet were nourished on her breasts all night.
> (23)

Love is a thirst (24, 32, 44); the hero of a French novel wards it off with rosbif (25). But the wife offers only poison wine. She is "barren" (6), she faints for the wrong reasons (21); she does not nurture, she gives no milk. There are only two extended depictions of nature in the poem, and they both culminate in moving images that suggest her failed motherhood:

> Look, woman, in the West. There wilt thou see
> An amber cradle near the sun's decline:
> Within it, featured even in death divine,
> Is lying a dead infant, slain by thee.
> (11)

> I have seen across the twilight wave
> The swan sail with her young beneath her wings.
> (47)

Between the bitterness of the first image and the calm sadness of the second has come the realization that one cannot drink transcendence in real life: Raphael's Michael is false because "That suckling mouth of his, upon the milk / Of heaven might still be feasting through the fray" (33). So the husband's last hope is for sensible, sexless communication between human equals, not communion with a nurturing angel. "Our inmost hearts had opened, each to each. / We drank the pure daylight of honest speech"; but "Alas! that was the fatal draught, I fear" (48). Both communion and communication come only with death: "Lethe had passed those lips, and he knew all" (49).

"But they fed not on the advancing hours" (50). The union they sought—murderous or nurturing, spiritual or rational—was a poetic absolute, a timeless certainty, but they lived in the world of change. And so the husband defines and becomes himself by testing the poetic images that embody his desires against the essentially novelistic reality of personal relationships in society and time. Since he has defined himself in relation to his wife (8), whom suddenly he no longer knows, his search for self-knowledge—the whole story, in fact—begins and ends with his knowledge of her, from "By this he knew she wept with waking eyes" (1) to "and he knew all" (49). It begins, that is, with him watching and interpreting her actions, and ends with her definitive self-revelation to him. Over and over again he watches her, responds in fantasy, words, or action, interprets and reinterprets to find out what she really is and what he really feels. In a typical stanza he will first describe her behavior, then elaborate a response to it, and end by addressing her (silently or aloud) or observing her again. His feelings are thus continually modified by her behavior, which they modify in turn.[39]

We are always aware, because the husband so acutely is, that his feelings exist and have meaning only in the ordinary world he inhabits with other people. Nearly every stanza in *Modern Love* begins and ends with an insistent sense of another person's presence, real or imagined. Many have a form of "you" in the last two lines. Particularly striking are the startling endings of a long discourse on life and love—"Lady, this is my sonnet to your eyes" (30)— and of the explication of Raphael's picture—"This to my Lady in a distant spot . . . If the spy you play, / My wife, read this!" (33). Sometimes when the situation provides no one to listen or speak, the husband drags someone in by the heels: dinner guests (17), rustic lovers (22), an inconsequential doctor (27), a vague "you" (29). Often a shadowy auditor is implied by a rhetorical question, and once the wife's response comes in his dream (23). Sonnets that generalize extensively end with vivid descriptions of people (19, 41) or direct address (30, 33), and in one that contains no people at all personifications interact instead (4).

The affair with the Lady falls into two parts which both separately and together have the same basic structure as most of the individual stanzas and the poem as a whole: encounter, imaginative elaboration, another encounter. Here most explicitly the theme is that when emotions are spurious in themselves or falsify their object, their enactment will reveal the falsity. This alters or extinguishes them, often in surprising ways. First the husband wants to make the Lady a sunflower reflecting his own satanic light for others to see and envy (28); and his first surprise is that his imagination will not work at command:

> Am I failing? For no longer can I cast
> A glory round about this head of gold.
> Glory she wears, but springing from the mould;
> Not like the consecration of the Past!
> (29)

The Wordsworthian vocabulary suggests that this is a failure specifically of the poetic imagination, of which "Love, the crowning sun" (30) is a similarly inconstant variant. Resigned to Epicurean darkness, then, and the skull beneath the skin (29), he looks at her again. The surprise this time is pleasanter: "This golden head has wit in it" (31), and her common sense and cool approbation seem even nicer than love. But sexual consummation brings a double surprise, for although he finds her quite splendid he still wants the consecration and the lover's dream. So, baffled, he turns back to his wife. They renew hostilities, the Lady reappears, and the affair recommences.

This time, however, he hopes to find light in her, not to cast it himself. He has learned a dark lesson:

> Give to imagination some pure light
> In human form to fix it, or you shame
> The devils with that hideous human game:—
> Imagination urging appetite!
> . . . .
> My soul is arrowy to the light in you.
>   (38)

But this is a game too, of course. His high-flown, obscurely allusive eloquence is histrionic, not disinterested, and collapses into irony: "So, therefore, my dear Lady, let me love! . . . 'Tis Love, or Vileness!" (38). Save me from myself—one of the oldest tricks in the seducer's book, as the irony acknowledges. But she "yields," and this time she is really perfect (39). By convincing her, furthermore, he finally convinces himself: "Belief has struck the note of sound" (39) and silent music is within him and without. Reluctant honesty and highly self-conscious imagination have created the Romantic vision to which Victorian poetry aspires, a universal harmony transfiguring lover, beloved, and nature, uniting earth and sky, shadow and living light, silence and song, waking and dream.

But social reality effaces the hard-won poetic vision. The wife appears with her lover—she is significantly and uncharacteristically defined in the merely social terms of "name" and "honour" (39)—and the sight of them shatters the harmony and thereby invalidates the love. The husband does not know what he wants, whom he loves (40), but he gives up the discredited "living passion" to take up the "lifeless vow" of marriage and the "spurious desire" of a social being (41). And when the desire is fully enacted at last, consummated, husband and wife both know that he does not love her. Their games and their fictions have all been played out. He loves no one.

This is reality, "tragic life," and it is only bare bones and shadows. They see each other clearly now, but as skeleton ("She sees through simulation to the bone," 44), and shadow (49). The consummation itself is expressed in the image of the wind's "skeleton shadow on the broad-backed wave" (43), and later there is a shadowy remarriage in the sunset: "Our spirits grew as we went side by side. / The hour became her husband and my bride" (47). Just as the moon of music became a "dancing spectre" (39), so now the lover is a shadow too, easily dismissed (46), and the Lady exists only in her emblem, the trampled rose (45). Clear-sightedness and unillusioned honesty do not bring marital happiness or even, except very briefly, peace; like Dorothea and Casaubon in *Middlemarch*, like Vittoria and Carlo Ammiami, the more husband and wife know each other, the more miserable they are and the more they diminish and harm each other.

Nor do they, in fact, really know each other. The husband's last words in the poem are triumphantly erroneous: "I feel the truth; so let the world surmise" (48). The "pure daylight of honest speech" (48) has been fatally unilluminating: she thinks he loves the Lady, he thinks she has done something desperate, and both are wrong (48). When she returns he sees no "wicked change" in her, she thinks "his old love had returned" (49), and both are wrong again. In fact the story has two successive and contradictory endings: the husband's mistaken interpretation of his wife's departure (48) and the narrator's account of her return and suicide (49). Most readers evidently take the motive the husband gives for her flight—to let him return to the Lady—as that of her later suicide, but in the penultimate sonnet the narrator tells us her real motive: she is afraid to see once more that he does not love her, and afraid to show her heart to him.[40] At the point when all remaining illusions are about to collapse, that is, the wife kills herself and the husband is silent, his voice displaced by the narrator's.

In *Modern Love* as in *Amours de Voyage* the relation of the narrator to the speaker is something of a problem. The transition from third person to first in the opening sections is particularly blurry and confusing.[41] We can partly explain this, of course, as a way of distancing autobiography; but the narrator's reappearance at the end suggests a more intrinsic function, and one that clearly marks the essentially novelistic quality of *Modern Love*: to tell us what the husband cannot and give us a wider vision than the husband's own. Since the poem presents a quest for knowledge of the self in relation to others, it matters very much that we be able to assess both the accuracy of the husband's interpretations of his wife and his sincerity about himself. So one function of the narrator is that served by Mary and Georgina's letters in *Amours de Voyage*: he tells us that the husband's first bitter and romantic picture of his wife is essentially accurate (1, 2), and when the third person shades into the first, the absence of clear demarcations validates the husband's reading of her even more broadly (3, 6, 9). The narrator guides our reading of the husband's self-analyses, too: he "ape[s] the magnanimity of love," but his pain is real (2, 4), and he does feel the fury of a wild beast despite the ironical overstatement that might make us doubt it (9). Such distinctions prepare us for the complex interdependence of acting and sincerity that follows. He warns us once against the husband's habitual distrust of his wife's sincerity: "he saw hypocrisy designed" (5) suggests that the husband is wrong. In addition, the narrator describes extended or unusually complicated circumstances. But at the end of the poem he reemerges as the fully omniscient narrator whom J. Hillis Miller has called "the most important constitutive convention for the form of Victorian fiction."[42] The husband has moved toward knowledge of himself and his wife, but he cannot possess his own life, cannot see himself separate, distinct, and whole.[43]

So the narrator tells us when and how husband and wife understand or misunderstand themselves and each other, and pronounces final, generalized, and scrupulously equal judgment on them both. He also frees the husband from having to respond, morally or emotionally, to his wife's death. The total lack of any such response is particularly striking since he has been quiveringly responsive to almost everything she does; but what could he say? We may guess that he is glad to be rid of her, but we never find out what he feels or— odder still—learns about his wife. "Pity pleads for Sin . . . and he knew all" (49), the narrator blandly tells us, and leaves it at that.

For while the husband has been obsessed with questions of guilt and innocence and the exact definition of his own feelings, the narrator is interested in the larger workings of fantasy and reality, love and change.[44] "Thus piteously Love closed what he begat," he says (50). Meredith described *Modern Love* as "a dissection of the sentimental passion of these days,"[45] and by "sentimental" Meredith means seeing things as more benign, simple, and innocent than they are. The sentimentality of husband and wife lies in their belief that love should not be subject to time and circumstance, but this illusion is itself natural, as Meredith's gloss on Nature's speech in Sonnet 30 explains:

while you lovers are acting Nature you are ignorant of her; and she has to cure you of your idealistic mists, by running the sharp thorn of Reality into your quivering flesh. Romance is neither in nor out of nature. It is young blood heated by Love or the desire for Love. It's true while it lasts—no longer.[46]

Modern Love, like Meredith's novels, has its roots in his early writings where Romance and Reality (using the terms as Meredith does in his letter) are in uncertain balance or bewilderingly collide: the poems of idealism and passion turned oddly off course by psychological acuity and social criticism, the prose concocted of unstable mixtures of romance, fantasy, irony, allegory, satire. *Modern Love* recognizes the truths of Romance—even the truths of its illusions—and gives it full play and the poetic richness that is its due. But the play falters and collapses, and the often strained and excessive quality of the language shows Meredith's awareness that some of his poetic battalions are tarnished tin soldiers. And when Romance has been battered to pieces by novelistic Reality, the final assessment is spoken by the only voice adequate to it, the narrator's:

> they fed not on the advancing hours:
> Their hearts held cravings for the buried day.
> Then each applied to each that fatal knife,
> Deep questioning, which probes to endless dole.
> Ah, what a dusty answer gets the soul
> When hot for certainties in this our life!—
> (50)

Only in the mind of an omniscient narrator can the past live on in the present, and certainty be attained without endless dole.

Conclusion

Amours de Voyage, Maud, Modern Love, and *Fifine at the Fair* combine lyrical and novelistic elements in essentially similar ways. The novelistic element appears as the pressure that the world of other people exerts on emotional and imaginative life;[1] it is the resistant medium in which the lyrical impulse has to operate and which constantly threatens to make poetic utterance either impossible or absurd. This social world is contingent, particular, and immediate; mid-Victorian fiction itself was often set a generation in the past, but these poems are exactly contemporary. Clough and Tennyson weave current public events into the basic fabric of their stories. Meredith's title announces his intention to analyze peculiarly "modern" ways of living and feeling, and even Don Juan writes under imaginative pressures indistinguishable from those exerted by contemporary England. The plots concern romantic love in terms of marriage: that is, love both as an exclusive personal emotion and as the basis of a formal bond linking individuals to each other and to the larger society. The hero's problem is less to win or keep the fruits of love than to ascertain the precise nature and degree of his own feelings, which are obscured by a bewildering interplay of personal and social motives. The main problem for the reader, correspondingly, is to assess the speaker's tone and the poet's attitude. This is made more difficult and more interesting by our knowledge that the poems are to a large but indeterminate degree autobiographical. In three of the four poems, moreover, the relation between poet and protagonist is mediated by an ambiguous third party who seems to be identified sometimes with one, sometimes with the other, of the two. Within all four poems the tone moves between the extremes of visionary lyricism and icy irony, with many abrupt and confusing transitions along the way. And finally, the quality of the poetry is extremely variable: it often seems flat or strained or excessive, some-times out of control and sometimes grimly self-parodic, and yet it can often astonish the reader with intensity or subtlety or wit or sheer lyrical beauty.

Marriage, or courtship with marriage in view, raises on the level of plot the same problems about poetry and poetic communication that Tennyson, Browning, and Arnold were concerned with in their shorter monologues. The double conception of love is precisely analogous to the double idea of poetry as both a spontaneous outpouring of individual feeling and a powerful agent to stir right feeling in many hearts and link individuals in social union. The task of each protagonist is the amatory counterpart of the Victorian poet's: to reconcile the two aspects of love without letting the public, pragmatic func-tion of marriage compromise the sincerity of the heart. Thus in the total movement of the plot the love story is primarily the means by which the pro-tagonist resolves—or tries to—the problem of his relations with society. All the wives or potential wives are disposed of, having served their purpose, be-fore the poems end. In the two earlier ones love brings the initially detached and lonely hero into a new relationship with society, a relationship sym-bolized in its ideal completeness by the unrealized potentiality of marriage. As Claude's love for Mary grows, so does his involvement with her family and friends, and his pursuit of her requires not only energetic traveling but an un-wontedly active sociability. Marriage would have meant settling into some definite position in England; as it is, however, he roams off instead toward Egypt and a more abstract, transcendent fulfillment. Maud's lover, who is at first more furiously alone than Mary's, moves uneasily toward reconciliation with his family and neighbors and achieves a grand if impersonal union at the end: "I have felt with my native land, I am one with my kind" (III.58). In these two poems both the initial situation and the resolution are defined in terms of the protagonists' relation to English society, and Maud and Mary serve as agents to change that relation. The two later protagonists, in contrast, chafe against the constraints of marriage. Husband and wife in Modern Love are forced into sexual proximity and immoral complicity by their social role as a married couple: they share a bedroom (not a bed) at a house party, kiss in a game of forfeits, and unite to deceive their friends. Don Juan starts and ends his long speech by defining Fifine as escape from society and Elvire as total imprisonment within it: such plot as the poem has concerns his oscillation between the two. And when the four protagonists draw back from the women, it is more often a revulsion against the social relations she involves him in than a response to any qualities of her own.

This is not to say that marriage is solely or even primarily symbolic of more abstract relationships. On the contrary: its symbolic force derives from the fact that marriage really is, in the poems as (to a lesser degree) in the world they represent, the single most important link between the individual and society. It is almost, in fact, the only link. The lot of the bachelor as Claude ironically describes it sounds nearly as dreary, although not as desperate, as the spinsterhood Charlotte Lucas marries Mr. Collins to escape. The protagonists seem to be related to the world solely in their roles as lovers or husbands. Whenever this becomes explicit, they see it as a mark of ignominy. They crave nobler activity, wider scope. But Claude participates in Rome's great struggle only as a potential protector of the British female and forms no ties to political or artistic Rome or even—except briefly, through Mary—to the English tourists. Maud's lover sees speculators and oppressors thrive while there is nothing for a decent young man to do. The husband in *Modern Love* nurses an ill-defined grudge against his wife for trying to keep him domesticated, lapdog size, a mere mincing Fairy Prince of a lover, when he "plotted to be worthy of the world" (10). And Don Juan attributes his interest in women to his failure to reach satisfactory terms with the world of men.

The best alternative to marriage is war, both as an outlet for emotional energy and as a mode of organized fellowship. *Amours de Voyage* ends with the thunder of French cannon, *Maud* with English guns and war cries, and even *Modern Love* with an image of martial thunder that generalizes the husband's distress into something representative and shared.

> In tragic hints here see what evermore
> Moves dark as yonder midnight ocean's force,
> Thundering like ramping hosts of warrior horse,
> To throw that faint thin line upon the shore!
> (50)

But war remains hardly more than a potent metaphor, offstage and distant even in *Amours de Voyage* and *Maud*. There were few opportunities for a pacific and impoverished Victorian gentleman to fight for his country—but he could always fall in love or get married. The parallel between love and war, moreover, is probably not fortuitous. The heroes have a lot of aggressive energy and no proper outlet for it, and when they affect other people at all they usually do harm. The women who are instrumental in their quests for self-knowledge come to grief: two end up disappointed and unhappy and the other two end up dead. Because they are driven by the need for fuller vision, more fundamental self-realization, and wider unity with mankind than either the social structure or, failing that, personal relationships alone seem able to give them, they cannot find peace in the world and are unable to give it to others.

Thus all merely personal feelings are open to suspicion. The contradictions between marriage as a moral and emotional ideal and as a definitive but commonplace social fact are at the center of these poems, as they are of much nineteenth-century fiction—in which ideal standards are more rigidly upheld than they appear to have been in life, even by moralistic novelists themselves. The four protagonists are as aware as George Eliot or Trollope are of the emotional self-mystification and moral self-deception that is likely to occur when love and baser interests seem to coincide, and less tolerant than an impersonal narrator would be of their own confusions. They want their love to be like a poem, spontaneous, self-generated, and sincere, and are afraid that it might be willed or even faked in response to external needs and pressures. So they are sharply watchful for any illicit influence on others' feelings or their own and are seldom sure what, if anything, they actually feel. Matters are complicated, too, by the fact that the women who are the objects of their doubtful love are also the most important of the people whose independent reality makes up their social world. All four protagonists define themselves, like characters in a Victorian novel, largely in terms of how others see them, and test their identities by the reflection in the eyes of others. The two earlier lovers are "self-conscious" in the simple sense of being prone to shyness, awkwardness, and embarrassment, anxiously mulling over the possible meanings of every sign of favor or disdain. The husband in *Modern Love* wants to win the Lady primarily so that others' envy will restore his self-esteem; "I do not know myself without thee more," he cries to his wife in dismay (8). Don Juan demands Elvire's moral approbation even while he teases and betrays her, and needs a woman—any woman—to prove his own reality. Maud's lover loses himself in madness when he loses her. Only Claude accepts the inevitable: since Mary, he assumes, is no longer who she was, "I will be bold, too, and change" (V. 58).

They think that love, like a poem, should be an eternal emotional truth that will give them access to their true selves, and they discover that such absolutist notions are inadequate in the ordinary world of marrying and being given in marriage. Much of what happens in the three earlier poems is that the speakers gradually cease to perceive the women as changeless types of the eternal feminine, stock figures from literature. Mary turns out to be not just sensible and nice but loving and clever too, Maud gradually becomes a girl of seventeen with a few quite ordinary dresses, and the story of *Modern Love* consists almost entirely of the reluctant dismantling of erotic stereotypes. The contrasting types in *Fifine* of whore and wife, soulless beauty and sexless virtue, are the most blatantly conventional and yield only in the epilogue to a more lifelike and original figure. The four heroes are particularly susceptible to stereotypes of wickedness—even Claude compares visiting the Trevellyns to landing on Circe's isle—and subject to fits of fantastic suspiciousness; but all they discover is simplicity and innocence. Mary did not want Claude teased about his "intentions," Maud is not calculating or proud, the wife is not adulterous. The most disconcerting quality to discover seems to be straightforward rationality, as Claude and the husband show in their almost identical irony:

> Oh, rare gift,
> Rare felicity, this! she can talk in a rational way.
> (II.253–254)

> Yet she has that rare gift
> To beauty, Common Sense. I am approved.
> It is not half so nice as being loved,
> And yet I do prefer it. What's my drift?
> (31)

The most interesting thing about the collapse of the stereotypes is that the heroes do not welcome it. Nor does it produce a happy ending, except where it suggests the reunion of lovers after death. Instead, it indicates that the root of failure is not in the object of love, but in the ideal of love itself. "Modern" love is like modern poetry as the central Victorian tradition defined it: it is expected to clarify, elevate, and purify social, imaginative, and even moral existence. Tested in these poems by experience, the ideal invariably fails, and the ideal of lyric poetry that it is bound up with necessarily fails too.

The failure of an imaginative ideal to stand the test of experience and the difficulty of evaluating what has happened and apportioning the blame are central in every way to these poems—to the tone especially, and also to the incidents in the poets' lives from which they arose. We hear a similar mixture of self-pity, self-disgust, self-doubt, and self-justification in the voices of all four protagonists, about whom the authors' feelings run a similar gamut from admiration to angry contempt. Each poem tempts informed readers to

149

identify the poet with his hero, and even when we resist the temptation in its cruder forms we cannot but see that the poems spring from major and essentially similar crises in the poets' personal and artistic lives. When Clough went to Rome in April 1849 he had come to realize that his high-principled departure from Oxford had barred him, perhaps forever, from his natural place in the world; he had formally resigned his Oriel fellowship just six months earlier, and was about to begin a job in London that would prove just as dreary and unsuitable as he expected it to be. Tennyson wrote *Maud* when he was able to look back from a position of emotional and financial security and assured artistic achievement on the excesses and miseries of earlier years (the poem's superb enactment of callow youth sometimes makes us forget that when Tennyson wrote it he was in his middle forties). Meredith was sorting out his feelings about the brilliant wife who had abandoned him and died unreconciled. Browning, whose nuptial bliss was legendary, had become the object of ill-natured gossip about a proposal of marriage with Lady Ashburton. These are all situations in which a man is likely to be fighting the conviction that he has been made a fool of—or worse, made a fool of himself. He would want to blame a world too crass to appreciate his generous, romantic impulses (Browning said that marriage with Lady Ashburton attracted him for his son's sake, but his heart was buried in Florence); he would fear that some weakness or falseness in himself had brought the disaster upon him.

This is the sort of uneasiness we hear in the poems—which is not to say that the events caused them. But the man who wrote the poem was also the man who mismanaged his private affairs, and it is reasonable to suppose that similar characteristics manifested themselves in both. The relevant crises in the writers' lives were the consequences of their own behavior, fruits of their own wills and personalities. Even falling unhappily in love is not, after all, something that just randomly happens to people—it seems at least as likely that poetic attitudes cause love affairs as that love affairs determine poems, and Tennyson's love for Rosa Baring, for instance, must have been as much effect as cause of his imaginative vision of the world. In these poems, at any rate, personal issues are also literary ones, treated on one level in the plot and argument, on another in tone, image, and style; and everywhere we hear the same note of self-doubt.

The speakers are particularly on the watch to spy out insincerity in their language. Sick from the disease of self-consciousness, with the usual mid-Victorian attendant evils of inability to act, self-disgust, and doubt of the reality even of one's pain, the qualities they are most self-conscious about are poetic as well as personal. They distrust the spontaneity of their feelings, actions, and language alike. They are tormented by the fact that their lives are neither really like, nor totally unlike, art: they cannot fill traditional literary roles, but they cannot escape them either. Similarly, they find traditional poetic language too grand for modern feelings and situations, and the language of contemporary speech not grand enough: there is always a disparity that threatens to produce irony, and they are noticeably aware of their diction as a matter of deliberate choice. Only at rare moments, or moments of very high or very low intensity, does a particular mode of feeling and speaking seem not only adequate but wholly unforced and necessary; and even the best moments are apt to end in self-revulsion or fastidious doubt.

The poems generate their atmosphere of distinctively literary self-consciousness partly through allusions, especially the numerous ones to Shakespeare which remind us that all Victorian indecisiveness aspires to the dignity of Hamlet. (The last, belated Victorian monologuist is in this tradition when he remarks sadly that he is not Prince Hamlet, nor was meant to be.) When Claude angrily imagines himself "the observed of such observers" (III.279), or the husband mocks his half-wish to play Othello, our attention is being called both to the fact that they conceive their own lives in terms of literary patterns, and to the poems themselves as existing in the context of literary tradition. The most blatantly sustained examples of such allusiveness are the near-parodies of current literary habits early in *Modern Love* and *Fifine* in which the speakers evoke the amoral, self-referential beauty of Pre-Raphaelite enchantresses to describe women who are not like that at all. On the largest scale, too, the poems are allusions of much the same sort. The most important ones—to Goethe, the Renaissance sonnet sequence, *Hamlet*, the Don Juan literature and legends—are mostly a matter of structure and plot and quite unobtrusive, so that we rarely notice them while we are actually reading. When we do think about them, what we mostly notice is what does not fit; but the discrepancies do not invite judgmental comparison—it is inconceivable, for instance, that Tennyson wants us to think about his poem's inferiority in breadth and dramatic characterization to Shakespeare's play, nor is there much point in comparing nineteenth-century marriage and the amorous conventions of Renaissance poetry. Like the heroes' own awareness of literary models for their behavior, these allusions suggest less an ironic undercutting of the speakers than an assertion that the models provided by literature are inappropriate for life.

None of the speakers, of course, is willing to assert the supremacy of art over life; they all have a strong moralistic bias and a diffuse but persistent sense of guilt. Although they worry about their sexual or aggressive impulses, what they fear most is being too self-involved, too self-conscious—too literary—to be responsible moral agents in society. The two later poems represent amoral aestheticism and irresponsibility chiefly in the image of the Pre-Raphaelite fatal woman who made her first and most suggestive appearance as William Morris's Guenevere in 1858. "The Defense of Guenevere" is a variant of the short auditor poem—a narrator introduces Guenevere, occasionally describes her or tells us what happens, but mostly just reports her speech to the knights who have accused her of adultery—and in it Morris exploits possibilities that the other poets who used the form deliberately restricted and resisted.

Guenevere never stops being aware of her auditors and of the effect her words are having on them. She speaks with a clear and urgent purpose (although we don't know its full extent until the end of the poem), and she achieves it. The only response the poem actually records is a negative one— "'Ah! God of mercy, how he turns away!'" (164)[2]—but she holds her accusers at bay until Launcelot arrives to rescue her, and that is all she wanted. She achieves this, however, by exploiting her extraordinary self-consciousness: her "defense" is the display of her beauty, not her paradoxical and unsatisfactory argument. She holds her hearers by drawing them to participate in her rapt self-admiration.

> "say no rash word
> Against me, being so beautiful . . .
>
> . . . .
>
> see my breast rise,
> Like waves of purple sea, as here I stand;
> And how my arms are moved in wonderful wise."
> (223–228)

When she looks at them, she sees herself reflected; they become her mirror, showing her what she could not otherwise see:

> "See through my long throat how the words go up
> In ripples to my mouth . . ."
> (230–231)

The wife in *Modern Love* has "Eyes nurtured to be looked at" instead of to see (5); Fifine shamelessly presents herself to be admired and seems to be saying,

"I call attention to my dress, / Coiffure, outlandish features, lithe memorable limbs, / Piquant entreaty" (399–401). But these descriptions are the speakers' interpretations, wishful thinking rather than fact: they express both speakers' ambivalent desire for a woman like Guenevere, their yearning to escape from an unsatisfactory reality into a prefabricated world of make-believe.[3] Guenevere is the personification of "art for art's sake" (Pater used the phrase at the end of a review of Morris's poems that became the famous conclusion to *The Renaissance*).[4] Sincerity is meaningless to her except as fidelity to her sensuous impressions and her sense of herself as a beautiful living object. She plays with the words "truth" and "lie" until they become a meaningless blur of sounds, and dismisses moral judgment as a matter of arbitrary designations, the choice between two pieces of colored cloth. Her aestheticism is rendered more distinctively perverse by a touch of cruelty: she reminds Gauwaine of his mother's severed head and recalls with languid pleasure, vivid imagery, and implied threat how Launcelot killed another accuser in a battle that ended in "'a spout of blood on the hot land'" (214). Nor is there any moral counter-pressure in the poem, although unlike strict dramatic monologues this one has a narrator who feels free to intervene at will. The narrator's voice does not provide a point of view that would create an ironic perspective on Guenevere, since he admires her even more than she admires herself: she "spoke on bravely, glorious lady fair" (56). He is pleased by the outcome, too: "The knight who came was Launcelot at good need" (295).

The poem itself is like Guenevere, with the intricate terza rima pattern, the slight, persistent archaisms of diction and style that retard its movement, the languor, and the creation of a self-enclosed world of its own. The use of auditors is distinctive in that the auditors, the narrator, and (if the poem works) the reader are drawn together into the circle of the speaker's self-fascination, becoming her mirrors rather than her judges. For the Pre-Raphaelite woman is a model for poetry as well as a subject for poems. The sonnet as Rossetti defines it in the introductory sonnet of *The House of Life* sounds just like Guenevere:

> *Look that it be,*
> *Whether for lustral rite or dire portent,*
> *Of its own arduous fulness reverent:*
> *Carve it in ivory or in ebony,*
> *As Day or Night may rule . . .*[5]

"A sonnet is a moment's monument," not more lasting than brass but small and self-worshipping. It is a monument to poetry for its own sake, indifferent whether it is for good or for evil, exclusively concerned to create a self-enclosed lyrical world of imaginative, emotional, and sensuous intensity. The speaker in "The Defense of Guenevere" is not, like earlier speakers, a figure for the poet; she is a figure for the poem.

And yet "The Defense of Guenevere" only exaggerates qualities that are already present in the early monologues of Tennyson, Browning, and even Arnold. Simeon, Tiresias, and Ulysses say in effect: look at me, admire me, follow me out of vulgar life into another world. Browning's speakers show the connection between aestheticism and cruelty when they flaunt their wickedness and defy judgment; Guenevere displays her beauty as the Duke displays his power. And though the world of Arnold's "Resignation" is more real and more austere than Guenevere's, it is also sad and strange and empty of everything but transient beauty and a sort of love. But in the works by the three major poets, the self-conscious aestheticism that Morris and Rossetti so thoroughly exploit is countered by other values and subordinated to a wider, saner, and more interesting vision; and the example of Morris's and Rossetti's brilliant but irredeemably minor poems can help us to see why Tennyson, Browning, and Arnold were so wary of the domination of art, and so dubious about the beneficence of poetry.

The Victorian poem with auditors culminates in *Amours de Voyage, Maud, Modern Love,* and *Fifine at the Fair,* which stretch the union of contradictory impulses it embodies to the breaking point or perhaps a little beyond. The half-veiled, half-open use of autobiographical material, the elusive irony, and the voices that mediate between poet and protagonist combine to leave us in considerable uncertainty about the poet's attitude and presence; these are signs of the same discomfort about the poet's relation to his readers that is central to the shorter poems, and of the same conflicting impulses both to reveal and to conceal his own experiences and feelings. The shorter poems are concerned with poetry as communication, incorporating the responses of possible readers through those of the auditors; they are concerned both about the speaker's effectiveness and about the value of his speech, and enact various ways in which things can go wrong, from the hearers' obstinacy or obtuseness at one extreme to the speaker's malice or duplicity at the other. The long poems use mimetic plots to figure forth a similar exploration of imaginative speech: to how the effect on others of the protagonists' communicated vision, and the ct on that vision of others' responses to it. Structuring the poems as a sequence of present-tense moments allows the responses to be continuously incorporated and lets the speakers watch their lyrical, imaginative, and visionary impulses work themselves out in the contemporary social world. The development of the plot shows what these impulses do to others and how experience modifies them. The question of sincerity arises explicitly and often as a fear of insincerity in others and a suspicious watchfulness for signs of it in oneself. And the dramatic situation that in the monologues defines the speaker's words as being uttered at a particular time and for a particular purpose is replaced or substantially augmented by the speaker's self-consciousness about his words whether anyone else hears them or not. The effect is the same: to test the possibility of poetic discourse in the alien world of prose.

There are very few dramatic monologues or other poems with responsive auditors, and there are even fewer of the long poems that extend their peculiar methods and concerns. They all arise from a brief confluence of literary streams that do not mingle and quickly flow apart again; it is the unusual combination of familiar elements that makes them seem both typically "Victorian" and highly idiosyncratic. In them, the currents that went to producing Victorian mimetic fiction on the one hand, and the poetry of aestheticism and decadence on the other, briefly coincide. Perhaps that is why this very small group includes so many of the poems that are generally agreed to represent Victorian poetry at its most characteristic, its most problematic, and its best.

Notes

INTRODUCTION

1. W. J. Fox, review of Tennyson's *Poems, Chiefly Lyrical, Westminster Review*, 14 (January 1831), 224; reprinted by Isobel Armstrong in *Victorian Scrutinies: Reviews of Poetry 1830–1870* (London: Athlone Press, 1972), p. 83.

2. E. D. H. Johnson defined the Victorian poets' problem as a "double awareness," a "tension originating in the serious writer's traditional desire to communicate, but to do so without betraying the purity of his creative motive"; *The Alien Vision of Victorian Poetry: Sources of the Poetic Imagination in Tennyson, Browning, and Arnold* (Princeton: Princeton University Press, 1952), pp. ix, xi. As Alba H. Warren says, Victorian "theorists are most likely to stand on the individualistic and subjective qualities of poetry, the expression of emotion, or the exercise of the feelings; but poetry, as sympathetic imagination or imaginative sympathy, is also conceived as a binding social and political force, as well as a powerful moral agent"; *English Poetic Theory 1825–1865* (Princeton: Princeton University Press, 1950), p. 212.

3. *The Mirror and the Lamp: Romantic Theory and the Critical Tradition* (New York: Oxford University Press, 1953). Carl Dawson says: "Expressive theories of literature, which are by mid-century the dominant theories, do not, in fact, fit comfortably with theories of social utility, and early Victorian critics struggle with apparently irreconcilable premises"; *Victorian Noon: English Literature in 1850* (Baltimore: Johns Hopkins University Press, 1979), p. 19.

4. Review of Tennyson's *Poems*, 1842, *Quarterly Review*, 70 (September 1842), 402; reprinted in *Victorian Scrutinies*, pp. 141–142. On the relation between content and communication in Victorian poetic theory see Armstrong, *Victorian Scrutinies*, p. 13.

5. Arthur Henry Hallam, "On Some of the Characteristics of Modern Poetry, and on the Lyrical Poems of Alfred Tennyson," *The Writings of Arthur Hallam*, ed. T. H. Vail Motter (New York: Modern Language Association of America, 1943), p. 192. John Stuart Mill, "What Is Poetry?" (1833), in *Mill's Essays on Literature and Society*, ed. J. B. Schneewind (New York: Collier Books, 1965), pp. 109–110, 103–104. Thomas

Carlyle, "The Hero as Poet," *Sartor Resartus, On Heroes and Hero Worship* (London: Everyman's Library, 1908), p. 323. *The Letters of Matthew Arnold to Arthur Hugh Clough*, ed. Howard Foster Lowry (Oxford: Clarendon Press, 1932), p. 146.

6. ["Poetry of the Year 1842"], *Christian Remembrancer*, 4 (July 1842), 49; quoted in *Victorian Scrutinies*, p. 5.

7. "What Is Poetry?," p. 109.

8. As Leon Gottfried says, romanticism "stood like the Chinese Wall separating the nineteenth century from the dominant literary tradition of the eighteenth century . . . and from the antecedent tradition of wit going back to Donne"; *Matthew Arnold and the Romantics* (London: Routledge & Kegan Paul, 1963), p. 3.

9. On nineteenth-century ideas of sincerity see Patricia M. Ball, *The Central Self: A Study in Romantic and Victorian Imagination* (London: Athlone Press, 1968), pp. 152–165; David Perkins, *Wordsworth and the Poetry of Sincerity* (Cambridge, Mass.: Harvard University Press, Belknap Press, 1964); Lionel Trilling, *Sincerity and Authenticity* (Cambridge, Mass.: Harvard University Press, 1972); Henri Peyre, *Literature and Sincerity* (New Haven: Yale University Press, 1963). Dawson discusses Victorian ideas about sincerity, truth, reality, and the speaking voice in *Victorian Noon*, pp. 161–167.

The cult of sincerity is deliberately and often ironically exploited for the purpose of persuasion in Victorian prose: in the simple and candid personae of Arnold and Huxley, the resonant preachments of Carlyle, and Newman's *Apologia Pro Vita Sua*, the most powerful autobiography of the century. Newman wrote with the avowed intention of proving that he was not a liar, and insofar as he succeeds it is because we feel that at the actual moment of writing (as opposed to the moments he writes about) he is sincere; we respond to the voice we hear, not to the story it tells us; to the man, not to the events of his life. But of course Newman was a master of rhetoric who knew very well what he was doing, and his deliberate enactment of sincerity can still make readers profoundly uneasy.

10. *On Translating Homer*, in *On the Classical Tradition, The Complete Prose Works of Matthew Arnold*, ed. R. H. Super, 11 vols. (Ann Arbor: University of Michigan Press, 1960–1977), I: 206, note.

11. *Edinburgh Review*, 77 (April 1843), 383; reprinted in *Tennyson: The Critical Heritage*, ed. John D. Jump (New York: Barnes & Noble, 1967), p. 147.

12. *Letters of Matthew Arnold 1848–1888*, ed. George W. E. Russell (New York: Macmillan and Co., 1895), I: 71–72.

13. See Kathleen Tillotson, *Novels of the Eighteen-Forties* (Oxford: Clarendon Press, 1954).

14. "On Art in Fiction" [1838], *Nineteenth-Century British Novelists on the Novel*, ed. George L. Barnett (New York: Appleton-Century-Crofts, 1971), p. 102.

15. On the changing relationship between novelist, narrator, and reader, see Kathleen Tillotson, *Novels of the Eighteen-Forties*, and "The Tale and the Teller," *Mid-Victorian Studies* (London: Athlone Press, 1965); Richard Stang, *The Theory of the Novel in England 1850–1870* (New York: Columbia University Press, 1959); George H. Ford, *Dickens and His Readers: Aspects of Novel-Criticism since 1836* (Princeton: Princeton University Press, 1955).

16. *Writings of Arthur Hallam*, p. 197; Spedding, *Edinburgh Review*, 77 (April 1843), 382, reprinted in *Tennyson: The Critical Heritage*, p. 146; Hunt, *Church of England Quarterly Review*, 12 (October 1842), reprinted in *Tennyson: The Critical Heritage*, p. 133.

17. "The National Gallery," II, *Politics for the People*, no. 3 (May 20, 1848), 38; reprinted in *Victorians on Literature and Art*, ed. Robert L. Peters (New York: Appleton-Century-Crofts, 1961), p. 186.

George Levine has memorably remarked that "all Victorian art aspired to the condition of fiction, not music, and where it swerved from this condition it tended to fail"; *The Boundaries of Fiction: Carlyle, Macaulay, Newman* (Princeton: Princeton University Press, 1968), p. 78.

18. George Eliot, *Middlemarch*, ed. Gordon S. Haight (Boston: Houghton Mifflin Co., 1956), p. 538 (chapter 72).

19. "The Three Voices of Poetry," *On Poetry and Poets* (New York: Farrar, Straus and Cudahy, 1957), p. 104. Eliot, who writes some of the closest twentieth-century equivalents to the Victorian dramatic monologue, sees the difficulties of characterization in terms of drama rather than prose fiction: "dramatic monologue cannot create a character. For character is created and made real only in an action, a communication between imaginary people"; ibid.

20. As Michael Mason says, "The response is a kind of delight, or glee, that any virtuoso performance gives, and, as with virtuoso performances, there is a close bond between the performer and the audience, a happy conspiracy of display on the one hand and applause on the other"; "Browning and the Dramatic Monologue," in Isobel Armstrong, ed., *Robert Browning*, Writers and Their Background (Athens: Ohio University Press, 1975), pp. 235–236.

21. Ina Beth Sessions, "The Dramatic Monologue," *PMLA*, 62 (1947), 508.

22. *The Poetry of Experience: The Dramatic Monologue in Modern Literary Tradition* (1957; reprinted New York: W. W. Norton & Co., 1963), p. 85.

23. *Browning's Characters: A Study in Poetic Technique* (New Haven: Yale University Press, 1961), p. 122. Honan analyzes the problem of definition, pp. 104–125. K. E. Faas surveys Victorian poems and definitions in "Notes towards a History of the Dramatic Monologue," *Anglia*, 88 (1970), 222–232.

Ralph W. Rader proposes a classification based on relationships between poet and speaker, in "The Dramatic Monologue and Related Lyric Forms," *Critical Inquiry*, 3 (1976), 131–151. In practice, however, the classification of many poems will inevitably seem arbitrary. Kristian Smidt points out that in a very large number of Victorian poems the relation of the poet to the speaker is unclear; "Point of View in Victorian Poetry," *English Studies*, 38 (1957), 1–12. And the reader's problem follows from the poet's: "the greatest difficulty for the Victorian writer," W. Stacy Johnson says, "is to know what his own voice is"; *The Voices of Matthew Arnold: An Essay in Criticism* (New Haven: Yale University Press, 1961), p. 6.

24. A. Dwight Culler, "Monodrama and the Dramatic Monologue," *PMLA*, 90 (1975), 366–385; Alan Sinfield, *Dramatic Monologue* (London: Methuen & Co., 1977), p. 76.

25. Langbaum, *Poetry of Experience*, pp. 190–191; Honan, *Browning's Characters*,

p. 156; Culler, "Monodrama," p. 383. Honan's formulation basically seems to mean that speaker and auditor have, at some level, something in common.

26. *Poetry of Experience*, pp. 182, 183.

27. *Dramatic Monologue*, p. 26.

28. Patricia M. Ball considers these and other long poems in *The Heart's Events: The Victorian Poetry of Relationships* (London: Athlone Press, 1976). She argues that "Victorian poets set up new concepts of the long poem, or the lyric group" to fit the ideas "that change . . . is integral to love and . . . that the inner life as it is affected by close relationships evolves with a logic of its own which is not merely that of temporal sequence"; p. 4. Sinfield discusses *Maud, Amours de Voyage,* and *The Ring and the Book* as "super-monologues"; *Dramatic Monologue*, pp. 35–41.

CHAPTER ONE

1. Evidence for dating Tennyson's poems is given in *The Poems of Tennyson*, ed. Christopher Ricks (London: Longmans, Green and Co., 1969).

2. Hallam Tennyson, *Alfred Lord Tennyson: A Memoir by His Son*, 2 vols. (London: Macmillan and Co., 1897), I: 43 (hereafter cited as *Memoir*).

3. Harvard Notebook 7. Hallam Tennyson printed a toned-down and abbreviated version (*Memoir*, I: 497–498). A facsimile of the manuscript appears in Edgar F. Shannon, Jr. and W. H. Bond, "Literary Manuscripts of Alfred Tennyson in the Harvard College Library," *Harvard Library Bulletin*, 10 (1956), 254–274 (Plate II).

4. Such stories give "a point of view to the imagination for the delineating of human passions more comprehensive and commanding than any which the ordinary relations of existing events can yield"; Mary W. Shelley, *Frankenstein or the Modern Prometheus*, ed. M. K. Joseph (London: Oxford University Press, 1969), p. 13. (Shelley wrote this preface in his wife's name.) Tennyson's storyteller, similarly, "stands as it were on a vantage-ground" and "becomes the minister & expounder of human sympathies." The glaciers of Chamouny may appear in the essay because of Shelley's "Mont Blanc," or because that is where Frankenstein reencounters his huge and terrible creature.

5. Ovid, *Fasti* II. 503 (London: Loeb Classical Library): "*humano maior.*"

6. Compare especially "some as they lived, seemingly pale . . . some as they died in a still agony" and "Adonais": "Chatterton / Rose pale, his solemn agony had not / Yet faded from him; Sidney, as he fought / And as he fell and as he lived and loved" (399–402).

7. *The Tempest*, IV.i.151.

8. Ricks notes the similarity; *Poems of Tennyson*, p. 556. All references to Tennyson's poems are from this edition.

9. *Memoir*, I: 72–73. Tennyson may have been thinking of the vain searches for ghosts that Shelley reports in "Hymn to Intellectual Beauty" 49 ff.

10. *Memoir*, I: 5. Philip Collins discusses Tennyson's readings in *Reading Aloud: A*

Victorian Métier, Tennyson Society Monographs, no. 5 (Lincoln: The Tennyson Society, Tennyson Research Centre, 1972).

11. *Memoir,* I: 48.

12. *Paradise Lost,* IV. 801–803. See Sir Charles Tennyson, "Tennyson as a Humorist," *Six Tennyson Essays* (London: Cassell & Co., 1954), p. 16, and *The Letters of Arthur Henry Hallam,* ed. Jack Kolb (Athens: Ohio University Press, 1981), p. 602, note 3.

13. Edward Gibbon, *The History of the Decline and Fall of the Roman Empire,* ed. William Smith, 8 vols. (London: John Murray, 1854), IV: 320, note 72 (chapter 37).

14. Critics have paid more attention to the first conception, although the poem has been read as a serious psychological study by Christopher Ricks in *Tennyson* (New York: Macmillan Co., 1972), pp. 107–111, and by W. David Shaw in *Tennyson's Style* (Ithaca: Cornell University Press, 1976), pp. 103–106. The fullest analysis of the poem is William E. Fredeman's "'A Sign betwixt the Meadow and the Cloud': The Ironic Apotheosis of Tennyson's St Simeon Stylites," *University of Toronto Quarterly,* 38 (1968), 69–83.

15. *The Poems of Tennyson* gives full information about these drafts, with one error: lines 143–157 (not 143–147) are missing from them.

16. Gibbon, *Decline and Fall,* IV: 321.

17. Trinity Notebook 20. The Harvard manuscripts include a very similar version of this passage.

18. As Ricks says, Tennyson was "haunted" by this cliché; *Tennyson,* p. 57.

19. Trinity Notebook 15; quoted in Ricks, *Tennyson,* p. 302. This phrase migrated to the 1842 version of "Oenone" as "gazing on divinity disrobed" (154).

20. *Inferno,* XXVI. 118–120, in *The Vision; or, Hell, Purgatory, and Paradise,* trans. H. F. Cary (London: John Taylor, 1831). Tennyson probably used Cary's translation. Ulysses' literary history is traced by W. B. Stanford in *The Ulysses Theme: A Study in the Adaptability of a Traditional Hero,* 2d ed. (Ann Arbor: University of Michigan Press, 1968).

21. *Memoir,* I: 214.

22. Stanford describes Ulisse as "a paradoxical, Janus-like figure: one face looks sombrely back to the conventional Latin conception of Ulysses as the treacherous conqueror of the Trojans; the other gazes, with astonishing radiance, on towards the spirit of the Renaissance and of nineteenth-century romanticism"; *Ulysses Theme,* p. 178. This is surely how Tennyson read the canto.

23. *Memoir,* I: 196.

24. "On Some of the Characteristics of Modern Poetry, and on the Lyrical Poems of Alfred Tennyson," *The Writings of Arthur Hallam,* ed. T. H. Vail Motter (New York: Modern Language Association of America, 1943), pp. 189, 190.

25. Ibid., p. 197.

26. Harvard Notebook 16.

27. John Pettigrew convincingly argues that the poem begins as soliloquy and shifts at line 33 ("This is my son") "from interior to exterior monologue"; "Tennyson's 'Ulysses': A Reconciliation of Opposites," *Victorian Poetry,* 1 (1963), 41. Pettigrew points

out that soliloquy is what readers would expect in 1842, and that Ulysses would be unlikely to speak of his "agèd wife" and a "savage race" if those he referred to were listening (he speaks more tactfully of a "rugged people" in the third paragraph); p. 40. A. Dwight Culler says that "Telemachus occupies the same position toward Ulysses that Menoeceus does toward Tiresias": he acts for him. Culler argues that since Tennyson elsewhere prefers action to contemplation, Ulysses cannot be "contemptuous" of Telemachus; *The Poetry of Tennyson* (New Haven: Yale University Press, 1977), pp. 89–90. But "action" and "contemplation" are not sufficient terms to describe either poem; they ignore speech.

28. "What . . . is Mariana repressing? Why, that she doesn't want or need the other who cometh not. What would she do with him, what mental space has she left for him?"; Harold Bloom, *Poetry and Repression: Revisionism from Blake to Stevens* (New Haven: Yale University Press, 1976), p. 153.

29. Valerie Pitt calls it his "central political poem" and "his last attempt to put across his social theories in a direct manner"; *Tennyson Laureate* (Toronto: University of Toronto Press, 1962), pp. 179, 181. A. S. Byatt, on the other hand, focuses on the lyrical element in "The Lyric Structure of Tennyson's *Maud*," in *The Major Victorian Poets: Reconsiderations*, ed. Isobel Armstrong (Lincoln: University of Nebraska Press, 1969). The point is that both views are valid.

30. See *Poems of Tennyson*, p. 1090. Ralph Wilson Rader discusses the circumstances of the poem's composition in *Tennyson's Maud: The Biographical Genesis* (Berkeley and Los Angeles: University of California Press, 1963), pp. 2–11.

31. *Memoir*, I: 396, 408; George Brimley, "Tennyson's Poems," in *Essays*, ed. William George Clark, 2d ed. (Cambridge and London: Macmillan and Co., 1860), pp. 75–84.

32. "Tennyson's Maud," *Fraser's Magazine*, 52 (September 1855), 267.

33. Tennyson's comment is recorded by Ricks in *The Poems of Tennyson*, p. 1040. Edgar F. Shannon discusses Tennyson's revisions in "The Critical Reception of Tennyson's 'Maud,'" *PMLA*, 68 (1953), 397–417. Critics still make similar judgments. Rader says that the hero's emotions are damagingly excessive to the story because Tennyson drew them from experiences he had not distanced or mastered; *Tennyson's Maud*, pp. 116–117.

34. Review of *Maud, and Other Poems*, *Edinburgh Review*, 102 (1855), 509, 510. (The attribution is made by Shannon, "Critical Reception," p. 415.) On Kingsley's dislike of *Maud* see Shannon, "Critical Reception," p. 405; on Patmore's, see Derek Patmore, *The Life and Times of Coventry Patmore* (London: Constable, 1949), p. 97.

35. Carol T. Christ finds a similar ambivalence in Tennyson's attitude toward precision of detail: he "values the intensity of feeling he gains in his microscopic eye," but associates such intensity with madness; *The Finer Optic: The Aesthetic of Particularity in Victorian Poetry* (New Haven: Yale University Press, 1975), p. 36.

36. Pitt points out that Tennyson "always thought of the marriage bond as the archetype and model for social relationship"; *Tennyson Laureate*, p. 181.

37. There are specific echoes of Spenser: "merry play" (I.629, *Epithalamion*, 368), "affright" (I.669, *Epithalamion*, 339)—as well as the more general ones: "twelve sweet hours that past in bridal white . . . But now by this my love has closed her sight"

(I.663, 665). Section XVIII may recall Adam's discovery of Eve in *Paradise Lost*, VIII, and the description of nature in terms of sweet odors, breezes, and precious stones (I.649–650) recalls Milton's descriptions of Eden in Book IV.

38. Robert James Mann, *Tennyson's "Maud" Vindicated: An Explanatory Essay* (London: Jarrold & Sons, [1856]), p. 76. James R. Kincaid defends the ending in terms not incompatible with Mann's: "War . . . is the nearly absurd but legitimate demand that society makes on those who would be accommodated to it; it stands as the final rebuke to all absolutists. The narrator can finally learn to live with his own dark self when he can learn to live with the darkness of war"; *Tennyson's Major Poems: The Comic and Ironic Patterns* (New Haven: Yale University Press, 1975), p. 132.

39. Cf. *Maud*, I. 648–650: "It seems that I am happy, that to me / A livelier emerald twinkles in the grass, / A purer sapphire melts into the sea."

40. *Memoir*, II: 125. This is an appropriate episode for the history of a poem about the dangers of poetic communication.

41. See A *Variorum Edition of Tennyson's Idylls of the King*, ed. John Pfordresher (New York: Columbia University Press, 1973).

42. Ibid., p. 734.

43. It is generally agreed that the grail quest represents the life of poetic imagination; see e.g. E. D. H. Johnson, *The Alien Vision of Victorian Poetry: Sources of the Poetic Imagination in Tennyson, Browning, and Arnold* (Princeton: Princeton University Press, 1952), p. 48. John D. Rosenberg notes the decisive importance of the nun's "myth-making powers" in the formation of both the grail legend and the quest: *The Fall of Camelot: A Study of Tennyson's "Idylls of the King"* (Cambridge, Mass.: Harvard University Press, Belknap Press, 1973), p. 143.

44. Kincaid points out that Arthur's final speech is "uttered by a king who no longer believes in the efficacy of utterance"; *Tennyson's Major Poems*, p. 198. Kincaid's discussion of "The Holy Grail" (pp. 192–198) provides a subtle account of the balance in the poem between Percivale's point of view and Ambrosius's: neither is wrong, but the views are irreconcilable.

45. In several other late monologues auditors are present only to be talked at. Many of these poems are in dialect, and typically though not invariably they are based on curious or pathetic incidents and the speakers are poor, ignorant, quaint, or mad. The auditors, like the cats in "The Spinster's Sweet-Arts," let the speaker tell a story or display his personality or the flavor of his speech.

46. The speaker in "Despair" flings back the words of the minister who rescued him from suicide: "Blasphemy! true! I have scared you pale with my scandalous talk" (111); but his speech too is mostly self-expressive and evidently does not persuade. In the slight and very disagreeable "Happy: The Leper's Bride," however, the wife convinces her husband to let her share his bodily decay and life of ritual death (she gloats over details of physical morbidity with Simeon's nastiness but not his unintentional humor). And Romney, recognizing the woman who has appeared to nurse him on his deathbed as the wife he had deserted years before, repents and is forgiven: in the course of the poem she evidently weeps, tends him affectionately, and urges him to hope. But she had forgiven him already.

CHAPTER TWO

1. *The Letters of Robert Browning and Elizabeth Barrett Barrett 1845–1846*, ed. Elvan Kintner, 2 vols. (Cambridge, Mass.: Harvard University Press, Belknap Press, 1969), I: 7. As Ian Jack points out, Browning regarded Elizabeth Barrett first of all as the "appreciative and understanding reader" that in 1845 he sorely needed; *Browning's Major Poetry* (Oxford: Clarendon Press, 1973), p. 110.

2. The Duke was identified before the Chatterton essay had been discovered by Louis S. Friedland: "Ferrara and *My Last Duchess*," *Studies in Philology*, 33 (1936), 656–684. The rise and fall in England of the Tasso legend are traced by C. P. Brand in *Torquato Tasso: A Study of the Poet and of His Contribution to English Literature* (Cambridge: University Press, 1965), pp. 205–225.

3. References to Browning's poetry are to *The Poems*, ed. John Pettigrew, 2 vols. (New Haven: Yale University Press, 1981), and *The Ring and the Book*, ed. Richard D. Altick (1971; New Haven: Yale University Press, 1981).

4. *Robert Browning and Julia Wedgwood: A Broken Friendship as Revealed by Their Letters*, ed. Richard Curle (New York: Frederick A. Stokes Co., 1937), p. 147.

5. *Browning's Essay on Chatterton*, ed. Donald Smalley (Cambridge, Mass.: Harvard University Press, 1948; reprint ed. 1970), p. 116.

6. The case against the Countess was first argued by John V. Hagopian, "The Mask of Browning's Countess Gismond," *Philological Quarterly*, 40 (1961), 153–155. Michael Timko tellingly defends the older readings of this and other Browning poems; "Ah, Did You Once See Browning Plain?," *Studies in English Literature*, 6 (1966), 731–742; but he does not explain the last stanza.

7. Kintner, *Letters*, I: 7.

8. "Introductory Essay" ["Essay on Shelley"], *Poems*, I: 1001.

9. W. G. Collingwood, *The Life of John Ruskin* (Boston: Houghton, Mifflin & Co., 1902), pp. 164, 166. For Ruskin's letter, see David J. DeLaura, "Ruskin and the Brownings: Twenty-Five Unpublished Letters," *Bulletin of the John Rylands Library*, 54 (1972), 324–327. Thomas J. Collins suggests that the dramatic monologue "is a retreat for Browning, not a victory," and that Browning used it because it allowed him "to reach an audience . . . to *be* a poet of his time"; "The Poetry of Robert Browning: A Proposal for Reexamination," *Texas Studies in Literature and Language*, 15 (1973), 332.

10. Robert Langbaum, *The Poetry of Experience: The Dramatic Monologue in Modern Literary Tradition* (1957; reprint ed. New York: W. W. Norton & Co., 1963), pp. 182–184.

11. Langbaum uses "Blougram" and "Sludge" as examples of the "disequilibrium" that, he says, characterizes all dramatic monologues; ibid., p. 188.

12. Most recent critics more or less accept F. E. L. Priestley's defense of Blougram's argument in "Blougram's Apologetics," *University of Toronto Quarterly*, 15 (1946), 139–147. The fullest rebuttal is Philip Drew's *The Poetry of Browning: A Critical Introduction* (London: Methuen & Co., 1970), pp. 124–143. Browning demands of his reader, Drew says, "that he shall be continually vigilant to distinguish between truth and sophistry, between deception and self-deception"; p. 119. Drew himself exercises

such vigilance, but it seems an odd demand for a poet to make. Julia Markus traces contemporary sources for the characters and issues in "Bishop Blougram and the Literary Men," *Victorian Studies,* 21 (1978), 171–195; Markus shows that Browning's sympathies were complex and many-sided.

13. *Poems,* I: 1006.

14. Ibid., p. 1009. For Browning's response to the substantiation of the charges, see William Irvine and Park Honan, *The Book, the Ring, and the Poet: A Biography of Robert Browning* (New York: McGraw-Hill, 1974), pp. 283–284, 553, note 23.

15. Matthew Arnold, "Wordsworth," *English Literature and Irish Politics, The Complete Prose Works of Matthew Arnold,* ed. R. H. Super, 11 vols. (Ann Arbor: University of Michigan Press, 1960–1977), IX: 53; Thomas Carlyle, *On Heroes, Hero-Worship and the Heroic in History,* in *Sartor Resartus, On Heroes and Hero Worship* (London: Everyman's Library, 1908), p. 302; Arnold, "The Study of Poetry," *Complete Prose,* IX: 183.

16. *Heroes and Hero-Worship,* p. 358. Smalley demonstrates that Browning's essay on Chatterton, like some of his plays, shows his interest in arguing hard cases, and particularly the cases of impostors; *Browning's Essay on Chatterton,* pp. 54–77. But the essay is above all a defense of Chatterton's sincerity against the notorious facts of his career, like Carlyle's defense of Mahomet and Cromwell—also notorious as impostors—in *Heroes and Hero-Worship.* In 1840 Browning had attended Carlyle's lectures on heroes; see *New Letters of Robert Browning,* ed. William Clyde DeVane and Kenneth Leslie Knickerbocker (New Haven: Yale University Press, 1950), p. 19.

17. The end of "Caliban upon Setebos" (also published in *Dramatis Personae*) is precisely the opposite: suddenly thinking his indiscreet soliloquy has been overheard, he starts to talk like Sludge with Hiram Horsefalls: "Lo! 'Lieth flat and loveth Setebos!" (292).

18. J. Hillis Miller remarks that Browning tries to "use point of view to transcend point of view"; *The Disappearance of God: Five Nineteenth-Century Writers* (Cambridge, Mass.: Harvard University Press, Belknap Press, 1963), p. 148. He is similarly trying, perhaps less successfully, to use speech to transcend speech.

19. Robert Langbaum discusses Balaustion as an interpreter of myth in "Browning and the Question of Myth," *The Modern Spirit: Essays on the Continuity of Nineteenth- and Twentieth-Century Literature* (New York: Oxford University Press, 1970). Clyde de L. Ryals says that Balaustion "sums up all that Browning had previously tried to say about both his artistic creed and his religious faith"; *Browning's Later Poetry, 1871–1889* (Ithaca: Cornell University Press, 1975), p. 41.

20. See Ryals, *Browning's Later Poetry,* p. 57.

21. As Roma A. King, Jr., says, the poem questions "the reality not merely of the act but of the actor"; *The Focusing Artifice: The Poetry of Robert Browning* (Athens: Ohio University Press, 1968), p. 171.

22. Drew describes the poem as "a record as it were of Browning's own difficulty in assessing Napoleon III"; *Poetry of Browning,* p. 297. Browning's attitude toward Napoleon III is traced by William Clyde DeVane in *A Browning Handbook,* 2d ed. (New York: Appleton-Century-Crofts, 1955), pp. 359–363; and Leo A. Hetzler in "The Case

of Prince Hohenstiel-Schwangau: Browning and Napoleon III," *Victorian Poetry*, 15 (1977), 335–350.

23. Charlotte Crawford Watkins studies the poem as an analysis of contemporary relativism in "The 'Abstruser Themes' of Browning's *Fifine at the Fair*," *PMLA*, 74 (1959), 426–437.

24. W. C. DeVane assumes that they are young in "The Harlot and the Thoughtful Young Man: A Study of the Relation between Rossetti's *Jenny* and Browning's *Fifine at the Fair*," *Studies in Philology*, 29 (1932), 463–484. The argument of this essay (that the poem refers, as Rossetti in his paranoia thought, to "Jenny") depends on this un-warranted assumption.

25. Barbara Melchiori, *Browning's Poetry of Reticence* (New York: Barnes & Noble, 1968), p. 183.

26. The poem is almost always discussed as if Don Juan's auditor were no more real than Hohenstiel-Schwangau's. Melchiori pays some attention to Elvire's dramatic presence in her chapter on *Fifine* ("Browning's Don Juan") in *Browning's Poetry of Reticence*. So does Isobel Armstrong, more briefly, in "Browning and Victorian Poetry of Sexual Love," in *Robert Browning*, Writers and Their Background Series, ed. Isobel Armstrong (Athens: Ohio University Press, 1975), p. 296. To dismiss Elvire and Fifine as simply abstractions or fantasy figures, to which Browning for mysterious and inade-quate reasons gave human names and dramatic roles, makes the poem's form seem arbitrary and capricious and slights half its meaning.

27. Sven-Johan Spånberg discusses the poem as part of the Don Juan legend in "The Don Juan Figure in Browning's *Fifine at the Fair*," *Comparative Literature*, 28 (1976), 19–33, emphasizing similarities between Browning's character and Molière's.

28. William O. Raymond uses the Lady Ashburton episode as a key to the poem in "Browning's Dark Mood: A Study of *Fifine at the Fair*," in *The Infinite Moment and Other Essays in Robert Browning*, 2d ed. (Toronto: University of Toronto Press, 1965). It has long been assumed that Browning clumsily proposed to Lady Ashburton and was rejected, but Maisie Ward persuasively suggests that Lady Ashburton invited Brow-ning's offer; *Robert Browning and His World: Two Robert Brownings?* (New York: Holt, Rinehart and Winston, 1969), pp. 70–72; and William Whitla argues that it was Lady Ashburton who proposed; "Browning and the Ashburton Affair," *Browning Society Notes*, 2 (July 1972), 12–41. Whoever initiated it, a discussion of marriage between them led to bitter ill feeling.

29. As Drew says, the poem "poses the crucial question 'What sort of terminus is possible to a man who does *not* find in love an abiding power?'"; *Poetry of Browning*, p. 307. Melchiori sees Elizabeth occasionally behind Elvire, but only when Don Juan seems to be thinking of her as dead; *Browning's Poetry of Reticence*, pp. 184–187. Sam-uel B. Southwell finds a "deep ambivalence toward Elizabeth" in the poem; its "funda-mental impulse," he says, "is male loneliness, the need of woman"; *Quest for Eros: Browning and "Fifine"* (Lexington: University Press of Kentucky, 1980), pp. 25, 29.

30. For discussions of Aeschylus see Kintner, *Letters*, I: 30 ff.

31. *Prometheus Bound. Translated from the Greek of Aeschylus. And Miscellaneous Poems* (London: A. J. Valpy, 1833), p. 8; *The Poetical Works of Elizabeth Barrett Brow-ning*, Cambridge ed. (Boston: Houghton Mifflin Co., 1974), p. 130.

32. Kintner, *Letters*, I: 303. Kintner points out that Browning read these letters over in later years and may have used them for his poems; II: 940, note 3.

33. Some critics think the speaker of the prologue and the epilogue is Browning, and some think he is Don Juan. Irvine and Honan call the two characters in the epilogue "Robert" and "Elizabeth"; *The Book, the Ring, and the Poet*, pp. 464–466. King finds the epilogue "either unrelated or tangentially related" to the poem as a whole; *Focusing Artifice*, p. 187. Ryals argues that the speaker is Don Juan throughout; *Browning's Later Poetry*, pp. 80–82. But Don Juan and the speaker in the epilogue have nothing in common except that they inhabit the same poem, use some similar imagery, and are married men. One is a weary and contemptuous husband, the other a widower filled with love and regret. Perhaps the Victorian delicacy of Mrs. Sutherland Orr put it best: "We may even fancy we read into the letters of 1870 that eerie, haunting sadness of a cherished memory from which, in spite of ourselves, life is bearing us away"; *Life and Letters of Robert Browning*, 2d ed. (London: Smith, Elder, & Co., 1891), p. 294.

34. DeVane and Knickerbocker, *New Letters*, p. 214.

35. Walter M. Kendrick reads it as a "deconstructive" poem that explores the impossibility of reaching through language to any nonlinguistic reality; "Facts and Figures: Browning's *Red Cotton Night-Cap Country*," *Victorian Poetry*, 17 (1979), 343–363.

CHAPTER THREE

1. Arnold may have taken Wordsworth's example. As David Perkins says, "Often the poems show Wordsworth speaking to his wife, his children, his sister, or other familiars. . . . As an audience, they would not inhibit or control the poetry in any way, and they would also bring to bear a protective sympathy"; *Wordsworth and the Poetry of Sincerity* (Cambridge, Mass.: Harvard University Press, Belknap Press, 1964), p. 160.

2. *Letters of Matthew Arnold 1848–1888*, ed. George W. E. Russell, 2 vols. (New York: Macmillan and Co., 1895), II: 10.

3. "Belles Lettres," *Westminster Review*, n.s. 8 (July 1855), 297; reprinted in *Matthew Arnold: The Poetry: The Critical Heritage*, ed. Carl Dawson (London: Routledge & Kegan Paul, 1973), p. 130.

4. "Recent English Poetry," *Selected Prose Works of Arthur Hugh Clough*, ed. Buckner B. Trawick (University: University of Alabama Press, 1964), p. 164; reprinted from *North American Review*, 77 (July 1853), 1–30. Arnold's poetry is quoted from *The Poems of Matthew Arnold*, ed. Kenneth Allott, 2d ed., ed. Miriam Allott (London: Longman, 1979).

5. Arnold's various attempts to find an appropriate voice or tone for his poems are subtly analyzed by W. Stacy Johnson in *The Voices of Matthew Arnold: An Essay in Criticism* (New Haven: Yale University Press, 1961).

6. The relevant comparison is to "Tintern Abbey"; see Leon Gottfried, *Matthew Arnold and the Romantics* (London: Routledge & Kegan Paul, 1963), pp. 219–223,

and M. G. Sundell, "'Tintern Abbey' and 'Resignation,'" *Victorian Poetry*, 5 (1967), 255–264.

7. *Unpublished Letters of Matthew Arnold*, ed. Arnold Whitridge (New Haven: Yale University Press, 1923), pp. 20–21; *Letters*, ed. Russell, I: 117; *Unpublished Letters*, p. 21. The evidence for the traditional association of Fausta with Jane Arnold Forster is set forth in Allott's notes to the poem. A. Dwight Culler's incisive comment on "Marguerite" could be applied to Fausta as well: we know that she existed both because of the abundant evidence and because "Arnold was incapable of inventing her": all Arnold's poems "involving character and incident . . . derive either from his own experience or from a literary or historical source"; *Imaginative Reason: The Poetry of Matthew Arnold* (New Haven: Yale University Press, 1966), p. 120.

8. *The Correspondence of Arthur Hugh Clough*, ed. Frederick L. Mulhauser, 2 vols. (Oxford: Clarendon Press, 1957), I: 251.

9. *Selected Prose*, pp. 153, 144.

10. Richard Holt Hutton, "The Poetry of Matthew Arnold," *Literary Essays*, 3rd ed. (London: Macmillan and Co., 1888), pp. 320, 337, 312.

11. *Unpublished Letters*, p. 18. Whitridge's tentative date of 1853 is generally agreed to be erroneous.

12. *The Letters of Matthew Arnold to Arthur Hugh Clough*, ed. Howard Foster Lowry (Oxford: Clarendon Press, 1932), pp. 86, 66, 81, 98–99, 99.

13. Russell, *Letters*, I: 72, 73.

14. *Unpublished Letters*, p. 17; *Letters to Clough*, p. 104.

15. Preface to first edition of *Poems* (1853), *On the Classical Tradition*, *The Complete Prose Works of Matthew Arnold*, ed. R. H. Super, 11 vols. (Ann Arbor: University of Michigan Press, 1960–1977), I: 10.

16. Isobel Armstrong discusses the Preface in the context of contemporary criticism in *Victorian Scrutinies: Reviews of Poetry 1830–1870* (London: Athlone Press, 1972), pp. 31–50. See also Sidney Coulling, *Matthew Arnold and His Critics: A Study of Arnold's Controversies* (Athens: Ohio University Press, 1974).

17. *Complete Prose*, I: 4.

18. Ibid., I: 2.

19. *Letters to Clough*, p. 128.

20. *Complete Prose*, I: 6.

21. On the romanticism of Victorian philology, see J. W. Burrow, "The Uses of Philology in Victorian England," in *Ideas and Institutions of Victorian Britain*, ed. Robert Robson (New York: Barnes & Noble, 1967), pp. 180–204.

22. *Complete Prose*, I: 7, 11.

23. Ibid., I: 2, 7, 12, 2.

24. Ibid., I: 7.

25. Ibid., I: 1, 2, 4.

26. Ibid., I: 8.

27. Russell, *Letters*, I: 34; see *Letters to Clough*, pp. 132–133 for a similar comparison to Thackeray.

28. *Complete Prose*, I: 10.

29. Ibid., I: 5.

30. Ibid., I:53.

31. "Dover Beach" probably refers to Arnold's wedding trip in June 1851. Certainly it sounds like such a poem: "the world, which seems / To lie before us like a land of dreams." The argument that it was written in the early 1850s is convincingly made by Kenneth Allott in "The Dating of Dover Beach," *Notes and Queries*, n.s. 14 (1967), 374–375. S. O. A. Ullmann makes a strong case for a date between June 1851 and April 1852 in "Dating through Calligraphy: The Example of 'Dover Beach,'" *Studies in Bibliography*, 26 (1973), 19–36. Ullmann suggests too that the manuscript which ends "Ah love &c" is probably an intermediate draft and therefore does not support the assumption traditionally based on it that the last paragraph was written earlier than the rest; pp. 34–35.

It is possible, of course, that Arnold did not mean us to think of the couple in the poem as married; but the Dover setting suggests that they are traveling together, and if they were not married that unconventional fact would have found expression in the poem.

32. The poem is usually read with little or no reference to the dramatic situation and as a statement of unmitigated pessimism. But as William Cadbury says, "The surprising thing about 'Dover Beach' is that . . . it is so cheerful"; he concludes that it "provides us cheer through the creation of a narrator whose gloomy thought is true, but whose action is so honest and so strong that it creates for us a perfect image of human worth"; "Coming to Terms with 'Dover Beach,'" *Criticism*, 8 (1966), 126, 138.

CHAPTER FOUR

1. Meredith's poems are quoted from *The Poems of George Meredith*, ed. Phyllis B. Bartlett, 2 vols. (New Haven: Yale University Press, 1978). Clough's poems, including manuscript variants, are quoted from *The Poems of Arthur Hugh Clough*, ed. F. L. Mulhauser, 2d ed. (Oxford: Clarendon Press, 1974).

2. *The Letters of Matthew Arnold to Arthur Hugh Clough*, ed. Howard Foster Lowry (Oxford: Clarendon Press, 1932), pp. 66, 95.

3. "Recent English Poetry," *Selected Prose Works of Arthur Hugh Clough*, ed. Buckner B. Trawick (University: University of Alabama Press, 1964), p. 144.

4. *Letters to Clough*, p. 132.

5. *The Correspondence of Arthur Hugh Clough*, ed. Frederick L. Mulhauser, 2 vols. (Oxford: Clarendon Press, 1957), II: 546.

6. See Kathleen Tillotson, *Novels of the Eighteen-Forties* (Oxford: Clarendon Press, 1954), pp. 122, 131.

7. *Poems of Clough*, p. 624, line 9.

8. J. C. Shairp responded with two letters of vehement dispraise and urged Clough not to publish it; *Correspondence*, I: 275–277. Katharine Chorley says that this is "the only serious contemporary criticism we have" of the poem; *Arthur Hugh Clough: The*

Uncommitted Mind: A Study of His Life and Poetry (Oxford: Clarendon Press, 1962), p. 200.

9. *Letters to Clough*, pp. 66, 99.

10. *Clough: The Critical Heritage*, ed. Michael Thorpe (New York: Barnes & Noble, 1972), p. 112.

11. "Recent English Poetry," p. 168.

12. "Matthew Arnold," in *Nineteenth-Century Essays*, ed. Peter Stansky (Chicago: University of Chicago Press, 1970), pp. 347, 348; reprinted from *The Nineteenth Century*, 38 (December 1895). As Robindra Kumar Biswas says, "Claude is defined by the personal letter, that oblique and yet most self-conscious of verbal forms. His existence is inseparable from his capacity for considered verbalization"; *Arthur Hugh Clough: Towards a Reconsideration* (Oxford: Clarendon Press, 1972), p. 310.

13. "Letters of Parepidemus, Number One," *Selected Prose*, pp. 175, 176, 177.

14. [Henry Sidgwick], "*The Poems and Prose Remains of Arthur Hugh Clough*," *Westminster Review*, n.s. 36 (1869), 381; reprinted in *Critical Heritage*, p. 286.

15. Clough's irony is subtle and perplexing, seldom purely negative and almost never simple. Barbara Hardy defines it as "the very rare kind that can live with strong feeling and does not shrivel it up by ridicule or criticism"; "Clough's Self-Consciousness," in *The Major Victorian Poets: Reconsiderations*, ed. Isobel Armstrong (Lincoln: University of Nebraska Press, 1969), p. 266.

16. *Correspondence*, I: 156.

17. Richard Holt Hutton remarks on similarities between *The Bothie* and *Hermann and Dorothea* in "Arthur Hugh Clough," *Literary Essays*, 3rd ed. (London: Macmillan and Co., 1888), pp. 290–295; reprinted in *Critical Heritage*, pp. 253–255. Clough speaks of *Evangeline* in a letter to Emerson; *Correspondence*, I: 240–241. John Goode notes the influence of the *Roman Elegies* in "*Amours de Voyage*: The Aqueous Poem," in Armstrong, *Major Victorian Poets*, pp. 285–286.

18. *Poems of Clough*, p. 619.

19. Ibid., p. 620.

20. "Recent English Poetry," p. 145.

21. *Correspondence*, II: 548.

22. *Poems of Clough*, p. 652, line 15.

23. *Correspondence*, I: 300, 301. As Walter E. Houghton says, Claude feels a "deep distaste for the unreal and distorted vision of life that love creates"; *The Poetry of Clough: An Essay in Revaluation* (New Haven: Yale University Press, 1963), p. 139.

24. *Poems of Clough*, p. 651, lines 4, 7–8.

25. On May 2, 1827, Thomas Arnold wrote: "I care very little for the sight of their churches, and nothing at all for the recollection of them. . . . Precious marbles, and precious stones, and gilding, and rich colouring, are to me like the kaleidoscope, and no more. . . . I declare I do not know what name of abhorrence can be too strong for a religion which . . . feeds the people with poison"; Arthur Penrhyn Stanley, *The Life and Correspondence of Thomas Arnold*, 6th ed. (London: B. Fellowes, 1846), p. 649. Walter E. Houghton finds Claude's fits of Protestant revulsion "in bad taste"; *Poetry of Clough*, p. 123; but Clough's "taste" in such matters was probably less delicate.

26. "Lecture on Wordsworth," *Selected Prose*, p. 121.

27. *Correspondence*, I: 278.

28. On the political motives and meaning of Clough's trip to Rome see Evelyn Bar-
ish Greenberger, *Arthur Hugh Clough: The Growth of a Poet's Mind* (Cambridge,
Mass.: Harvard University Press, 1970), pp. 126–130. John Goode discusses the politi-
cal context of Clough's poetry in "1848 and the Strange Disease of Modern Love,"
Literature and Politics in the Nineteenth Century, ed. John Lucas (London: Methuen
& Co., 1971), pp. 45–76.

29. *Correspondence*, I: 242–243.

30. The story of the marriage is told by Lionel Stevenson in *The Ordeal of George
Meredith: A Biography* (New York: Charles Scribner's Sons, 1953), and by Diane Johnson in *The True History of the First Mrs. Meredith and Other Lesser Lives* (New York:
Alfred A. Knopf, 1972). Phyllis Bartlett shows how Meredith uses his early chivalric
love poetry for satiric purposes, in "Richard Feverel, Knight-Errant," *Bulletin of the
New York Public Library*, 63 (1959), 329–340; she briefly considers his writings on
fallen women. Gillian Beer discusses Feverel in terms of the complex relationship between experience and literary pattern in the chapter on that novel in *Meredith: A
Change of Masks: A Study of the Novels* (London: Athlone Press, 1970).

One literary pattern that is less relevant than it seems is the traditional sonnet sequence. Discussions of the poem in that context add up mostly to an extensive cata-
logue of differences and an unpersuasive assertion that Meredith consistently and ironically alludes to those differences. See Arline Golden, "'The Game of Sentiment':
Tradition and Innovation in Meredith's *Modern Love*," *English Literary History*, 40
(1973), 264–284, and Cynthia Grant Tucker, "Meredith's Broken Laurel: *Modern
Love* and the Renaissance Sonnet Tradition," *Victorian Poetry*, 10 (1972), 351–365.
The clearest echo of a Renaissance sonnet in the whole poem is the ugly archaism
"God wot" (43)—which unfortunately does not seem to be ironical at all.

31. *The Letters of George Meredith*, ed. C. L. Cline, 3 vols. (Oxford: Clarendon
Press, 1970), I: 160.

32. *The Shaving of Shagpat: An Arabian Entertainment*, *The Works of George Meredith*, 29 vols. (New York: Charles Scribner's Sons, 1909–1912), I: 189.

33. Ian Fletcher stresses the sympathy and complexity of the treatment of fatal
women in *Shagpat* in "*The Shaving of Shagpat*: Meredith's Comic Apocalypse," *Meredith Now: Some Critical Essays*, ed. Ian Fletcher (London: Routledge & Kegan Paul,
1971). A poem deploring prostitution, "London by Lamplight," appeared in *Poems*
(1851).

34. *Letters*, I: 262.

35. For studies of the imagery of *Modern Love* see Norman Friedman's "The Jan-
gled Harp: Symbolic Structure in *Modern Love*," *Modern Language Quarterly*, 18
(1957), 9–26; and Elizabeth Cox Wright's "The Significance of the Image Patterns in
Meredith's *Modern Love*," *Victorian Newsletter*, 13 (1958), 1–9.

36. "The Defense of Guenevere," 60; "Body's Beauty," *The House of Life*, Sonnet
78, in *The Pre-Raphaelites and Their Circle*, ed. Cecil Y. Lang (Boston: Houghton
Mifflin Co., 1968). "The Defense of Guenevere" had been published in 1858.

37. J. Huizinga, *Homo Ludens: A Study of the Play-Element in Culture* (London:
Routledge & Kegan Paul, 1949), p. 43.

38. Meredith's fullest exploration of the value and meaning of role playing comes in the two novels about Sandra-Emilia-Vittoria, whose three names correspond to her three major roles. Both novels are filled with dramatic performances, on and off the stage, of different kinds: deceptive, self-deceptive, self-expressive, self-realizing. The climax is Vittoria's appearance at La Scala as a role-playing heroine who represents Italy and expresses Vittoria's own deepest feelings. When the opera ends, she and Carlo declare their love, there is a popular uprising, and she becomes the heroine of the risorgimento. But love and politics—her private self and the public role that springs from both her self and her art—conflict; the resolution comes only with the death of Carlo and the end of her operatic career.

Jonas A. Barish has ascribed the nineteenth-century dislike of acting to the Romantic and Puritan "belief in an absolute sincerity which speaks directly from the soul, a pure expressiveness that knows nothing of the presence of others"; "Antitheatrical Prejudice in the Nineteenth Century," *University of Toronto Quarterly*, 40 (1971), 288. From *Modern Love* and his novels we can see that Meredith both shares and fights this prejudice.

39. Graham Hough compares *Modern Love* to the traditional sonnet sequence and points out that the stanzas are "far more like episodes in a narrative poem, and far more of them are concerned with specific scenes and incidents than is usual with the individual sonnets of a sequence . . . The method is actually more like that of the cinema . . . crucial scenes . . . interspersed with passages of atmosphere and reflection"; *Selected Poems of George Meredith*, ed. Graham Hough (London: Oxford University Press, 1962), pp. 8–9.

40. C. Day Lewis expresses the majority view: "So, mistakenly thinking he still hankers after the other woman, he releases him and herself, takes poison"; *Notable Images of Virtue: Emily Bronte, George Meredith, W. B. Yeats* (Toronto: Ryerson Press, 1954), p. 32. Long before this view became established, E. K. Chambers recognized the problem of the disparate endings and concluded that the wife really had been physically unfaithful; "Meredith's *Modern Love*," A *Sheaf of Studies* (Oxford: Oxford University Press, 1942), p. 82.

41. Willie D. Reader finds no real difference between husband and narrator; "The Autobiographical Author as Fictional Character: Point of View in Meredith's *Modern Love*," *Victorian Poetry*, 10 (1972), 131–143. Phillip E. Wilson identifies the narrator with the husband and finds the organizing principle of the poem to be the narrator's difficulty in establishing his own innocence; "Affective Coherence, a Principle of Abated Action, and Meredith's *Modern Love*," *Modern Philology*, 72 (1974), 151–171. Carol L. Bernstein analyzes the instability of the self in the poem and suggests that we can "see the self taking different stances, trying out different roles," and able sometimes to "know itself as an other"; *Precarious Enchantment: A Reading of Meredith's Poetry* (Washington, D.C.: Catholic University of America Press, 1979), p. 12.

42. *The Form of Victorian Fiction: Thackeray, Dickens, Trollope, George Eliot, Meredith, and Hardy* (Notre Dame: University of Notre Dame Press, 1968), p. 11.

43. Henry Esmond, J. Hillis Miller says, "claims to be . . . in full possession of himself by way of a full possession of all the times of his life"; *Form of Victorian Fiction*, pp. 23–24. The limits of his self-knowledge suggest that "omniscience is possible

only to a narrator who is a collective mind rising from the living together of men and women in a community"; ibid., pp. 24–25. The consciousness of the narrator in *Modern Love* seems to develop from, along with, and beyond the consciousness of the characters. Both *Henry Esmond* and *Modern Love* are explorations of deep personal experience that are also explorations of the meaning of fictional form.

44. At the end of *Feverel*, too, the speaker changes: we learn about the tragedy from Lady Blandish. As Beer says, "The self-protecting irony with which Meredith has masked his relationship to his work means that he cannot find a narrative tone for the conclusion except through the dramatic voice of Lady Blandish. This also releases him from any need to force home an unequivocal judgment"; *Meredith*, p. 15.

45. *Letters*, I: 160.

46. Ibid., p. 129.

CONCLUSION

1. "Not isolated consciousness, not consciousness at grips with natural objects, not consciousness face to face with God in meditation, but consciousness of the consciousness of others—this is the primary focus of fiction"; J. Hillis Miller, *The Form of Victorian Fiction: Thackeray, Dickens, Trollope, George Eliot, Meredith, and Hardy* (Notre Dame: University of Notre Dame Press, 1968), p. 2.

2. *The Pre-Raphaelites and Their Circle*, ed. Cecil Y. Lang (Boston: Houghton Mifflin Co., 1968).

3. Meredith and Browning may actually have been thinking of Morris's poem, since they had both read the volume. Browning admired it very much: see Delbert R. Gardner, *An "Idle Singer" and His Audience: A Study of William Morris's Poetic Reputation in England, 1858–1900* (The Hague: Mouton, 1975), p. 25. The poem itself, of course, draws on Browning's example.

4. "Poems by William Morris," *Westminster Review*, n.s. 34 (1868), 312. Jonathan F. S. Post says that "Guenevere's defense seems also a young author's defense of poetry, while the most basic denial of Gauwaine and his accusations, whatever they are, is the poet's refusal ever to let him speak"; "Guenevere's Critical Performance," *Victorian Poetry*, 17 (1979), 327.

5. "*A Sonnet is a moment's monument*," Lang, *Pre-Raphaelites*.

Index

Abrams, M. H., 4
Aeschylus
   Prometheus Bound, 75–77, 78–79
Allott, Kenneth, 169 n.31
Apostles, The (Cambridge Conver-
   sazione Society), 17
Arabian Nights, The, 39, 129, 131
Armstrong, Isobel, 157 n.4, 166 n.26,
   168 n.16
Arnold, Jane. *See* Forster, Jane Arnold
Arnold, Matthew, 1, 3, 4, 5, 6, 7, 8, 12,
   13, 14, 54, 60–61, 83–108, 117,
   119, 122, 146, 154, 158 n.9
   on Clough's poetry, 91–92, 102, 111,
      114
   and his audience, 8, 53, 83–85, 88
   and irony, 90–91
   and lyric, 7, 90, 102
   and "Marguerite," 8
   and myth, 99–101, 103, 104–105
   Works by:
      "The Buried Life," 7, 14, 83–84,
         91–98, 99, 100–101, 104, 105,
         107, 117, 138
      "Destiny," 96, 97
      "Dover Beach," 3, 13, 83–84,
         106–108
      "Empedocles on Etna," 95, 97, 98,
         99–100, 105–106

*Empedocles on Etna, and Other
   Poems*, 83, 94–98
"Euphrosyne," 96
"Excuse," 96
"Faded Leaves," 95–96
"The Forsaken Merman," 84, 85,
   86, 94
"To a Friend," 85
"The Future," 98, 101
"To George Cruikshank," 85
"To a Gipsy Child by the Sea-
   Shore," 85
"In Harmony with Nature," 85
"Indifference," 96
"Longing," 95, 96
"To Marguerite—Continued," 95,
   96, 100, 104
"Meeting," 95
"Memorial Verses," 95
"A Memory Picture," 118
Merope, 103, 106
"On the Modern Element in Liter-
   ature," 99
"Morality," 95
"Mycerinus," 85, 86
New Poems, 83
"The New Sirens," 86
"Parting," 96
"Philomela," 83–84, 104–106, 122

Arnold, Matthew (*continued*)
   Poems (1853), 83, 99, 104, 105
   Preface (1853), 5, 83, 98–103, 104,
     105, 106
   Preface to *Merope*, 106
   "Progress," 95
   "A Question," 85
   "Quiet Work," 85–86
   "Religious Isolation," 94
   "To a Republican Friend," 85
   "Resignation," 1, 2, 6, 83–84,
     86–91, 92, 93, 96, 97, 104, 107,
     154
   "On the Rhine," 96
   "The River," 96
   "The Scholar-Gipsy," 107
   "The Second Best," 95
   "Self-Dependence," 95, 97
   "Shakespeare," 85
   "The Sick King in Bokhara," 85, 86
   Sohrab and Rustum, 103
   "Stagirius," 85
   "Stanzas in Memory of the Author
     of 'Obermann'," 95
   "The Strayed Reveller," 86
   *The Strayed Reveller, and Other
     Poems*, 83, 85, 86, 94
   "A Summer Night," 95
   "Switzerland," 8, 14, 95–96, 109
   "Thyrsis," 105, 107
   "Too Late," 96
   On Translating Homer, 7
   "Tristram and Iseult," 95
   "Urania," 96
   "*In Utrumque Paratus*," 86
   "The World and the Quietist," 85
   "Written in Emerson's Essays," 85
   "Youth and Calm," 95
   "The Youth of Nature," 95
Arnold, Thomas (poet's father), 120, 170
   n.25
Ashburton, Louisa, Lady, 78, 150, 166
   n.28
Audience, 5, 7, 8–9, 66, 99–100
   Arnold and, 8, 53, 83–85, 88

Browning and, 8, 50, 53–54
Clough and, 114, 125–126
   of Greek drama, 100
   Tennyson and, 7, 8, 9, 17–19, 53
Auditor element, 11, 13, 14, 35, 109
Auditors in Victorian poetry, 1, 2–3,
   8–15, 19, 23, 154, 155
Austen, Jane
   Pride and Prejudice, 147
Autobiography in poems, 12, 125–126,
   127–128, 130–131, 145,
   149–150, 154

Ball, Patricia M., 158 n.9, 160 n.28
Baring, Rosa, 150
Barish, Jonas A., 172 n.38
Barrett, Elizabeth. *See* Browning, Eliz-
   abeth Barrett
Bartlett, Phyllis, 171 n.30
Beer, Gillian, 171 n.30, 173 n.44
Bentham, Jeremy, 3
Bernstein, Carol L., 172 n.41
Biswas, Robindra Kumar, 170 n.12
Bloom, Harold, 162 n.28
Brand, C. P., 164 n.2
Brimley, George, 36, 162 n.31
Brontë, Charlotte
   Villette, 102
Browning, Elizabeth Barrett, 48, 53, 66,
   78–79, 82
Browning, Robert, 1, 3, 4, 5, 6, 7, 8,
   12, 13, 15, 47–82, 92, 93, 119,
   125, 146, 173 n.3
   and his audience, 8, 50, 53–54
   and Lady Ashburton, 78, 150
   obscurity of poems, 53
   on Shelley, 60
   on speaking out, 48, 82
   Works by:
     "Amphibian," 79
     "Andrea del Sarto," 7, 9, 54–55,
       57, 59
     "Any Wife to Any Husband," 54
     Balaustion's Adventure, 65–67,
       76–77

In a Balcony, 61
Bells and Pomegranates, 47, 53
"Bishop Blougram's Apology," 7, 54, 58–64, 67, 81
"The Bishop Orders His Tomb at Saint Praxed's Church," 9, 47, 51, 52, 55, 59
A Blot in the 'Scutcheon, 48, 61
"Caliban upon Setebos," 165 n.17
"Christina and Mondaleschi," 82
"Count Gismond," 1, 47, 50–51
"*Dîs Aliter Visum*," 3, 58–59, 61, 63–64
Dramatis Personae, 58, 64
essay on Chatterton, 48, 49–50, 65, 165 n.16
essay on Shelley, 60
Fifine at the Fair, 3, 11–12, 15, 66, 68–80, 109, 110, 125, 145–151, 152–153, 154–155
"By the Fireside," 54, 59
"Fra Lippo Lippi," 8, 54, 55–58
"House," 8
"The Householder," 79–80
"James Lee's Wife," 14
"Johannes Agricola in Meditation," 2
"The Laboratory," 47, 51, 52, 82
Luria, 61
"Martin Relph," 82
Men and Women, 53, 54, 58, 64
"Mr. Sludge, 'The Medium'," 3, 7, 13, 58–60, 61, 62–63, 67
"My Last Duchess," 1, 2, 6, 7, 16, 47, 48–50, 51, 52, 82, 154
"One Word More," 8, 78, 82
Pauline, 50
"Pheidippides," 82
"Pictor Ignotus," 54
Pippa Passes, 6, 61, 66, 67
"Porphyria's Lover," 49
Prince Hohenstiel-Schwangau, 65–66, 67–68, 69, 78
Red Cotton Night-Cap Country, 66, 80–82

The Return of the Druses, 61
The Ring and the Book, 47, 49, 64–65, 66
"A Serenade at the Villa," 54
"Soliloquy of the Spanish Cloister," 49
Sordello, 53, 54
A Soul's Tragedy, 61
"Two in the Campagna," 7, 54
"Youth and Art," 63
Bulwer-Lytton, Edward, 9
  My Novel, 102
Burrow, J. W., 168 n.21
Byatt, A. S., 162 n.29
Byron, George Gordon, Lord, 3, 18, 135

Cadbury, William, 169 n.32
Carlyle, Thomas, 3–4, 5, 8, 28, 107, 115, 158 n.9, 165 n.16
  on sincerity, 6, 61, 62
  Works by:
    Heroes and Hero-Worship, 61
    Sartor Resartus, 131
Chambers, E. K., 172 n.40
Characterization, 9–11, 12–14, 132, 138, 148
Chatterton, Thomas, 48, 49–50
Chorley, Katharine, 169 n.8
Christ, Carol T., 162 n.35
Clough, Arthur Hugh, 5, 15, 91–92, 97, 109–126
  on Arnold's poetry, 85, 88, 111, 122
  autobiographical elements, 125–126
  on love, 120
  on poetry and novels, 111, 119
  on Wordsworth, 122
  Works by:
    Ambarvalia, 114
    Amours de Voyage, 11–12, 102, 109–126, 142, 145–152, 154–155
    The Bothie of Tober-na-Vuolich, 102, 113, 115, 116
    Dipsychus, 116
    "Letters of Parepidimus," 115

Clough, Arthur Hugh (*continued*)
  "Recent English Poetry," 85, 111,
    114, 119
Coleridge, Samuel Taylor, 3
  conversation poems, 5
  Works by:
    "The Eolian Harp," 2
Collins, Philip, 160 n.10
Collins, Thomas J., 164 n.9
Communication, poetry as, 1–11 *pas-
    sim*, 146, 154
  in Arnold, 94, 96, 98–100, 106–107
  in Browning, 47, 53, 54–58 *passim*,
    66, 68
  in Tennyson, 1, 17, 18, 24–25, 32,
    42–46 *passim*
Coulling, Sidney, 168 n.16
Crimean War. *See* War.
Culler, A. Dwight, 13, 162 n.27, 168 n.7

Dante
  Inferno, 16, 27–29, 30
Dawson, Carl, 157 n.3, 158 n.9
DeVane, William Clyde, 165 n.22, 166
    n.24
Dickens, Charles
  Bleak House, 40
Donne, John, 5
  "The Flea," 2
  "The Sun Rising," 2
Dramatic lyric, 14, 15
Dramatic monologue, 1, 2, 14, 15, 16,
    24, 43, 48, 68, 106, 153, 155
  and characterization, 10–11, 159 n.19
  and communication, 11
  definitions, 12–13, 159 n.23
  and dramatic situation, 13–14, 55,
    155
  extended or sequence, 11, 112, 126,
    154–155
Drew, Philip, 164 n.12, 165 n.22, 166
    n.29

Eliot, George, 84, 148
  Middlemarch, 10, 60, 142

Eliot, T. S.
  on dramatic monologue, 11, 159 n.19
  on myth, 103
  Works by:
    "Gerontion," 2
    "The Love Song of J. Alfred Pru-
      frock," 16, 151
Emerson, Ralph Waldo, 119
Epistolary literary forms, 114
Euripides, 66–67
  Alcestis, 66, 76–77
Expressive theory, 4, 5, 12, 56, 102

Faas, E. K., 159 n.23
Fatal woman, 126–130, 131–135,
    137–138, 149, 151, 152–154
Fiction. *See* Novel, Victorian
Fletcher, Ian, 171 n.33
Ford, George H., 158 n.15
Forster, Jane Arnold, 87–88, 91, 168 n.7
Fox, W. J., 4
Fredeman, William E., 161 n.14
Friedland, Louis, 164 n.2
Friedman, Norman, 171 n.35
Froude, James Anthony, 88

Garden, Francis, 5
Gibbon, Edward
  *The History of the Decline and Fall of
    the Roman Empire*, 21, 22–23
Goethe, Johann Wolfgang von, 116–117,
    151
  Faust, 91, 116
  Hermann and Dorothea, 116
  Italian Journey, 116–117
  Roman Elegies, 116–117
Golden, Arline, 171 n.30
Goode, John, 170 n.17, 171 n.28
Gottfried, Leon, 158 n.8, 167 n.6
Greenberger, Evelyn Barish, 171 n.28

Hagopian, John V., 164 n.6
Hallam, Arthur
  death of, 16, 23, 29
  theory of poetry, 4–5, 7, 10

Hardy, Barbara, 170 n.15
Hetzler, Leo A., 165–166 n.22
Honan, Park, 13, 159 n.23, 167 n.33
Hone, William
  Every-Day Book, 22–23
Hough, Graham, 172 n.39
Houghton, Walter E., 170 n.23, 170
  n.25
Huizinga, J., 137
Hunt, Leigh, 10
Hutton, Richard Holt, 90, 170 n.17
Huxley, Thomas Henry, 158 n.9

Irony, 5, 30, 90–91, 113, 115, 122, 123,
  135–136, 145, 149, 151, 154
Irvine, William, 167 n.33

Jack, Ian, 164 n.1
Johnson, Diane, 171 n.30
Johnson, E. D. H., 157 n.2, 163 n.43
Johnson, W. Stacy, 159 n.23, 167 n.5
Joyce, James, 103

Keats, John, 3, 36, 60, 103
  "Ode to a Nightingale," 105
Kendrick, Walter M., 167 n.35
Kincaid, James R., 163 n.38, 163 n.44
King, Roma A., 165 n.21
Kingsley, Charles, 10, 36, 37

Langbaum, Robert, 12–13, 164 n.11,
  165 n.19
Language. *See* Poetic language
Levine, George, 159 n.17
Lewis, C. Day, 172 n.40
Longfellow, Henry Wadsworth
  Evangeline, 116
Lyric, 7, 14, 102, 145, 149, 155
  in *Amours de Voyage*, 111, 112, 114,
    123
  in *Maud*, 35, 36–37, 40
  in "Resignation," 90

Macaulay, Thomas Babington, 3
Mann, Robert James, 42

Markus, Julia, 165 n.12
Marriage, 11–12, 38, 69, 119–120, 145,
  146–147, 148
Marvell, Andrew
  "The Nymph Complaining for the
    Death of Her Faun," 39
Mason, Michael, 159 n.20
Mazzini, Giuseppe, 121, 125
Melchiori, Barbara, 166 n.25, 166 n.26,
  166 n.29
Meredith, George, 15, 125, 126–144,
  173 n.3
  and acting, 172 n.38
  on fatal women, 126–130, 131–135,
    137–138
  and his wife, 127–128, 130–131, 150
  transition from poet to novelist, 127
  Works by:
    Evan Harrington, 127, 138
    Farina, 127
    "Josepha," 128
    "Marian," 128
    Modern Love, 11–12, 109, 110,
      126–144, 145–153, 154–155
    Modern Love and Poems of the Eng-
      lish Roadside, 127
    The Ordeal of Richard Feverel, 127,
      130, 138, 173 n.44
    Poems (1851), 127
    Sandra Belloni, 172 n.38
    The Shaving of Shagpat, 127, 128,
      131, 133–134, 138
    "Shemselnihar," 129–130, 131
    "Song: Come to me in any shape,"
      128
    "The Song of Courtesy," 128
    Vittoria, 142, 172 n.38
Meredith, Mary, 127–128, 130, 150
Mill, John Stuart, 5, 6, 7, 93
Miller, J. Hillis, 143, 165 n.18, 172–173
  n.43, 173 n.1
Milton, John
  Paradise Lost, 19, 27, 39, 163 n.37
Molière, Jean Baptiste
  Don Juan, 69, 75

Monodrama, 13
Morley, John, 114
Morris, William
  "The Defense of Guenevere," 3, 133,
    152–154
  The Defense of Guenevere, 3
Mozart, Wolfgang Amadeus
  Don Giovanni, 69, 75
Myth, 67, 99–101, 103, 104–105

Napoleon III, 67, 68, 165 n.22
Narrators, 122–125, 127, 142–144, 145,
  153
Newman, John Henry
  Apologia Pro Vita Sua, 158 n.9
Novel, Victorian, 3, 102, 111, 119, 155
  as literary norm, 9–12, 15, 155
  novelistic aspects of poems, 10–11,
    40, 69, 70–71, 107, 112,
    126–127, 138, 139, 142, 143, 148
  novelistic element defined, 145

Orr, Mrs. Sutherland, 167 n.33
Ovid, 18

Palgrave, Francis, 114
Pater, Walter
  The Renaissance, 153
Patmore, Coventry, 37
  The Angel in the House, 14
Perkins, David, 158 n.9, 167 n.1
Pettigrew, John, 161–162 n.27
Peyre, Henri, 158 n.9
Pitt, Valerie, 162 n.29, 162 n.36
Poetic language, 12, 30–31, 109–110,
  115, 151
Poetry, Victorian theories of, 4–7, 9–10
Popularity
  of fiction, 9
  of poetry, 5, 29
Post, Jonathan F. S., 173 n.4
Pragmatic theory, 4, 12, 101–102, 146
Pre-Raphaelite woman. *See* Fatal
  woman
Priestley, F.E.L., 164 n.12

Rader, Ralph Wilson, 159 n.23, 162
  n.30, 162 n.33
Raymond, William O., 166 n.28
Reader, Willie D., 172 n.41
Ricks, Christopher, 161 n.14, 161 n.18
Rome, siege of. *See* War.
Rosenberg, John D., 163 n.43
Rossetti, Dante Gabriel, 154
  "Body's Beauty," 133
  "Jenny," 166 n.24
  "*A sonnet is a moment's monument,*"
    153–154
Ruskin, John, 53, 72, 107
Ryals, Clyde de L., 165 n.19, 167 n.33

Scott, Sir Walter, 9
Self-revelation, poets', 8
Senancour, Étienne Pivert de, 97
Sessions, Ina Beth, 12, 159 n.21
Shairp, John Campbell, 169 n.8
Shakespeare, William, 8, 62, 101, 151
  Hamlet, 151
  King Lear, 22
  Much Ado about Nothing, 61
  Othello, 61, 135, 136, 151
  The Tempest, 18
Shannon, Edgar F., 162 n.33
Shaw, W. David, 161 n.14
Shelley, Mary W.
  Frankenstein, 18, 160 n.4
Shelley, Percy Bysshe, 3, 6, 18, 36, 60,
  160 n.4
  "Adonais," 18, 160 n.6
  "Hymn to Intellectual Beauty," 160
    n.9
  "Mont Blanc," 160 n.4
  "The Triumph of Life," 18
Sidgwick, Henry, 115, 170 n.14
Sincerity, 6–7, 12, 47, 59–64, 67, 68,
  69, 92–97 *passim*, 108, 111, 114,
  115, 117–118, 142–143, 146, 148,
  150, 153, 155, 158 n.9
Sinfield, Alan, 13, 14, 160 n.28
Smalley, Donald, 165 n.16
Smidt, Kristian, 159 n.23

Smith, Alexander, 88, 119
  A *Life Drama*, 102
Sonnet sequence, 151, 171 n.30, 172
    n.39
Sophocles, 99, 103
Southwell, Samuel B., 166 n.29
Spånberg, Sven-Johan, 166 n.27
Spedding, James, 7, 10
Speech, 2, 8, 47, 49, 50, 52, 58, 66,
    81–82, 154
  and action, 16–17, 24, 81–82
  as aggression, 15, 82, 83
  as power, 8–9, 15, 18, 47, 49, 50, 52,
    53, 68
Spenser, Edmund
  Epithalamion, 37, 39, 162 n.37
Stanford, W. B., 161 n.20, 161 n.22
Stang, Richard, 158 n.15
Sterling, John, 4
Stevenson, Lionel, 171 n.30
Sundell, M. G., 168 n.6

Tasso, Torquato, 48, 164 n.2
Tennyson, Alfred, 1, 2, 3, 4, 5, 6, 7, 8,
    9, 10, 13, 15, 16–46, 54, 71, 92,
    146
  comic performances, 19
  fear of blindness, 25
  and ghosts, 18–19
  and his audience, 8, 17–19, 53
  and isolation, 32–34, 40–41, 42
  political poetry, 31, 35–36
  telling stories, 19
  Works by:
    "The Charge of the Light Brigade,"
      36
    "Despair," 45, 163 n.46
    "The Epic," 19
    essay on ghosts, 17–18, 49
    "A Farewell," 7
    "Godiva," 10
    "Happy: The Leper's Bride," 45,
      163 n.46
    "Hark! the dogs howl," 18
    "The Holy Grail," 3, 43–45

Idylls of the King, 42
"The Lady of Shalott," 32
"Lilian," 10
"Locksley Hall," 113
"The Lotos-Eaters," 32
"Mariana," 10, 32, 33
Maud, 3, 11–12, 13, 15, 34–42,
    43, 45, 102, 109, 110, 125, 126,
    145–152, 154–155
Maud, and Other Poems, 35
In Memoriam, 7, 8, 18, 37, 38
"Morte d'Arthur," 19
"Ode on the Death of the Duke of
    Wellington," 36
"Oenone," 31
"Oh! that 'twere possible," 34–35
"The Palace of Art," 31, 32–34
"The Poet," 9
"The Poet's Mind," 9
The Princess, 38
"To the Rev. F. D. Maurice," 36
"Rizpah," 3, 45–46
"Romney's Remorse," 45, 163 n.46
"St. Simeon Stylites," 1, 2, 6, 15,
    16–17, 19–23, 24, 26, 27, 29,
    31, 33–34, 42–45 *passim*, 51,
    154
"Semele," 25
"Sir Galahad," 44
"The Spinster's Sweet-Arts," 163
    n.45
"Tears, Idle Tears," 92
"Tiresias," 1, 2–3, 13, 16–17, 19,
    23–26, 27, 33–34, 42, 43, 45,
    154
"Tithonus," 2, 31–33
"The Two Voices," 30–31
"Ulysses," 1, 2, 4, 7, 13, 16–17, 19,
    23, 26–31, 33–34, 42, 43, 45,
    51, 154
Tennyson, Hallam, 17, 36
Thackeray, William Makepeace
  Henry Esmond, 172–173 n.43
  Vanity Fair, 119
Tillotson, Kathleen, 158 n.13, 158 n.15

Timko, Michael, 164 n.6
Trilling, Lionel, 158 n.9
Trollope, Anthony, 148
Tucker, Cynthia Grant, 171 n.30

Ullmann, S.O.A., 169 n.31

Wallis, Henry, 127
War, 147, 163 n.38
   Crimean, 36, 41–42, 126
   Siege of Rome, 120–121, 126

Ward, Maisie, 166 n.28
Warren, Alba H., 157 n.2
Watkins, Charlotte Crawford, 166 n.23
Whitla, William, 166 n.28
Wilson, Phillip E., 172 n.41
Wordsworth, William, 3, 6, 60–61, 87,
   94, 122, 140, 167 n.1
   Preface to *Lyrical Ballads*, 5
   "Scorn Not the Sonnet," 8
   "Tintern Abbey," 2, 91, 93
Wright, Elizabeth Cox, 171 n.35